SMEs and European Integration

In easily accessible language, this book analyses the impact of Economic and Monetary Union on Small and Medium-sized Enterprises (SMEs) in Europe. This over-arching and widely researched study first of all explains in a jargon-free manner the mechanisms of EMU and its likely effect on SMEs' internationalisation strategies. This empirical study explains and examines seven case studies of SMEs located in industrial districts in Germany and France and a questionnaire sent out to SMEs located outside industrial districts in Germany, France and Italy. Answers to many questions that have arisen over the years regarding SMEs and European integration can be found in the pages of this study. In a remarkably well-written and researched book, Birgit Hegge has succeeded in bringing together two interesting areas of research in an original and insightful manner.

This book will be incredibly useful as a background reference for international economics and business students at an advanced level. The evidence and conclusions of this book will also no doubt make extremely interesting reading for European policy-makers, along with those involved in European business.

Birgit Hegge holds a masters degree in international economics. She has completed a Ph.D. in Management at the University of Geneva.

Routledge studies in the European economy

1 **Growth and Crisis in the Spanish Economy, 1940–1993**
Sima Lieberman

2 **Work and Employment in Europe**
A new convergence?
Edited by Peter Cressey and Bryn Jones

3 **Trans-European Telecommunication Networks**
The challenges for industrial policy
Colin Turner

4 **European Union – European Industrial Relations?**
Global challenges, national developments and transnational dynamics
Edited by Wolfgang E. Lecher and Hans-Wolfgang Platzer

5 **Governance, Industry and Labour Markets in Britain and France**
The modernizing state in the mid-twentieth century
Edited by Noel Whiteside and Robert Salais

6 **Labour Market Efficiency in the European Union**
Employment protection and fixed-term contracts
Klaus Schömann, Ralf Rogowski and Thomas Kruppe

7 **The Enlargement of the European Union**
Issues and strategies
Edited by Victoria Curzon-Price, Alice Landau and Richard Whitman

8 **European Trade Unions**
Change and response
Edited by Mike Rigby, Roger Smith and Teresa Lawlor

9 **Fiscal Federalism in the European Union**
Edited by Amedeo Fossati and Giorgio Panella

10 **European Telecommunications Liberalisation**
Edited by Kjell A. Eliassen and Marit Sjøvaag

11 **Integration and Transition in Europe**
The economic geography of interaction
Edited by George Petrakos, Gunther Maier and Grzegorz Gorzelak

12 **SMEs and European Integration**
Internationalisation strategies
Birgit Hegge

SMEs and European Integration

Internationalisation strategies

Birgit Hegge

Routledge
Taylor & Francis Group
London and New York

First published 2002
by Routledge
11 New Fetter Lane, London EC4P 4EE

Simultaneously published in the USA and Canada
by Routledge
29 West 35th Street, New York, NY 10001

Routledge is an imprint of the Taylor & Francis Group

Typeset in Times by Keyword Typesetting Services Ltd.
Printed and bound in Great Britain by MPG Books Ltd, Bodmin

British Library Cataloguing in Publication Data
A catalogue record for this book is available
from the British Library

Library of Congress Cataloging in Publication Data
Hegge, Birgit, 1968–
SMEs and European integration: internationalisation strategies/Birgit Hegge.
p. cm. – (Routledge studies in the European economy; 12)
Includes bibliographical references and index.
1. Europe – Economic integration. 2. Small business – Europe – Finance – Case studies. 3. Economic and Monetary Union. 4. Euro. 5. Currency question. 6. Medical instruments and apparatus industry – France. 7. Medical instruments and apparatus industry – Germany. I. Title. II. Series.
HC241 H37 2002
337.1′4 – dc21

2001056889

ISBN 0-415-27739-6

Contents

Illustrations

Figures

Tables

Preface

This book is about integration, internationalisation and location of Small and Medium-sized Enterprises (SMEs). The idea to write about this topic dates back three years. At that time I was working as an assistant on a collection of articles on International Economic Integration, published in four volumes (General Editor: Miroslav Jovanovic; 1998, London: Routledge). Among the four volumes one was about general issues and we were looking for articles connecting integration, internationalisation and SMEs. Then, and during my three-year research, we discovered almost nothing. But the topic for my Ph.D. was born.

It is my opinion that research on international economics and international management has a chance to enrich the discussion only if it is written in a language that is understood by the majority of the audience. Therefore I have written this book in English even though this is not my native tongue. There may remain some mistakes regarding grammar and spelling for which I will have to ask for tolerance.

Acknowledgements

Unfortunately, it is impossible to mention everyone who contributed to this research with material or other useful inputs, so I will restrict my acknowledgements to those who were particularly helpful and highly valued.

I want to acknowledge the assistance of Carol Cosgrove Sacks, Carlos Jarillo, Miroslav Jovanovic and Charles Ricq. They all gave me some important ideas and comments for the book. Robert Langham and Heidi Bagtazo favoured this project from the outset. There were also two anonymous reviewers who gave me some useful advice. In particular, I would like to thank Victoria Curzon Price for reading and reading again the whole book. She continously supported my work and corrected my English – a very difficult task!

I would like to acknowledge the Department of Management of the University of Geneva for its kind financial assistance during my empirical research.

I also wish to express my appreciation to the owners of the firms and the corporate executives who participated in the interviews and completed our questionnaires. Without this support the research and the book would not have been possible. I sincerely hope that the result will meet with their approval.

Finally, I owe a great debt of gratitude to my family, and in particular to Gael and Kilian who kept me from taking my work too seriously. I dedicate this book to them.

Introduction

The objective of the 1992 Programme was to remove non-tariff barriers (NTBs)[1] on internal trade in the European Union (EU). In addition, it prepared the ground for monetary integration. The establishment of the Economic and Monetary Union (EMU) led to an enlarged market. This can be extremely profitable for firms involved in international transactions. In a majority of cases these firms are small and medium-sized. It is therefore interesting to find out how they reacted to this enlarged market access. Did they increase their international operations within the EU? Did they change their internationalisation strategies?

There are books and articles dealing with integration issues and there are others about internationalisation of Small and Medium-sized Enterprises (SMEs).[2] It may therefore be new and interesting to put the two topics together.

In many industries there are SMEs both inside and outside agglomerations.[3] Are they affected in the same way by the establishment of the EMU? By including some basics of the new economic geography a comparative study of SMEs located inside agglomerations and those located outside became feasible.

The objective of this book is therefore to analyse the impact of the EMU on international strategies of SMEs in and out of agglomerations or industrial districts. The topic is a connection between integration, internationalisation, location and SMEs. The term EMU is used throughout the book, as a clear separation between European Single Market and EMU would be difficult and as the EMU will be the 'last consequence'.

The framework

The Single Market Programme of 1992 (or Maastricht Treaty) prepared the ground for the establishment of the EMU. From 1992 the majority of NTBs were removed and the introduction of the single currency in 1999 was prepared, using a step-by-step approach. Major NTBs were border controls, red tape and differences of technical standards.

In addition to the abolition of NTBs there were special cooperation programmes for EU firms and changes in anti-trust policy, which stimulated trans-border transactions and cooperation among firms. We will, however, see that physical and technical barriers in particular hindered trade among SMEs within the EU. Our empirical study will show that the promotion of internationalisation and cooperation through national and EU programmes was less important for the SMEs of our sample.

The enlarged market modified not only country-specific advantages, but also firm-specific advantages. By following the comparative advantage theory of Ricardo such policy modifications change the price/quantity relations of the production factors and lead to changes regarding the industry structure, the degree of product differentiation and specialisation. Firm-specific advantages, such as a superior technology, business know-how, a special design or a superior production process,[4] can be exploited better in an enlarged market. In some cases this provokes the development of new firm-specific advantages.

Modifications of country- and firm-specific advantages influence the internationalisation of firms. SMEs doing business within the EU had to adapt their international strategies to the enlarged market in order to exploit efficiently their firm-specific advantage(s) and to fight increased competition. This meant an increase of international transactions for a majority of cases. But, for some SMEs, it also signified changes regarding their foreign-market entry strategy. Cooperation agreements with other EU firms became an attractive means of internationalisation. Even if some hindrances persisted, firms were able to benefit from the market opening. There were new opportunities, but also new challenges that created a healthy dynamic.

Country- and firm-specific advantages determine the location of firms. According to the new economic geography, lower trade barriers lead to the concentration of each industry in a single location. At a certain level this encourages industrial agglomeration.[5] In this sense, the removal of NTBs led to lower trade costs in the EU which reinforced the position of industrial districts.

Lower trade costs lead to an increased product differentiation and specialisation which is closely connected to SMEs' competitive advantage(s). This is very important for highly internationalised firms. SMEs located in industrial districts are, however, able to specialise 'better' than SMEs located outside as they benefit from proximity advantages. More specialisation within an industrial district also leads to more cooperation between the firms.

Figure 0.1 illustrates the main points of the book. Built upon this analytical framework, the three hypotheses in the first part are developed. During our research, these were simplified for ease of confirmation or rejection.

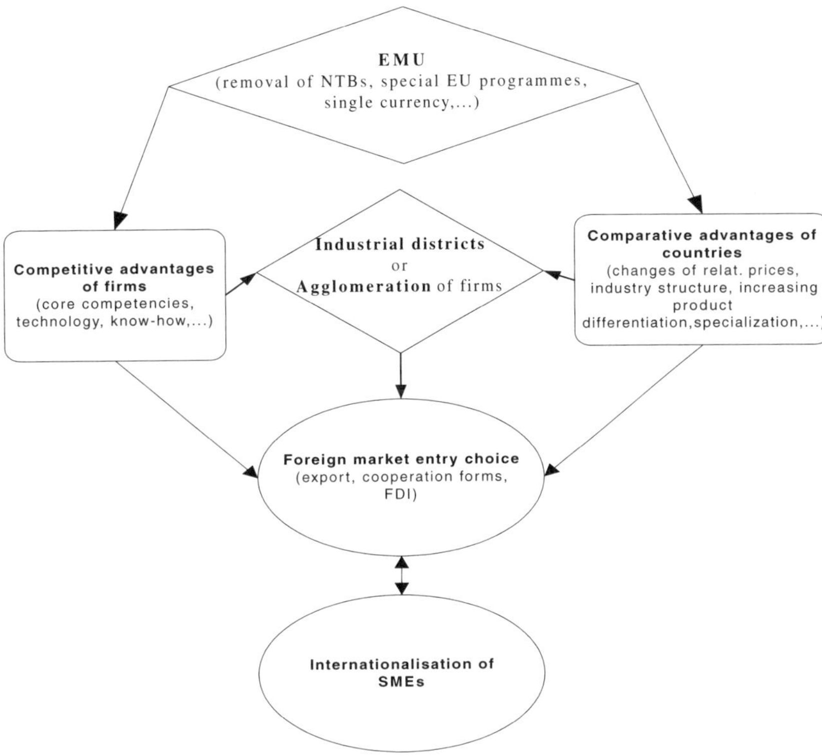

Figure 0.1 An analytical framework.

The empirical study

The tendency to claim universality from case-study research and to formulate innovative concepts based on one case study is common. The formulation of a universal method was not an objective of our empirical study. But, as case studies are relatively unexplored, it is a very appropriate research method. Case-study interpretations are rather qualitative, so it was decided to complete the empirical study through questionnaire research in order to obtain some quantitative results.

In order to answer the hypotheses, the empirical study (Part 2) of the research is based on seven case studies and a questionnaire. The research is concentrated on France, Germany and Italy, in order to find out if SMEs in the same industry react in a similar manner to the removal of NTBs in the different countries. All three countries are characterised by a high percentage of SMEs.

To obtain comparable results an industry has to be chosen where SMEs in the respective countries are highly represented. SMEs specialising in the medical and surgical equipment industry are predisposed to a certain degree of internationalisation. In addition, one finds them located both inside and outside industrial districts.

Agglomerations of firms or industrial districts exist in the region of Tuttlingen (Germany), in the region of Nogent (France) and in the region of Lecce (Italy). But, compared with Tuttlingen and Nogent, it was impossible to establish contact with SMEs in the region of Lecce despite numerous efforts.

The seven case studies are written with the cooperation of the five SMEs in Tuttlingen and with two SMEs in Nogent. The questionnaire was sent out to 100 French, 100 German and 100 Italian SMEs which are not located in industrial districts. This enables the comparison of the internationalisation strategies of SMEs located in and out of industrial districts after the establishment of the EMU. In addition there will probably be some differences from one country to another.

Definitions

There are different definitions of SMEs depending on authors and countries. For the EU, a SME is a firm which has fewer than 500 employees, an annual turnover of less than EUR 38 million and is no more than 33 per cent owned by a firm which is not a SME.[6] In the present research, and particularly in the empirical part, the SMEs of the case studies fulfilled these conditions. However, it cannot be guaranteed that the SMEs of the questionnaire also fulfilled them, in particular regarding ownership. In addition, in the literature survey some reference is made to firms with a higher turnover than that defined by the EU and to firms having more than 500 employees. But these examples help to illustrate some important points and in general the EU classification is used.

In this context it might therefore be interesting to find an economic definition of the SME. In general the SME is highly specialised on one or two product lines. This high specialisation might enable the SME to reap economies of scale. In some cases the firm finds itself in a situation of a quasi-monopoly. Competition with large enterprises becomes possible. The location in agglomerations (or industrial districts) enables SMEs to reap to a higher extent not only economies of scale, but also economies of scope due to proximity advantages. This facilitates their internationalisation.

A major point of the research is *firm-specific or competitive advantages*. According to Porter, a competitive advantage in either cost or differentiation is a function of a company's value-chain.[7] The activities performed by a firm in designing, producing, marketing and distributing its product are therefore important. There are two strategies by which a firm can obtain a competitive advantage: (1) cost leadership and (2) differentiation. In this sense cost leadership

> requires aggressive construction of efficient scale facilities, vigorous pursuit of cost reductions from experience, tight cost and overhead control, avoidance of marginal customer accounts, and cost minimization in areas like R&D, service, sales force, advertising and so on.... Low cost relative to competitors becomes the theme running through the entire strategy.... Having a low-cost position yields the firm above-average returns in its industry despite the presence of strong competitive forces.
>
> (Porter 1980: 35)

Differentiation is a strategy of

> differentiating the product or service offering of the firm, creating something that is perceived industrywide as unique. Approaches to differentiating can take many forms: design or brand image,... technology,... features,... customer service,... dealer network,... or other dimensions. Differentiation provides insulation against competitive rivalry.
>
> (Porter 1980: 37–8)

Thus a competitive advantage grows out of the value a firm can create for its buyers that exceeds the firm's cost of creating it.

Overview of the book

The book is organised as follows. Altogether there are three parts. Part I contains a literature survey in order to develop the three hypotheses of the research. Chapter 1 deals with the establishment of the EMU and the expected benefits for SMEs. An overview of major NTBs and programmes promoting cross-border cooperation among European SMEs precedes the discussion of short-term and medium-term effects of the establishment of the EMU. A special point will be monetary integration.

Internationalisation models are the subject of chapter 2. Classic internationalisation models such as the models of Hymer and Vernon, the internalisation theory and Dunning's eclectic paradigm of international production are related to the issue of integration. A critical description of internationalisation models in the business literature completes the chapter.

Chapter 3 traces the different foreign-market entry strategies such as exporting, contractual agreements and Foreign Direct Investment (FDI). These strategies are critically reviewed by putting them in context with the establishment of the EMU. Special attention is given to subcontracting activities as SMEs favour this strategy internationally and within industrial districts.

The mechanisms of location, covered in chapter 4, conclude Part I. This chapter begins with an introduction to the mechanisms of location, then describes the virtuous circle of cooperation and competition in industrial districts that lead them to international success. The last section of the chapter deals with transaction cost theory and game theory. Rather complementary, both of them deliver the basis for cooperation on an international and local level.

Part II contains the description of the empirical research. Industry choice is extremely important as there may be some characteristics that are industry-specific. Therefore Part II begins with an analysis of the European medical and surgical equipment and orthopaedic appliances industry (MSE) in chapter 6. By calculating the trans-border flows in France, Germany and Italy one realises that there has been a '1992 effect'. The industry description covers in particular the profile and market forces.

The field research is the subject of chapter 7. First, there is the questionnaire research with 300 SMEs in France, Germany and Italy located outside industrial districts. The situation of the SME sector in each country is shown. Second, there are the seven case studies provided by two SMEs in the industrial district of Nogent in France and five SMEs in the industrial district of Tuttlingen in Germany. The majority of SMEs wished to change their names in order to remain anonymous.

Part III contains the results of the field research and conclusions. Chapter 8 deals with the results of the questionnaire and the interpretation of the case studies. This leads to the first conclusions. Regarding the questionnaire, the main results are SMEs' increased export activities from 1992 on, and a growing number of cooperation agreements and FDI within the EU. A large majority of SMEs felt affected by the removal of NTBs within the EU. Also, SMEs in industrial districts felt affected by the removal of NTBs, but only those specialising in R&D-intensive instruments. They increased their international transactions within the EU and some of them changed their internationalisation strategy by going a step further.

Chapter 9 answers the three hypotheses by trying to approach economic and business concepts of internationalisation. In the last section a concept is provided that is valid for this empirical research. Further research may show if it can also be applied to other industries that resemble the one chosen in this research.

As the subject matter of the book spans a number of areas, it will be interesting as a background reference for international economics and international business students. In addition, it will be of interest to students following courses on European economic integration. But there may also be some interesting case studies for economic geographers.

Part I

Literature survey

1 1992 and beyond – market opening within the EU?

The objective of the 1987 Single European Act was to eliminate all barriers to the movement of goods, people and capital within the EU. With the 1992 Maastricht Treaty (or Single Market Programme) the ideas of the Single European Act became concrete. First, the main aspects of the Maastricht Treaty, having an impact on SMEs' internationalisation strategies, are described. Second, first results of the removal of NTBs are examined. Regarding the introduction of the new currency, the euro, possible consequences can only be supposed. It may be interesting to find out if SMEs are able to exploit their competitive advantage(s) better after the 1992 market opening.

The EMU – what does it mean?

First, the elimination of barriers to trade in the Single Market Programme should be understood as a removal of NTBs such as national standards, regulations and subsidies, which hindered trade because they enforced a difference between the nationals of the EU countries.

Second, there were special trans-border cooperation programmes and changes in anti-trust policy, leading to further openings and cooperation between firms within the EU.

The third important point of the Single Market Programme (and perhaps the most important hurdle!) was the establishment of the monetary union with the introduction of the single currency, the euro from January 1999 on.

There were three major NTBs that constituted important obstacles for SMEs following international strategies within the EU. First, there were *physical* border checks on goods crossing the internal EU border for statistical purposes, VAT adjustments and conformity with certain sanitary and health standards. Delays, unnecessary formalities and handling charges raised the costs for the firms.[1] These extra burdens were industry-specific as the check for conformity was, for example, especially pronounced in the food industry where standards differed from one country to another. There were many laws defining what could be sold as 'sausage', 'cheese', 'wine', or 'pasta'.[2]

Second, there were different national product or service regulations and standards, constituting *technical* barriers, which added some extra costs. According to the Cecchini Report,[3] manufacturing with the existence of these different national standards implied a loss of some 60 billion euros a year. Increased unit costs, increased stock-holding costs, distorted production and less business cooperation were some of the consequences. Testing and certification procedures were cumbersome, time-consuming and expensive. These costs had to be born by the exporter.[4] In Belgium, for example, lifts have to be equipped with a 'stop' button to permit handicapped or elderly people to leave them in safety, whereas in Britain a 'stop' button is prohibited. Most national standards are developed, however, by industry and on a voluntary basis.[5] Concerning the medical and surgical instrumentation industry these technical barriers, under the form of certifications or administrative procedures, were extremely high before 1992. Firms that specialise in producing 'new' and innovative medical instruments were hardest hit.

Third, there were *fiscal* barriers such as different VAT rates and excise duties. As there was no agreement on an approximation of the rates between the countries, the principle of origin was adopted.[6] Tax frontiers moved inwards and firms complained about the high administrative burden. Even if it is difficult to measure, it certainly constitutes an obstacle to intra-EU transactions and reduces their number and value.

Other NTBs were state aids,[7] different intellectual and industrial property laws and national public procurement policies which had a negative impact on enterprises wishing to treat the EU as a single environment.[8]

The Single Market Programme, with its new approach,[9] tried to remove the remaining obstacles to completing the internal market. It concerned SMEs, strongly involved in the development and distribution of products with a high technological standard.

- First, physical border controls were abolished, which facilitated and accelerated trans-border transactions.
- Second, there was a distinction as to which standards should be harmonised and which could be left to the principle of mutual recognition (mutual recognition and selective harmonisation).[10]
- Third, harmonisation of industrial standards was enforced by the intermediary of the Comité Européen de la Normalisation (CEN)[11] or the CENELEC in the electro-technical industry.[12] They can act on qualified majority votes.[13] It is up to the Community to prescribe some minimal legal rules, leaving the bigger part to these two instances where associations and entrepreneurs can influence the establishment of convenient standards.

The second important aspect of the Maastricht Treaty that may provoke an increasing internationalisation of SMEs is the establishment of special trans-border cooperation programmes and a favourable anti-trust policy. In both cases the EU favours SMEs considerably. Whenever there is any danger of SMEs getting caught in the net, the Commission usually makes an explicit exception in their favour.

The cooperation programmes are aimed at firms that are highly involved in R&D activities. Programmes such as ESPRIT[14] and BRITE,[15] that have as a precondition the participation of two or more firms from at least two different EU countries, show an increasing number of participating SMEs. Technology spill-overs and a higher degree of information exchange between geographically dispersed innovators become possible. Krieger-Mytelka and Delapierre[16] argued that the ESPRIT programme offered new possibilities for SMEs to become independent members of consortia. A disadvantage of the ESPRIT programme is, however, that it does not focus on long-term contractual arrangements. But, compared to large firms, the participation of SMEs in these programmes is still proportionally low.

Another interesting programme is JEV.[17] It concerns only SMEs and aims to promote cross-border activities among them. The concept of 'joint venture' covers any form of consortium, partnership or joint venture of an industrial, service, commercial or craft nature, which results in a new legal entity.[18]

The EU legislation favours cooperation agreements among European SMEs. Cooperation agreements that should normally be prohibited by virtue of Articles 81 and 82 of the EC Treaty were permitted through the Single Market Programme and notification was no longer required if the firms had a market share of less than 5 per cent and if their total turnover for one financial year did not exceed 300 million euros. These agreements were considered of minor importance. But SMEs complained about expensive and time-consuming multiple requests for information and filing requirements. They would prefer a 'one-stop shopping' at the EU merger control.[19]

In 1997, the Commission raised the market share threshold for notification from 5 per cent to 10 per cent for vertical agreements (linking companies along the supply side), while leaving it at 5 per cent for horizontal agreements (between competitors). In addition, agreements between SMEs with up to 40 million euros sales or 27 million euros assets and 250 employees were exempted even if the thresholds for market share were exceeded.[20]

To base the inter-firm cooperation on a legal platform, the Commission had already in 1985 introduced the European Economic Interest Grouping (EEIG), which is the only legal instrument whose structure is specially adapted to help transnational and interprofessional cooperation between economic operators, and particularly SMEs.[21]

In relation to the Single Market Programme and its effects of restructuring within the EU economy, Panic predicted an increase in SME mergers and acquisitions.[22] Even if mergers and acquisitions in industries

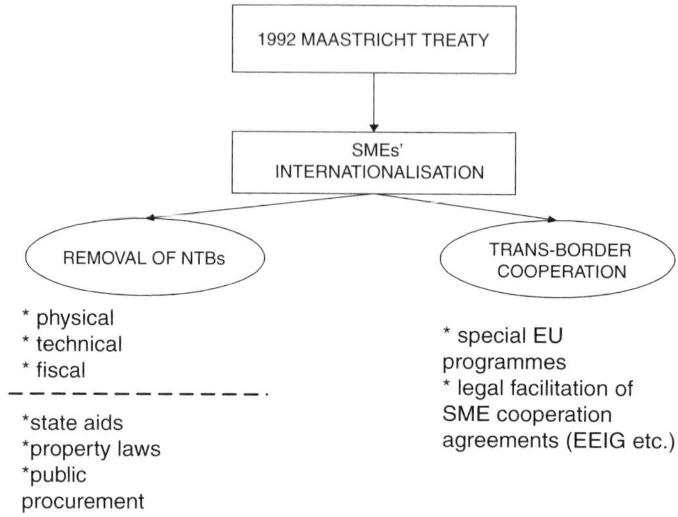

Figure 1.1 Maastricht Treaty and SMEs.

increased between 1986 and 1995 from 720 to 2,296, there were about 70 per cent domestic operations. World-wide there were about forty-five cross-border mergers and acquisitions deals worth over $1 billion in 1996. Among those forty-five deals there were about seven EU deals and thirty-three deals involving one EU firm.[23] This means that small- and medium-sized transnational corporations (TNCs) concluded the majority of the deals. SMEs therefore accounted for 94.3 per cent of all international merger and acquisition activity. A growth of trans-border mergers and acquisitions and cooperation agreements among European SMEs is supposed to increase their critical size. This is necessary to exploit their competitive advantage within a larger market.

The third and perhaps most important aspect covered by the Maastricht Treaty is the establishment of the monetary union. From January 1999 on, a core of EU members adopted a unified monetary policy and payment system based on the euro. It corresponds to the last of three stages in the creation of an economic and monetary union.[24] Possible effects of the introduction of the euro on SMEs' international strategies will be examined separately.

Removal of NTBs: expected benefits for SMEs?

The objective of this section is to find out if the removal of NTBs within the EU led to increasing international operations of SMEs. First, general microeconomic literature is analysed to get an idea of the benefits expected and realised. Second, short- and medium-run impacts on SMEs' international strategies within the EU are investigated. It may be SMEs that are the winners of this market opening and others that feel rather indifferent.

General economic repercussions

Economic analysis of the benefits of the establishment of the EMU distinguishes static and dynamic effects. Static analysis treats the completion of the internal market essentially as a one-off set of institutional changes, whereas dynamic analysis takes into account the medium- and long-term effects of the Single Market Programme. In general, the static effects may be more important in the early years, but the dynamic effects will take on increasing importance later.[25] These dynamic effects are expected to become important after the introduction of the single currency.

The Cecchini Report[26] as a static analysis estimated that by allowing a more efficient allocation of resources the programme will lead to a one-off rise in EU GDP of about 7 per cent. The direct costs of frontier formalities, and associated costs for the private and public sector before the Single Market Programme, were estimated to be about 1.8 per cent of the value of goods traded within the EU.[27] For several industries, such as the food and beverage industry, construction materials, textiles and clothing, the removal of technical barriers was supposed to lead to cost reductions of about 1 to 2 per cent.

Other consequences expected through the establishment of the EMU were a reduction in costs due to a better exploitation of economies of scale associated with the size of production units and enterprises, improved efficiency within enterprises and increased flows of innovation.[28] This static analysis mentioned the increased competition between enterprises within the EU and possible adjustments between industries, without recognising its whole medium- and long-term amplification.

The Cecchini Report neglected some important dynamic effects of the Single Market Programme as they are difficult to explain and to quantify.[29] It is hard to know which changes in the economy and its influences on enterprises are due to 1992 and which are due to the general globalisation of business and competition.[30] Cecchini, who based his estimate on traditional growth theory, assumed that the liberalisation of markets cannot permanently raise the rates of growth of the participating countries. He treated the 'question of how the internal market will alter the level, not the rate of growth, of output'.[31]

Baldwin[32] stated that the largest gains of the establishment of the EMU would not come from a one-time increase in income due to a reallocation of resources, but rather from dynamic effects. These expected dynamic effects were a higher growth of output, and increases in investment, productivity and innovation. In addition to the initial static effect, Baldwin predicted a 'medium-run growth bonus'. Higher investments and savings would be provoked through higher gains in efficiency. This growth bonus would increase the long-term growth rate of the EU permanently by 0.2 to 0.9 per cent.[33] But an increase in investments and savings is also furthered by the introduction of the single currency, as flexible exchange rates lead firms to require a higher rate of return on investments.

In contrast, Peck[34] argued that the potential gains of the EMU were overestimated, which was confirmed by an ex-post study of the European Commission in 1996. The main reason for such an overestimation was that the adaptation of economic actors to the regulatory and commercial environment needs time and, while some points of the EMU were implemented in 1995, others will not be implemented until after the year 2000.[35]

On an enterprise level, both short- and medium-run consequences of the Single Market Programme must be taken into consideration. These potential consequences are, however, dependent on each SME's approach towards internationalisation, on the industry and on its initial competitive advantages.

Short-term effects on SMEs

A first short-run impact of the establishment of the EMU on SMEs was expected to be on their costs, which decreased due to the reduction in delay and red tape when exporting goods. In addition, the harmonisation of technical standards facilitated a faster and cheaper handling of international operations within the EU. These costs were believed to add significantly to the firm's transportation and production costs.[36] Although some formalities shifted from customs offices on to the firms and new formalities arose, SMEs have acquired strong incentives and facilities to internationalise within the EU. SMEs were able to follow their customers across the border with less costs than before the Single Market Programme. In addition, it opened possibilities to gain new customers. An increased internationalisation of SMEs, exploiting their firm-specific advantages across the borders, can therefore be expected within the EU.

To get some results of the impact of the Single Market Programme, a 1997 ENSR survey investigated to what extent the harmonisation of technical standards, the abolition of border controls and changes in VAT regulations affected EU enterprises.[37]

Figure 1.2 shows us that the impact of the Single Market Programme becomes stronger with increasing firm size. Medium-sized firms felt strongly affected by the removal of fiscal barriers. One realises that for large firms fiscal barriers were less of a problem, even before 1992. Very small firms felt affected by the abolition of technical barriers, and these

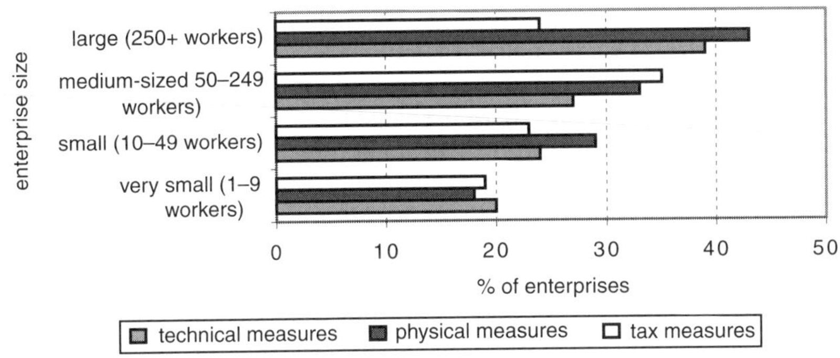

Figure 1.2 The impact of the Single Market Programme on enterprises in the EU by size class in 1997 (%). Source: European Commission (1997), 'The European Observatory for SMEs' (ENSR Enterprise Survey 1997), p. 271.

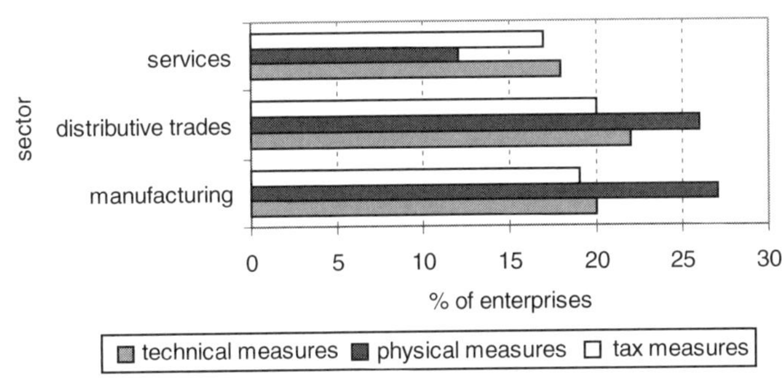

Figure 1.3 The impact of the Single Market Programme on enterprises in the EU by sector in 1997 (%). Source: European Commission (1997), 'The European Observatory for SMEs' (ENSR Enterprise Survey 1997), p. 271.

are generally highly specialised firms with a certain level of R&D. Firms of all size classes strongly felt the removal of physical barriers.

Another investigation (Figure 1.3) shows the impact of the Single Market Programme by sector of activity. Only 38 per cent of firms with twenty to forty-nine employees agreed that the Single Market Programme had successfully eliminated the obstacles to EU trade. In the detergent and cosmetics sector, for example, SMEs had better market access within the EU and 29 per cent of SMEs in the construction sector admitted that the European single market encouraged them to sell abroad.[38] Enterprises in the service sector were affected to a lesser extent than manufacturing and distributive trade enterprises, mainly as a result of the adoption of technical standards. Concerning other measures, the difference between sectors was not substantial.

In a majority of cases a firm that intends to go international wants to exploit its firm-specific or competitive advantage(s) in another country. The reduction of NTBs permitted a larger market access and the opportunity to benefit efficiently from the exploitation of a competitive advantage abroad. STRATEGOR[39] argued that a firm's competitive advantages, such as its core competencies (technological, industrial, organisational and managerial), are essential for its internationalisation process. In reality, the perceived competitive advantage of a firm can change during its internationalisation process. Jarillo and Martinez[40] investigated a sample of Spanish SMEs three years after the Spanish entry into the EU and during the time when the Single Market Programme was being implemented. They found out that costs of production were declining as a competitive advantage, whereas superior technology, style and design had gained importance.[41]

Even if some aspects of the Single Market Programme, such as the removal of border controls and the harmonisation of technical standards, permitted SMEs to exploit better their competitive advantages, some problems remained. In 1998, major problems regarding the adoption of the Single Market Programme still persisted in the areas of company law and corporate taxation. There is an absence of a common system of EU-wide consolidation of losses within groups, an unequal tax treatment of permanent establishments compared to domestic firms, and the persistence of withholding taxes on interest and royalty payments within groups of firms as well as for inter-firm dividends.

Despite these environmental changes that reduced transaction costs for certain EU firms, one should not neglect the reasons why the majority of SMEs internationalise in reality. In practice, around 40 per cent of first moves abroad are estimated to be unplanned responses to export opportunities.[42] This can take the form of faxes or other offers coming in from abroad. Aerts[43] examined the benefits and pitfalls affecting SMEs in Belgium that became international, and found that 93 per cent of the firms in the sample had an order from abroad. According to Root,[44] the most frequently mentioned reason for going international is the prospect of profit on immediate sales.

Medium-term effects on SMEs

The first medium-term results of the removal of NTBs was an increase in trade volumes by 20–30 per cent in manufacturing products among EU countries.[45] This increase in intra-EU trade due to the removal of NTBs was already predicted by Dunning.[46] He argued that intra- and inter-firm costs are reduced and enable the firms to exploit better the economies of plant specialisation and of vertical and horizontal integration.

The increase in intra-EU trade and trans-border investments brought about a high involvement of SMEs.

Ohlsson[47] pointed out that there are trade-intensifying effects in the former trade-exposed industries, trade-extending effects in industries and service sectors that were earlier sheltered by national policies, and direct factor mobility effects. Industries that suffered a lot from NTBs, such as food, mechanical engineering and chemicals, were especially affected.

The nature of trade flows has changed as the Member States' enterprises specialised increasingly within industrial sectors in certain price-quality ranges.[48] There was no increased sectoral specialisation of Member States concentrating on certain activities due to shifted comparative advantages as initially expected. There was an increasing convergence of industrial structures of the different Member States that differentiated themselves from each other by price-quality market niches. This can be illustrated by the intra-industry trade growth within the EU, which is an indicator of fragmentation. On average, intra-EU trade was about 10 percentage points higher for imports in 1990 than in 1980 and nearly 6 percentage points higher for exports.[49]

The specialisation in certain price-quality niches is very attractive for SMEs because the majority of them are highly specialised in one or two product lines. When a firm finds a niche in its domestic market, this same niche can be available in other countries, especially if this strategy is not hindered by NTBs. Medium-sized enterprises' search for a market niche in an international context is emphasised by Ohlsson, as they felt the strongest pressure to revise their strategy.[50] Also, Buckley and Brooke[51] argued that smaller firms, which would like to avoid competition with larger firms, can use their niche both within the domestic market and internationally when it is perceived that the same niche is available in other countries. In his analysis of SMEs' foreign investment behaviour, Buckley[52] stressed the importance of market niches in explaining their distribution and pattern of foreign activities. Aerts, who analysed the success factors and pitfalls of Belgium SMEs during their internationalisation process, argued that for 71 per cent of them specialisation was the main factor determining their international success.[53]

Through its specialisation on price-quality niches a firm has to configure its value-chain according to the new market structure. Configuration refers to the physical positioning of the value activities.[54] In some cases, therefore, it becomes necessary to change the international entry strategy. The result is an increased specialisation within the value-chain that permits SMEs to capture economies of scale and scope.[55] Baldwin listed three standard sources of economies of scale and their implications for 1992.[56] The first are specialised inputs: a larger market increases efficiency and profitability and therefore leads to a faster introduction of new specialised inputs. The second source of economies of scale is the number of technological spill-overs due to a higher degree of information exchange and informal contacts, maintained by innovators who are geographically dispersed. The third source is a profit-motivated innovation and growth: the potential innovator can spread the R&D costs over more units of output.

SMEs' obligation to specialise further is enforced through their confrontation with increasing competition from new entrants, often larger firms, in their traditional markets. Due to the 1992 market opening, SMEs are forced to make their own strategic decisions on how to counter competition, how to grasp new market opportunities and whether to enter into international cooperation agreements. In order to increase their critical size, SMEs have to follow first-mover advantages and niche strategies may be a means to build them up.[57] Within the 1997 ENSR survey previously mentioned, more than one-third of all respondent enterprises have faced increased foreign competition over the last five years. For about one-quarter of enterprises, foreign competition was not relevant.[58] Figure 1.4 shows that large firms feel international competition more than small firms because most if not all of them are already in several countries, while SMEs are nowhere near this level of internationalisation.

Another important effect of the specialisation in price-quality niches may be the evocation of agglomeration tendencies among enterprises within the EU. In this context, Jovanovic argued that through the Single Market Programme clusters of firms and industries in the EU became more visible.[59] Puga and Venables pointed out that a move towards a free trade area pulls industry into the integrating countries. Input–output linkages between the firms amplify this effect and if trade barriers fall below a certain level, this may lead to agglomeration tendencies.[60]

An increasing integration due to several EU policies makes a spatial reallocation of firms within the EU likely.[61] Major parts of the competition and industrial policy passed from the national to the EU level, which

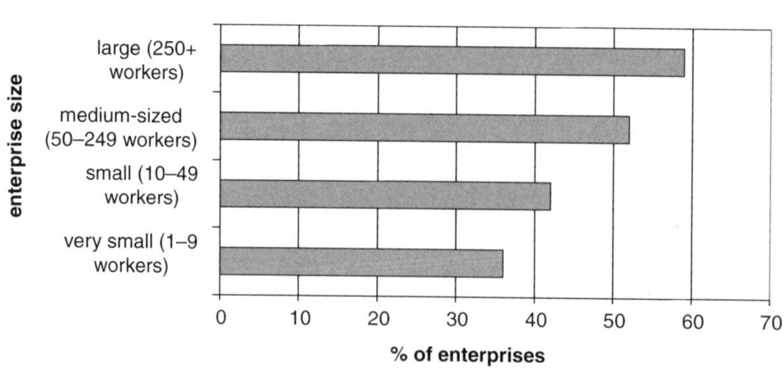

Figure 1.4 Percentage of enterprises with increased foreign competition from 1992 until 1997 (%). Source: European Commission (1997), 'The European Observatory for SMEs' (ENSR Enterprise Survey, 1997), p. 273.

leads to a reallocation of resources within the EU. This was reinforced through important changes in the EU regional policy.[62] The reduction of trade costs through the removal of NTBs and their further reduction through the introduction of the single currency may lead to the concentration of industrial output in distinct locations (similar to the US). Firms within those agglomerations are supposed to increase their critical size due to the enlarged market access.

It is also possible to argue that the abolition of NTBs favours SMEs in particular by emphasising the specialisation within the industries and less-large firms that benefited from the existence of those barriers by reaching strong economies of scale. A long-term consequence will be that internal trade among EU countries will be less intra-industry, but rather more inter-industry.

However, the argument that a firm can gain efficiency through international operations by taking into consideration country-specific comparative advantages[63] was still persistent within the EU in 1998. This means that a country's human capital, natural resources, know-how and technological advantages are still reasons for a firm to change its international strategy. In 1997, the major trends in European location choices were the shift of manufacturing out of Germany and to a lesser extent France, and into the UK, Ireland and occasionally Portugal, together with a new disinclination to invest at all in peripheral regions of the EU, notably Spain and Southern Italy.[64] The UK attracted corporate investment through cheap labour costs, a flexible market structure and incentives. Even if Germany was no longer considered as a manufacturing site of choice because it had become too expensive and inflexible, Southern Germany continued to be successful in attracting R&D investments.

The ENSR enterprise survey previously mentioned investigated the way enterprises perceive the completion of the European Single Market.[65] More than two-thirds of the respondent firms stated that they have been affected by the Single Market Programme. A 'larger selling market' and 'simplified international collaboration' represented major opportunities.

A major threat was 'greater competition'. Less important threats have been 'increased regulation' and 'increased production costs'. Relatively more manufacturing SMEs saw no threats at all, whereas trade enterprises tended to see more threats.

Table 1.1 shows that most firms, large and small, saw more threats than opportunities in the larger and more integrated Single Market. However, medium-sized firms were an exception to the rule.

The single currency: removal of a strong hurdle

The establishment of the EMU shows its main influences from 1999 on with the introduction of the *single currency*.[66] Despite the transition phase from 1999 until 2002, some potential influences on SMEs' international

Table 1.1 Single Market opportunities and threats by size of enterprises in 1997 (percentage of enterprises)

Larger market	*10–49 employees*	*50–249 employees*	*250+ employees*	*Average (total)*
Opportunities seen	28	39	27	16
Competition feared	46	26	49	34

Source: own estimate (based on ENSR Enterprise Survey 1997).

strategies can be previewed, based on existing literature. In addition, it is possible to investigate SMEs' attitude towards the introduction of the single currency as some enterprises had already prepared themselves for the transition period whereas others were rather indifferent.

One can expect that the monetary union could lead to further trade integration between the EU countries due to the elimination of exchange-rate costs. The resulting reduction in transaction costs may further promote intra-European trade.[67] A large part of this increasing intra-European trade is supposed to be among SMEs. Exchange-rate uncertainties inhibit firms from competing on foreign markets. A reduction in this uncertainty will not only promote trade, but also cross-border competition. This increasing competition may be high in industries asking for after-sales service networks.

Firms are able to reallocate resources to producing goods and services that are used for money-changing. In addition, a single currency frees up resources within those firms that are devoted to foreign-exchange hedging linked to intra-EU trade transactions.[68] SMEs can use the liberated money for further specialisation. The previous specialisation through the removal of physical, technical, fiscal and other NTBs therefore becomes reinforced.

The introduction of a single currency does not only influence trade flows between the EU firms, but also their investment decisions. McKinnon[69] stated that flexible exchange rates distort real investment decisions of enterprises. This was confirmed by an empirical study of Molle and Morsink,[70] who investigated intra-European FDI flows. Greater uncertainty, as given in the situation of flexible exchange rates, leads firms to require a higher rate of return on investments. Firms therefore react in a risk-averse manner. Without a single currency, for example, a French firm views an investment in Italy as riskier than a project in France.[71] It can therefore clearly be argued that exchange-rate uncertainty discourages long-term cross-border investments within the EU.

Lefebvre analysed the influences of the introduction of the single currency on an enterprise level. The changeover of national prices into the euro shows its impact on three levels within each enterprise: First of all, the conversion of national currencies into the euro leads to changes in

Table 1.2 Impact of the euro on EU enterprises in 1997

Products and services	*Distribution channel*	*Customers and market*
Entry of new competitors	Coherent management of distribution channels	New market development
New product creation	New (electronic) distribution channels	Increasing pressure on prices by direct customers
Changes in existing products	Control of the distribution channel	Communication in favour of final customers
'European' promotion		Management of disparities between prices
New prices		

Source: Lefebvre, F. (1998), *L'Euro*, p. 201.

prices. Depending on the industry, large currency fluctuations led to high price differences from one EU country to another.[72] These changes in prices influence to a large extent the creation of new products, modifications of existing products and promotion of activities.

An initial problem encountered by the enterprises is the determination of new prices. Indications in euro will lead to an increasing transparency across European countries as they can be compared from one country to another.[73] Due to consumer pressure, a certain price harmonisation will be a consequence across the EU countries.[74] The price harmonisation will be faster and more pronounced for high-technology products as they are relatively similar from one country to another.[75] The resulting intensified competition will increase the pressure to innovate new products or to improve old ones. It is, however, important to note that even before the introduction of the euro, prices across the EU had been converging slowly but constantly in certain industries as a result of deregulation, the removal of formal trade barriers, the harmonisation of regulatory ones, and the reduced ability of manufacturers to influence retailers' prices.[76]

Price transparency within the EU will intensify the firms' tendency to concentrate their ventures in one place within one country or region where they have the most advantages. By doing so, they will be able to reap increased economies of scale due to high volumes. On the other hand, the price transparency also increases the opportunities of supply for enterprises operating within the EU.[77] In some sectors it becomes profitable to replace a national supplier by a foreign EU supplier.

Due to the facilitated circulation of products and services and the reduction of the importing firm's exchange risk, the introduction of the single currency will increase competition between enterprises' distribution channels. A firm that harmonises its distribution channel across the EU countries may obtain lower margins in some countries[78] as it does not entirely eliminate the risk of parallel imports by important customers who buy large volumes.

An interesting distribution opportunity for SMEs is the area of direct sales via the Internet. Electronic distribution channels become attractive due to the increased transparency of the single currency across the EU countries. It is possible to reach new customers and to introduce new products. SMEs which have been active on a local or national level will be able to develop international operations with minimal adaptation (packaging, for example). Due to the larger volume, product profitability will increase. The use of the Internet as a distribution channel depends, however, on the sector of activity and the technological level of the products. For some firms, the Internet offers less security to guarantee the sustainability of the competitive advantage of their high-tech products.

Firms trading and investing throughout the EU may find it attractive to denominate their transactions in the single currency. Simplified internal accounting and reporting becomes possible as all subsidiaries use a single denomination. The consequences, especially for larger decentralised firms, are organisational changes to more centralised units.[79] But outstanding foreign-exchange positions in participating currencies will crystallise the moment that exchange rates are locked. This could lead to profits or losses due to exchange-rate movements between the time when the foreign-exchange position was acquired and the start of the monetary union.

The introduction of the single currency leads to greater depth and liquidity compared to existing national currencies, which is likely to provoke the development of new financial instruments. The enhanced liquidity and availability of new financial instruments could mean lower financing costs for SMEs. Financial instruments that will gain in attractiveness are the EASDAQ[80] market and the French Nouveau Marché[81] (Euro-NM initiative). These markets are for SMEs which need capital to grow, either in greater amounts or at lower costs than banks will provide because of the risk associated with smaller growing companies.[82]

It was primarily the advent of the single market in the securities field on 1 January 1996, with the entry into force of the Investment Services

Table 1.3 Overview of European 'baby bourses' in 1997

	Location	*Market capitalisation ($bn)*	*Number of listed companies*
Alternative Investment Market (AIM)	London	9.3	265
Nouveau Marché	Paris	1.5	22
EASDAQ	Brussels	1.4	7
Neuer Markt	Frankfurt	0.3	2

Source: *The Economist*, 15 March 1997, p. 88.

Directive and the Capital Adequacy Directive, which made possible the creation of new European capital markets for growing internationally oriented SMEs. These directives came into force after the abolition of controls on financial operations and exchanges in 1993 as the Maastricht Treaty previewed the complete liberalisation of capital flows in the EU.

EASDAQ, especially, is destined for fast-growing SMEs with a strong transnational vocation. Based on their growth, their potential profitability and strategic development, SMEs are selected for a quotation. There are only about 500 European SMEs that could take the opportunity of being quoted at EASDAQ. Nevertheless, the experience of NASDAQ in the United States shows that it can take a certain time for a new market to become highly successful. For the French Nouveau Marché, there were about 4,500 European SMEs that were identified as potential candidates for a quotation. EASDAQ and the Nouveau Marché therefore do not enter into competition. However, both became specialised in software, biotech and microelectronics firms.[83]

In reality, SMEs' attitude towards those new finance opportunities is still underdeveloped in Europe compared to the USA. In 1995, about 65 per cent of all European SMEs still used ploughback of profits as a financing method. There were only about 3 per cent that used the form of equity issue.[84] This low percentage of external equity financing may increase with the introduction of the single currency.

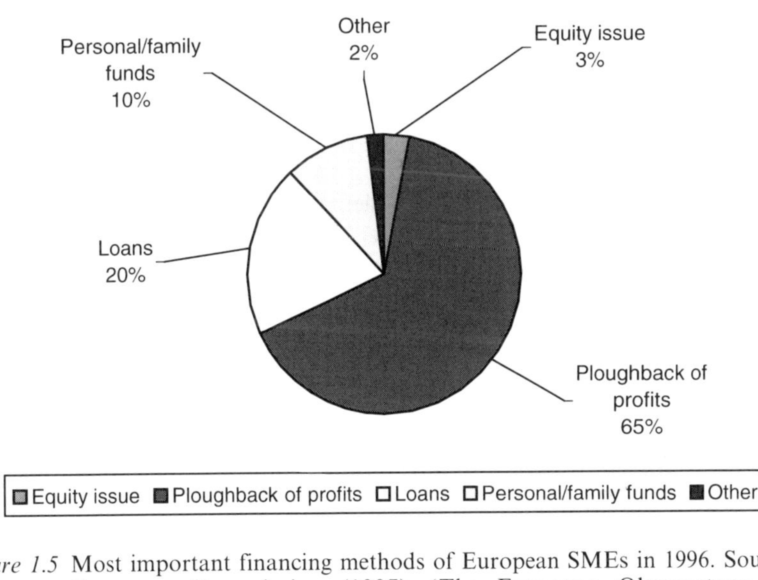

Figure 1.5 Most important financing methods of European SMEs in 1996. Source: European Commission (1997), 'The European Observatory for SMEs' (ENSR Enterprise Survey, 1997), p. 173.

Before firms can reap the described potential advantages of the introduction of the euro, they are confronted with the transition period during which each enterprise has the choice between a once-and-for-all changeover on 1 January 2002 or the use of the euro for some operations between 1999 and 2002.

SMEs face the problem of conversion of their financial systems to an entirely new currency during the transition period. This can be a time-consuming and costly process. A lot of SMEs think that in this context their software systems can be adapted to the use of the euro without any problems. According to a study by Ernst & Young, it needs at least fifteen days of preparation and development and four months for the changeover of all customer statistics, tariffs, prices and stocks.[85] In France, for example, only about one-third of SMEs contacted their computer specialist regarding the changeover before March 1998, and all of these firms were in the North-eastern trans-border region.[86] In addition, one-third of the firms that had not been informed about the conversion rules contacted their computer specialist. According to a study by Price Waterhouse Coopers, many SMEs are convinced that the key date is not 1999, but 2002. The information technology giant IBM conducted a study in 1998 and found an 'alarmingly low level of preparation for the new currency' among SMEs. Out of the 18,000 firms with fewer than 1,000 employees questioned, only 12 per cent had begun their transitional work, with German SMEs lagging well behind their French and Italian counterparts.[87] But once the software systems are changed to match those of suppliers and customers, it will lead to advantages as inter-firm communication will be facilitated.[88]

The problems encountered with such a conversion can be illustrated by the efforts of Daimler, the German multinational. In May 1999, the euro became their official 'house currency'. The changeover cost Daimler about 200 million Deutsche marks. But with the Euro in place, Daimler saves about 100 million Deutsche marks currency-exchange charges every year. Emerging problems are the supplying firms and the customers of the enterprise who have other timetables in switching over to the new currency. Also, paycheques continued to be issued in Deutsche marks until 2002 because of 'Germany's bureaucrats who refuse to accept tax and social security payments in euros'.[89] Compared with SMEs, large corporations are confronted with organisational changes.

The majority of SMEs that operate internationally and on domestic markets will be partial euro users. Most of them have retained their accounts and retail transactions in the national denomination until 2002, whereas they have used the euro for certain activities such as cross-border trade, long-term projects and transactions with TNCs.[90] SMEs, especially those acting as subcontracting firms for larger subcontractors, were urged to go for an early changeover.[91]

With the introduction of the single currency, perhaps the most important hurdle hindering trade within the EU was abolished. Among its multiple effects on firms are the elimination of money-changing transaction costs, improved allocation of EU capital (with the introduction of new financial services), intensified cross-border competitive pressures and a greater output through the reduction and harmonisation of inflation rates. Of the listed effects, only the first may be quantifiable. In 1998/1999, initial results were apparent from the way in which European SMEs tackled the transition period, while other effects could only be estimated based on the literature of currency areas.

The first phase of the Single Market Programme with its removal of NTBs clearly led to decreasing transaction costs within the EU. The reduction in transaction costs led to an enlarged market for firms and in some cases forced them to increase their optimum size. Depending on the sector, increased international flows between the EU firms became unavoidable.

Even if the most cited reason for a firm's internationalisation is the expectation of higher profits through increased sales, there are also other reasons such as the access to or the exploitation of superior technology and business know-how, design, etc. These competitive advantages or core competencies, which have only partially been exploited across the borders prior to 1992, could have been exploited efficiently due to the Single Market Programme. Despite some persisting inconveniences, a lot of SMEs gained through the market opening.

Hypothesis 1: Decreasing NTBs led to increased internationalisation of SMEs within the EU. This increased internationalisation is based on the exploitation of the SMEs' firm-specific competitive advantages rather than their country-specific advantages.

A firm can consider the different possibilities of going international once it is clear regarding the reasons leading to such a decision. A firm's decision to go international is therefore based on serious economic reasoning.

2 SMEs and internationalisation models

Even if each firm has its own reasons why internationalisation may be advantageous to its future, different economists and business scholars have found models to explain the internationalisation process and the existence of TNCs, in the hope of finding some common features. As SMEs involved in trans-border business activities can be considered as small TNCs, a critical presentation of the different models may be interesting.

There are different theoretical approaches to a firm's internationalisation and only the most important models or concepts are described in this chapter. First, authors such as Hymer and Vernon have focused on the structures of market oligopolies and imperfect competition. Second, Coase, Williamson, Buckley, Casson and Rugman considered different types of organisation related to relative costs. Applied to international firms, this signifies the choice between foreign-market serving by integration or not. Third, Dunning's eclectic paradigm explained the existence of a transnational enterprise by considering simultaneously ownership, location and internalisation advantages. The fourth approach, the Uppsala stage model, was less an explanation of international production. It rather explained the process of internationalisation. The fifth approach is derived from business and strategic management literature.

'Classic' internationalisation models

The model of Hymer (1970)

Hymer based his internationalisation model[1] on the theory of the firm. The main idea is that in the early stages of growth a firm increases its domestic-market share steadily by mergers and capacity extension. However, it is possible to increase industrial concentration and market power within the domestic market only to a certain level. At this stage the profits earned by the monopoly (or oligopoly) power in the domestic market are invested abroad.

The model advances two major reasons why firms would move beyond their original national borders. One is buying up another firm or displacing their own plant or parts of the production process. The other is to employ abroad the firm's special advantages, such as skills, entrepreneurship or access to capital. Ownership advantages are emphasised to compensate for disadvantages in competition with domestic firms. But a firm can also export the commodity in which the advantage is embodied, or it could license it to a foreign enterprise. It would, however, prefer FDI rather than licensing to avoid bilateral monopoly situations, technological misappropriation and the costly licensor and licensee relationship.

This 'market-power approach'[2] does not take into account the fact that, measured by their absolute number, most TNCs world-wide and within the EU are SMEs. To become a TNC a firm need not be an oligopolist or a monopolist at home before trying to exercise that power internationally.[3] The Single Market Programme led to stronger competition in the market for differentiated goods and an easy substitution is possible. Therefore, the market-power argument for transnationalisation is weakened. A lot of SMEs are highly specialised in niche products and the precondition of becoming an oligopolist in the home market before going international became obsolete.

The model of Vernon (1966)

The second theory of international production is the *internationalisation model of Vernon*.[4] The model was originally developed to explain US investment in Europe and in countries with relatively low labour costs. It is based on the monopolistic theory of international production.

In adapting to its market the firm moves through different stages according to the development of supply and demand for its product: innovation, maturity and standardisation.

Innovation and production take place in the home country. At first, consumption is weak, but becomes strong if the product enters the phase of maturity. From the first phase on there are exports to less advanced countries. In the phase of maturity, there are followers on the home market producing the same product and also starting to export. The phase of standardisation is first characterised by a production site abroad and exports from the home country. This changes in the later phase of standardisation as there are imports only from the less advanced country to the home country. Production stops entirely at home for cost reasons.

Vernon's product-cycle model emphasises less comparative costs and more location-specific advantages, the timing of innovation and the effects of scale economies. Recognising its shortcomings, Vernon proposed a modified version in 1974.[5] Even after the initial innovation phase, firms

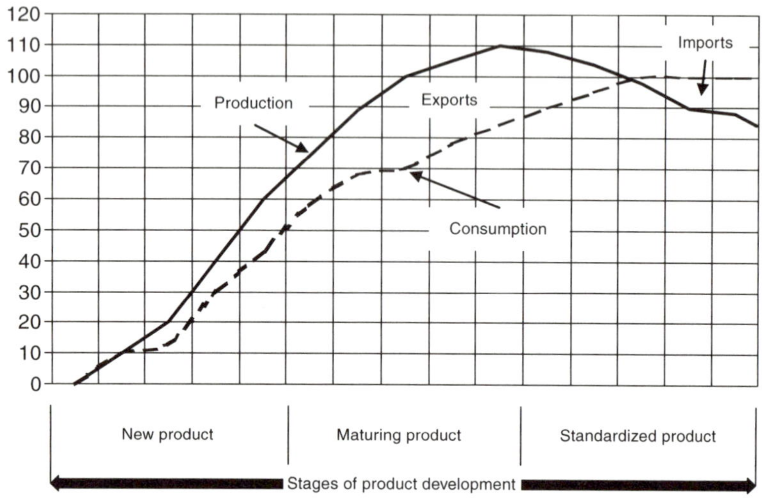

Figure 2.1 United States: product cycle and internationalisation. Source: Vernon, R. (1966), 'International investment and international trade in the product cycle', p. 201.

were able to preserve their position through economies of scale due to technological leadership. Locating the production abroad was seen as a risk-minimising strategy to avoid a price war in a mature oligopoly.

Despite its advantages in integrating supply and demand factors, the model has been overtaken by events as TNCs are now capable of developing, maturing and standardising products almost simultaneously, differentiating the product to suit a variety of needs without significant time-lags.[6]

In addition, a large majority of SMEs locate their foreign affiliates in developed countries. Firms from Western Europe invest especially in other European countries.[7] Vernon's model is of little use within the EMU, which is characterised by an increasing product differentiation and a market which became more homogeneous through the removal of NTBs and a common EU legislation. Traditional location-specific advantages therefore lost their initial importance and firm-specific advantages, neglected by Vernon, became important.

The internalisation theory

The third theory of international production is the internalisation theory, which purports to explain the existence of TNCs in terms of the failure of markets to efficiently transfer intermediate products between independent buyers and sellers located in different countries.[8]

It is based on Coase's[9] criticism of neoclassical economists who introduced transaction costs to measure the exchange between individuals or groups. According to Coase, a firm is likely to emerge, or in other words internalisation may take place, in cases where a short-term contract would be unsatisfactory between the partners on the market.[10] Through one single firm, the costs of negotiating and concluding a separate contract for each exchange transaction which takes place on the market are reduced or eliminated. If transaction costs are high enough, they justify 'the substitution of managed coordination for price-guided coordination'.[11]

The internalisation model claims the existence of both an external and an internal international market. The external international market is the traditional one and contains the following market imperfections imposed by governments: tariffs, quotas and NTBs. The internal international market covers all efforts connected with establishing and maintaining a relationship with a foreign partner.

Authors such as Williamson, Buckley and Casson derived their framework from Coase and considered the choice of different types of organisation in light of relative costs. If the transaction costs of undertaking an exchange through the market outweigh the bureaucratic costs of management within a hierarchy, according to the transaction-cost theory it is more efficient to coordinate everything within a hierarchy.[12] The market will be used if a transaction does not involve a high degree of asset specificity, or if a contract can be designed that diminishes the risk of opportunistic behaviour by the exchange of hostages. By transforming independent agents into employees, they reduce their incentive to cheat.[13] As specific assets have economic rents, a situation of bilateral monopoly is created when two parties engage in a transaction. The internal international market therefore covers all costs of finding an appropriate partner, of negotiating a contract or of opportunism.

The avoidance of the costs of repeated transactions within the marketplace is the primary motivation for internalising transactions. Transaction costs arise through people's inability to analyse everything in advance, through an uncertain business future, through the presence of few players for a given kind of transaction, and through the possibility that some players may be opportunistic. According to Williamson (1985, p. 47), opportunism refers 'to the incomplete or distorted disclosure of information, especially to calculated efforts to mislead, distort, disguise, obfuscate, or otherwise confuse'. But Williamson believes that exchange across markets is a more productive form of cooperation if opportunism is absent.[14] For Coase, opportunism does not offer a 'special' justification for vertical integration as there are a wide range of coordination problems of which opportunism is only one. It is necessary to compare transaction and management costs.[15]

Profits are maximised by an intra-firm trade in intermediate goods and services which eliminates transaction costs, rather than through the exclusion of rivals in the final product market (such as the Hymer model). The structure of the final product market is in the transaction-cost approach of secondary importance.[16]

Even if the model itself remains useful, there are two shortcomings concerning its application. First, a transaction-cost theory of international organisation should deal simultaneously with the costs of conducting market exchange and those effecting exchange within the firm.[17] These internal organisation and coordination costs can often be higher than initially calculated on the basis of market transaction costs.[18] In addition, transaction costs within the local environment are lower than the transaction costs with an 'unknown' firm abroad. Therefore, firms end up with FDI to internalise some of those foreign transaction costs.

Second, the internalisation model does not explain the structure and location of FDI flows, as it neglects ownership-specific and location advantages of FDI in addition to the internalisation possibilities.[19]

For internalisation theorists, ownership-specific and location advantages are considered as given and exogenous. Using the theory of the firm as a basis, they do not stress the interaction between the growth of the firm and possible changes of location. The existence of the transnational firm is explained as a special case by the general theory of the firm.[20] Location advantages, such as cheap labour costs, attractive taxes and special incentives, are still the main reasons for firms to dislocate within the EU. In a survey of 8,000 transnational firms conducted by the European Commission in 1992, 48 per cent of the firms said that taxation was always an important factor in deciding where to locate a production plant.[21]

Ownership-specific advantages are a necessary condition to guarantee a firm's survival *vis-à-vis* its rivals and to increase its market share within an industry. Sometimes, ownership-specific advantages may constitute a barrier to entry. Cantwell (1991: 45) defined ownership-specific advantages as 'advantages which lower the unit costs and raise the profit margins of given firms relative to others in the same industry'. In this context, innovation and the accumulation of technology are important factors enabling a firm to stay in business. This argument holds especially for SMEs that are highly specialised niche producers. To grow on a European and international level at the expense of competitors, strong ownership-specific advantages are necessary. It may be considered as a kind of precondition in order to internalise successfully.

Another argument, limiting the explanation of international activities through the internalisation theory, was the relatively recent development of transnational SMEs. In many cases they became international without an entire integration and control of their activities.[22] In accordance with their ownership or competitive advantage(s) they preferred either to export or to have a contractual agreement.

Dunning's eclectic paradigm of international production

The fourth international theory of production – in fact a combination of the most popular existing theories – is Dunning's eclectic paradigm of FDI, which distinguished three elements of the transaction-cost theory of the transnational enterprise.

- First, there are firm-specific or ownership-specific advantages (such as market access, patents, trademarks, economies of joint supply, international arbitraging) that also include proprietary know-how (unique assets) and transactional advantages. The latter reflect the enterprises' capabilities of economising on transaction costs as a result of the transnational coordination and control of assets. The advantages are therefore of two kinds: first, the privileged possession or access to specific assets, and second, the opportunity and ability to coordinate these assets across national boundaries.[23]
- Second, there are country-specific or location advantages (such as transport costs, production costs, tariff barriers, psychic distance, investment incentives) which state that some benefits are associated with locating certain activities in particular countries. Due to the adaptation to local opportunities it is possible to economise transaction costs provoked by structural market imperfections such as government regulation.[24]
- Third, there are internalisation advantages (such as effective management control, assurances of quality control, avoidance of buyer uncertainty, avoidance of property right infringement), which refer to the relative benefits associated with different entry modes. The advantages and disadvantages of internalisation have been described on pages 28–30.

Jacquemot summarised the eclectic paradigm of Dunning in Table 2.1. The three advantages were related to their respective theories.

Because of transaction costs, some benefits can be reaped only through coordination within the firm, rather than by market coordination. Dunning indicated three transactional market failures: first, the risk and uncertainty firms encounter when they carry out operations abroad; second, by arm's length relationships some external benefits cannot be captured; third, through the direct coordination of interrelated activities economies of scope can emerge.[25]

There is a progressive interaction between the OLI advantages. For example, due to an ownership advantage through an established technology and innovative strength in electronic engineering, a German SME may set up production in France and initiate a new research programme. The firm can gain internalisation advantages through its coordination of R&D activities in Germany and in France which extends its original ownership advantage by innovating in both countries.

Table 2.1 The three main questions and the different existing theories

	Response	*Theory*
Why undertake a direct investment?	Ownership-specific advantages	Market theory and theory of industrial organisation
Where should the plant be?	Location advantages	Theory of international specialisation and theory of capital
How should it be organised?	Internalisation advantages	Management theory and organisation theory

Source: Jacquemot, P. (1990), *La Firme Multinationale: Une Introduction Economique*, p. 123.

Table 2.2 OLI advantages and entry modes

	Ownership advantage	*Internalisation advantage*	*Location advantage*
Direct investment	Yes	Yes	Yes
Export	Yes	Yes	No
Contractual agreement	Yes	No	No

Source: Dunning, J.H. (1988), *Explaining International Production*, p. 28.

According to Dunning, the eclectic paradigm of international production

> embraces the three main vehicles of foreign involvement by enterprises, that is, direct investment, trade and contractual resource transfers, e.g. licensing, technical assistance, management and franchising agreements, and suggests which route of exploitation is likely to be preferred.
>
> (Dunning 1988a: 28)

For further details, see also Table 2.2.

However, the scheme does not explain cooperation forms such as minority and majority participation and common enterprises. The latter can be considered both as direct investments and contractual organisation forms. Mucchielli[26] emphasised this point and argued that technological competition through their accumulation within TNC networks and all forms of inter-firm cooperation are neglected. These inter-firm cooperation agreements are, however, very important instruments for the internationalisation process of SMEs.

Critical approaches also came from authors such as Buckley and Brooke,[27] who criticised the static character of the model. Buckley and

Brooke argued that the relationship between the three advantages and their development over time is unclear.

But Dunning also recognised that the eclectic paradigm does not explain complex strategic alliances:

> while the conceptual and analytical structure of the paradigm remains largely unimpaired its operational usefulness decreases as the complexity of the variables making up the OLI configuration increases. It is one thing, for example, to explain a discrete foreign investment by a rubber type of a tobacco company in terms of fairly specific and readily identifiable ownership, location and internalization advantages; it is quite another to model the extent, pattern and growth of international production of a company like Philips of Eindhoven, which owns 350 wholly or jointly owned subsidiaries, has over 800 strategic alliances, one or other of which involve most of the leading electronics and telecommunication companies in the world, and thousands of licensing or technical servicing agreements with industrial customers and subcontracting arrangements with its suppliers. And this is just one large MNE.
>
> (Dunning 1988a: 342)

To counter those shortcomings, Dunning updated his initial model by adapting it to the new environmental conditions which included the existence of strategic alliances. In this context, he acknowledged that the traditional assumption that the capabilities of the firm are limited to its ownership boundaries and that, outside these boundaries, factors influencing the competitiveness of the firm are exogenous, is no longer acceptable. This holds whenever collaborative agreements with other firms influence the firm's decisions.[28]

Dunning's OLI model found much recognition as it interconnected the three earlier models. Teece,[29] for example, became inspired by the model and pointed out that there are three factors that must be present to explain why a firm is likely to become a multinational and therefore to explain FDI. First, it must have certain special assets which give it a competitive advantage over indigenous firms; second, these assets are more economically utilised in production facilities in parts of the world beyond the firm's domestic market; and third, the best way to obtain value from employing the asset in foreign markets is to transfer the asset internally within the firm to another affiliated business unit.

The models of the following section (pp. 34–39) are different from the preceding ones, as they are used more in business than in economics. But they may be a means to complete the described models or to discover some additional interesting points regarding the internationalisation of SMEs.

'Alternative' internationalisation models

The model of the Uppsala school

The fifth model described is the Uppsala or stage-theory model referring to the process of internationalisation. It is therefore different from the preceding models, which described the existence of the transnational enterprise.

Within the stage-theory model, firms internationalise because other competitors in their national network internationalise. The relationships between the firms are described as a network and the firms in such networks are dependent on each other, so their activities need to be coordinated.

The model originates from the 1970s when Johanson and Wiedersheim-Paul[30] examined the internationalisation process of four multinational Swedish firms. They found that a firm progresses through five stages (see Figure 2.2).

It is further assumed that most obstacles to internationalisation are due to a lack of knowledge and resources. Lack of knowledge due to differences between countries, for example with regard to language and culture, constitutes an important obstacle to decision-making within the development of international operations. Learning about the foreign markets and operations by moving from the position of an 'early starter' to the position of an 'international among others' can reduce these obstacles.[31]

Different authors based their analysis of a firm's internationalisation on the stage-theory model. Unfortunately, the majority of them did not put the model in relation to the EMU.

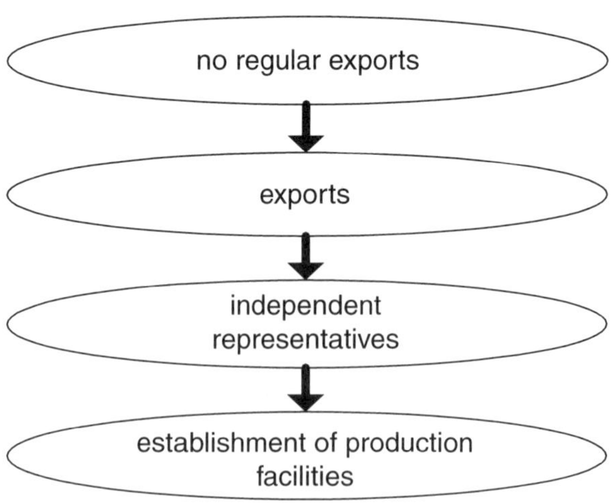

Figure 2.2 Stages model.

Table 2.3 The firm and the industrial system

		degree of internationalisation of the industrial system	
		Low	*High*
degree of internationalisation of the firm	Low	the early starter	the late starter
	High	the lonely international	the international among others

Source: Johanson, J. and Mattsson, L.-G. (1988), 'Internationalization in industrial systems – a network approach', p. 210.

According to Bamberger and Evers,[32] the process of internationalisation of a firm passes through several successive phases, generally starting with exporting. They assumed also that the series of internationalisation strategies is based on effects of learning and experience. The authors delivered some empirical results for eight European countries and concentrated their research especially on the initial phase of exporting.

Buckley[33] obtained similar results by examining the direct investment behaviour of SMEs. He drew out special factors that led to smaller firms influencing FDI, and found that the key constraints were the relationship between firm and market, shortages of capital and management time and the role of uncertainty. He sees exporting as a process that leads finally to FDI. Buckley gave two reasons for following intermediary stages: the first is that each stage allows a learning process to take place and the second is that the unsuccessful firm can drop out at any one of the intermediary stages.

Joynt[34] analysed the international strategy of Norwegian firms by using the stage-model approach and pointed out that learning is the key element in the internationalisation process. Internationalisation is examined according to production methods, sales objectives, organisation structure, market-servicing methods, markets and personnel. He found that, due to their small size, most Norwegian firms follow niche strategies, including on the world market.

Aerts, who examined the internationalisation process of Belgian SMEs, found that 62 per cent of the firms in his sample exported directly to neighbouring countries. In addition, he argued that exporting and importing are still the most common form of international business for SMEs. According to the author, expanding into international markets should be a gradual process.[35]

However, the stage-theory model also gives rise to considerable controversy regarding the applicability of the findings and the theory behind them. In practice, firms jump stages and transfer learning acquired in one market to another market.

Turnbull[36] stated that an 'orderly and progressive sequence' cannot be observed in many cases of internationalisation. He illustrated it empirically by a sample that portrayed the international expansion of British firms in Europe.

Petersen and Pedersen[37] achieved similar results from empirical studies and argued that the propensity to leapfrog is not particularly low among SMEs compared to larger firms. In this context, Zaby[38] criticised the Uppsala School model by pointing out that firms have leapfrogged intermediate stages of the internationalisation process. He emphasised that the internationalisation process cannot be generalised across industries.

In their empirical study on the influence of the Single Market Programme on international strategies of Spanish medium-sized enterprises, Jarillo and Martinez[39] found that half the firms did not follow the stage-theory model. They did not start selling their products to Latin America due to similarities with Spain in terms of culture, education and language. In addition, although Portugal's economic and cultural environment is similar to that of Spain, Spanish firms did not start their international operations in Portugal. Fifteen out of thirty-five firms started their international operations in an advanced stage by setting up sales offices or production subsidiaries at the beginning.

A United Nations survey[40] on small and medium-sized TNCs confirmed these findings. They found that fully 70 per cent of all foreign affiliates established by SMEs had no previous relationship with their parent firm.

A major criticism of the stage-theory model is that it is based on only two empirical studies: the mentioned research of the export behaviour of four Swedish firms and research on Australian firms.[41] But a further criticism could be that the stage-theory model deals with only the early stages of internationalisation. Therefore the model may be of some use for SMEs starting their internationalisation process. There are, however, arguments against this hypothesis. In his empirical analysis Cavusgil[42] found that export experience is not a strong predictor of internationalisation. Despite a greater experience gained over the years, many firms prefer to stay at the experimental level.

Another example of firms that might stay at stage one for a long time are the SMEs that start their international experience as a subcontractor for a foreign firm. They often stay on the export level because of country-specific advantages rather than firm-specific advantages. But if they develop their own firm-specific advantages, they can change their strategy by starting to expand outside. They can do so by finding other clients, then expanding abroad either to produce more cheaply or to follow the market, etc.

Another argument against the model is that the world has become more homogeneous and psychic distance has decreased. This is even more pronounced in the case of the establishment of the EMU, where markets became more homogeneous due to the removal of NTBs. A certain psychic distance is likely to persist between the EU countries, however. There has been a general internationalisation of industries and markets and therefore the lack of market knowledge is no longer a factor limiting the pace and patterns of internationalisation of firms. Petersen and Pedersen[43] pointed out that it seems difficult to justify why accumulation of market knowledge should be the sole explanation of incremental entry-mode behaviour, which is assumed by the Uppsala internationalisation model. By empirical studies among SMEs they found that the increase in sales volume precedes the acquisition of knowledge about foreign markets. In addition, the observed firms did not enter foreign markets in accordance with successively increasing psychic distance.[44]

But one of the strongest shortcomings of the stage-theory model may be that it does not take into account external forms of foreign-market operations such as licensing, subcontracting, franchising, joint ventures, and other strategic alliances. These means of internationally exploiting a firm's competitive advantage gained in importance, especially after the establishment of the enlarged EU market, as described in chapter 1. Therefore, to explain or predict the behaviour of particular TNCs or groups of TNCs, the different models should be supplemented by an appreciation of firm-specific, strategic-related variables. Here the business strategy literature is especially helpful.[45]

Internationalisation strategy in business literature

According to business strategy literature there are two factors a firm has to take into account when developing an international strategy:

- First, the firm has to take into consideration the costs based on the minimum size for efficiency[46] to be able to compete. If the minimum size of efficiency is large compared with the size of the domestic market as a whole, the enterprise may be a TNC since, to stay competitive, it must be large enough to go abroad. Every industry has its minimum efficient scale below which it is difficult to operate because fixed costs become too high.

  In this context a survey by the United Nations[47] found that many small and medium-sized TNCs had a market share of about 30 per cent at home in terms of their primary product and about 15 per cent abroad. The critical size on a national market is soon reached in highly specialised industries such as, for example, the MSE.
- Second, the firm has to investigate the opportunities for product differentiation in different locations to find out where it can compete successfully. If the firm is highly specialised, internationalisation becomes

necessary in order to realise a certain sales volume. This factor is especially important for SMEs following a niche strategy.[48]

Based on these two factors, a firm can decide whether the market is global, European, or if it is possible to follow a local strategy. Decreasing NTBs within the EU led to an increased market access and therefore to an increasing optimum size of SMEs. To stay competitive, they had to go abroad or enlarge their existing international operations.

An internationalised firm has the possibility of weighing the degree of integration of the activities of different units against the localisation of activities of different units.[49] This positioning has two reasons: First, it is dependent on the different industries. The food industry, for example, demands a low degree of integration and a high degree of local responsiveness as tastes vary between the different countries within the EU. Second, governments can press firms to invest locally, to transfer advanced technology or to create employment. These pressures often take the form of NTBs. With respect to these two dimensions, enterprises can adapt a multidomestic, a global or a transnational strategy.[50] The lowering of trade barriers within the EU allows TNCs to capture more economies of scale through a higher level of integration. Firms rationalise manufacturing by specialising in the production of a few items for national consumption and export the rest in Europe. Therefore, Jarillo and Martinez[51] argued that the trend will change from an autonomous to a more receptive strategy.

To complete the two dimensions of integration and localisation, another article by Jarillo and Martinez[52] included the 'externalisation dimension'. The externalisation dimension includes the amount of external resources used through licensing, franchising, strategic alliances, joint ventures and other cooperation agreements. By these means, firms operating on an international level were able to follow the strategy of cost leadership and differentiation. To illustrate their arguments, Jarillo and Martinez described the case of Benetton and McDonalds. Benetton shops are spread all over the world, owned by independent owners who have franchise relationships with the firm. There is a high degree of externalisation and coordination of activities, but a medium degree of localisation. McDonald does manufacture abroad, but the operations are carried out by franchisees.

The exposure of different internationalisation models demonstrated the economic reasoning behind each internationalisation process. The models were analysed empirically by many economists and business scholars to test their reliability. Their positioning has taken place in favour of one of the models or against it. In practice, it is almost impossible to find a general valid model. Each model must be put in the context of the time it was developed. In this sense, one or another aspect of a firm's internationalisation is emphasised. If one takes them altogether they can be considered as complementary rather than substitutes.

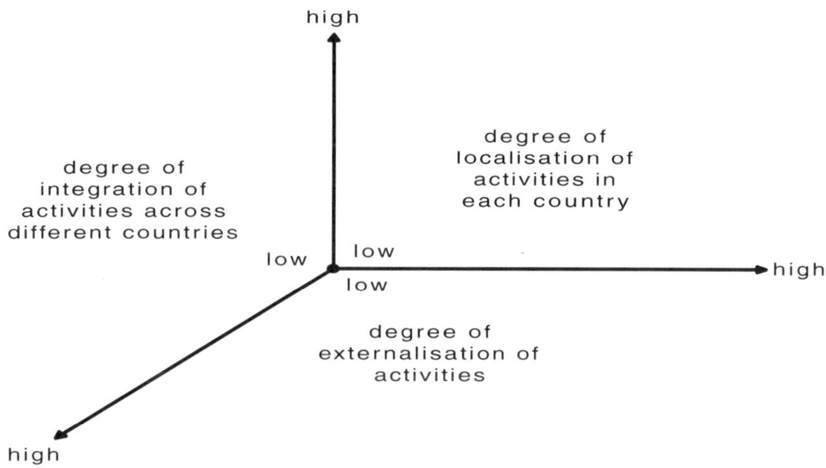

Figure 2.3 The three dimensions. Source: Jarillo, J.C. and Martinez, J.I. (1991), 'The international expansion of Spanish firms: towards an integrative framework for international strategy', p. 296.

To add some missing points to the internationalisation models and to complete potential open questions behind the internationalisation process of firms, an investigation of the different foreign-market entry strategies becomes necessary.

3 The 'right' entry choice within the EMU

The foreign-market entry choice is dependent on country- and firm-specific factors. The removal of NTBs between the EU countries led to an increased internationalisation of SMEs. This may have changed SMEs' foreign-market entry strategies. To investigate potential changes theoretically, major foreign-market entry strategies such as exporting, FDI and contractual agreements are related to the removal of NTBs. Some foreign-market entry strategies may have proved more convenient for the exploitation of firm-specific advantages than others.

Before analysing exporting strategies versus FDI and cooperative forms of going international, it is helpful to look at the main internationalisation strategies:

- First, a firm can export by producing at its home-base location. Exporting is separated from other ways of foreign-market servicing by the location factor as most of the value-adding activities take place in the home market. Associated risks are low because little capital is involved compared to other market entry strategies.[1]

  There are different export modes or channels a firm can choose, such as exporting through domestic intermediaries, called indirect exporting, or direct exporting by a foreign agent or distributor channel. When choosing the direct-export channel, managers need to make decisions on the channel performance specifications, the channel type and the channel members. The choice of an agent or distributor involves the drawing up of his profile, locating prospects, evaluating prospects and finally his choice.
- Second, a firm can enter a trans-border cooperation agreement with one or more firms abroad. Cooperation agreements, such as licensing, franchising, subcontracting and other alliances, are an important means to internationalise. SMEs, often characterised by shortages in capital, management time and human resources, can go international without losing their independence as in the case of a merger.
- Third, a firm can produce through a foreign subsidiary for local sale and exports. FDI is a management- and capital-intensive activity

as moving involves risks. However, many SMEs are confronted with limited financial and human resources and little international experience.

Exporting or FDI

FDI requires the freedom of establishment and national treatment in foreign markets. Compared to exports there is no FDI in perfectly competitive markets as its existence is explained by market imperfections. These market imperfections include the avoidance of tariffs and NTBs, the integration of operations at different locations, economies of scale, externalities, market presence, expected profits and differences in taxation.[2]

If the potential small and medium-sized TNC wants to choose the cost-minimising way to serve a foreign market, it has to take into consideration all the factors favouring one or the other way of going international. When deciding between FDI and exporting, a firm must take into account the following factors:

- location factors of a potential foreign market
- possible internalisation advantages
- firm-specific factors.

Location factors

Location factors or advantages especially include foreign country factors, but also home country factors, both of them having an economic, political and socio-cultural character.[3]

One important target-country factor is the present size of the target-country market as relatively small markets favour exporting and large markets favour FDI. Through the internal market, however, small European countries lost this disadvantage. The Netherlands and Belgium, for example, became attractive places for FDI.

Another factor is the competitive situation in the target market. An atomistic market may be served best through exports and an oligopolistic one through FDI as it enables firms to compete better against dominant rivals. This factor is strongly dependent on the industry where the firm operates. The food and drink industry is a good example of an atomistic market.

Target-country environmental factors, such as restrictive government policies and regulations, discourage exporting. An example may be the Japanese response to European import restrictions on cars as they started to produce them in the EU. Within the EU, the implementation of the Treaty of Rome eliminated tariffs and quotas on internal trade in 1968. The Single Market Programme abolished most NTBs.

Also, Dunning[4] argued that the relative size and growth of the foreign market, the relative costs of supplying this foreign market through imports or local production and the relative advantage of establishing a local production or licensing influenced FDI. He named it 'import-substituting investment' as it seeks new markets, but replaces trade. In this sense, the establishment of the EMU was supposed to lead to decreasing intra-EU imports, substituting investments and increasing trade as market imperfections sloped down. A condition was, however, that the existence of NTBs induced FDI.

Target-country production factors influence the location of a firm to a large extent. These factors include the availability and costs of natural resources and labour in the foreign market, its transport costs and general economic climate. Dunning[5] named the FDI induced by these factors 'resource and efficiency based'. Hennart (1991: 85), stated that the decision to export or to locate a foreign production abroad is 'based on a comparison of delivered costs and is a function of the relative production costs of a domestic and foreign location, of transport costs and of tariff and non-tariff barriers to trade'.

Low production costs in the target country favour FDI and discourage exports. In addition to the quality, quantity and costs of the input factors, the quality and cost of the economic infrastructure plays a role.

Labour costs are still different in the EU countries, which encourages a firm to invest where labour is less expensive or where labour laws are less strict. Portugal, Spain and the UK, for example, are very attractive regarding labour costs and the UK is well known for its friendly labour laws.

When deciding between FDI and exporting, transport costs may play a role. This point, however, is strongly dependent on the character of the product. Highly differentiated products can absorb higher unit transportation costs and still remain competitive in a foreign market.[6] Therefore niche producers may use exporting more often than firms that produce standardised products. Transport costs are less important in the case of after-sales services as they demand a high proximity to the customer and sometimes some local adaptation. In this case a FDI may be the preferred mode (examples can be found in computer services, banking, etc.).

Other target-country factors relevant to a firm's decision between FDI and exporting may be the geographical and cultural distance between the home country and abroad. Some geographical distance may make it impossible for a firm to compete against local firms abroad because of high transport costs. Other problems are different cultural values, language, social structure and ways of life.[7] Molle and Morsink[8] investigated FDI and trade within the EU and found that physical and cultural distance constitute a barrier for FDI as each country within the EU is characterised by a different history, customs and laws.

In addition to these target-country factors, home-country factors such as the home market's competitive structure, the production costs and special governmental incentives have to be taken into consideration when choosing between FDI and exporting. Low production costs at home and special subsidies, for example, may favour exporting.

Internalisation factors

Internalisation factors or advantages are essential factors in a firm's decision between exporting and FDI as transaction costs may be reduced through horizontal or vertical integration.

First, benefits from internalisation arise through gains in time because bypassing the market involves higher coordination efforts.[9] These coordination costs may be even higher in cases of geographical and cultural distance between the cooperation partners. A firm located in Italy has different working conditions from a firm in Germany, because each firm's business culture reflects to a large extent the culture of the firm's country.

Second, transfer pricing between the integrated parties permits it to capture benefits as nominal prices can be altered without affecting revenues. A TNC can manipulate prices of intra-corporate transactions such as royalty payments and inter-affiliate goods movements by moving tax profits to low-tax countries and reporting higher profits in such countries. TNCs also use transfer-pricing to control and evaluate the performance of the firm.[10] As there is still a lack of tax harmonisation within the EU, TNCs can profit from the different national systems.

Third, buyer uncertainty can be eliminated when buyer and seller are part of the same organisation. This buyer uncertainty may be especially high in the case of technological knowledge owned by one of the participating firms. Other cases of buyer uncertainty are quality control and the long-term functioning of the distribution system. A lot of firms exposed to this situation prefer forward integration, rather than passing through an arm's length transaction.[11]

Fourth, by internalisation a firm can avoid being the victim of a cartel and/or a monopoly.[12] Stigler's classical argument deals with firms which want to integrate backward in order to negate the cartel prices.

Fifth, joint production in marketing and manufacturing permits gaining economies of scale and scope.[13] This depends, however, on the ease with which intermediate or final products can be traded internationally.[14]

As the Single Market Programme led to a removal of border stoppages and harmonisation of technical standards, trade of intermediate and final products was facilitated within the EU. Industries where NTBs were high, such as food, chemicals, office equipment, motor vehicles, mechanical and electrical engineering, felt this facilitation strongly.[15]

High transaction costs are not a sufficient condition for the existence of TNCs as the internalisation of market failures can lead to higher internal organisation costs than by an arm's length relationship. A firm has to consider both the costs that emerge when conducting market exchanges and the internal organisation costs. According to Buckley and Casson (1979: 3), the optimum size of a firm is reached 'where the costs and benefits of further internalisation are equalised at the margin'.

Very often vertical integration is seen as a means to capture the margins of the suppliers or the distributors without taking into account the profitability.[16] Profitability is not only a question of margins but also one of investment, which is necessary if a firm integrates vertically. Often a supplier is more cost-effective than an internal corporate division and profitable parts of the firm end up subsidising inefficient ones. According to Jarillo, these considerations are especially relevant for SMEs as they have limited resources and need to specialise in a specific asset of the business. Integration would cause them to lose their flexibility and their specialisation which are their best competitive weapons.[17]

Another problem for one single organisation is that of increased communication costs. Contrary to the internal market, the external market is characterised by an information exchange in prices and quantity. Internal exchanges, however, demand formal and informal communication. Formal mechanisms include formalisation by a contract, standard routines, the planning process and control. Less formal communication relates to the development of a common organisation culture based on socialisation and the communication of values and objectives to individuals.[18] These informal communication mechanisms are extremely important as internalisation reduces the individual's incentive to exert initiative and effort.[19]

By the use of an arm's length relationship the agent's effort is constrained by a price system that is proportional to the output. The internalised firm has to replace the price system of the external market through behavioural constraints in the organisation. In this context, Hennart[20] stated that internalisation takes place if the transaction costs of the market for goods and services are higher than those of labour.

Also, one single organisation does not always reduce opportunistic behaviour. Despite managerial solutions to the problem of coordination there are situations where internalisation is not better than an arms' length relationship.[21]

Firm-specific factors

Firm-specific factors or a firm's proprietary assets may represent a certain knowledge of how to produce a cheaper or better product at given input prices, or how to produce a given product at a lower cost than competing firms.[22] These advantages could be a firm's special skills regarding technology, management, promotion or something else that differentiates it from its competitors. For STRATEGOR,[23] these firm-specific factors consist of 'costs' such as economies of scale, the experience curve, decreasing transport costs and cost differences between countries. The advantage may vary strongly in tangibility and specificity. It can emerge in the form of a firm-specific know-how or as a patent.

Compared to exports, FDI allows the transfer of a firm's managerial, technical, marketing, financial and other skills to a target country under the firm's own control.[24] By this means the firm is able to exploit fully its competitive advantages abroad and to keep entire control over its intangible assets. Firms that would like to serve a foreign market with technology-intensive products, for example, may instead consider FDI (or licensing/franchising/subcontracting) as a foreign-market entry mode. Measured with the horizon of a firm's investment decision, these competitive advantages are medium- to long-term. FDI might even improve these advantages.

A firm that exports is not able to profit entirely from its competitive advantage abroad. By using indirect exporting, it has no influence on its marketing activities abroad. Even if it may be a cheap means to serve a foreign market, the firm does not learn anything as it insulates the manufacturer from the foreign market. Direct exporting, however, has higher start-up costs, greater information requirements and a higher risk as it links a domestic firm through a chain of marketing agencies to the final customer.[25] The control over firm-specific advantages is higher than in the case of indirect exporting.

Firm-specific advantages become important relative to location and internalisation advantages at a time when they are no longer limited within the boundaries of the firm.[26] Decreasing NTBs within the EU changed the attractiveness of locations and firms are now able to exploit these firm-specific advantages to a larger extent. Export activities or other contractual agreements are preferred means to export these firm-specific advantages to other countries because of reduced market failures. This preference is particularly strong if the existence of NTBs induces FDI activities.

But FDI and exporting are no substitutes for most firms as they are complementary international strategies. Molle and Morsink[27] investigated FDI and trade flows within the EU (and to and from third countries) and emphasised their complementarity. Sleuwagen confirmed this[28] by examining the FDI behaviour of Belgium firms in the EU. He stated that in most cases subsidiaries are started by acquisitions which receive heavy imports through their parent companies. The principal role of those subsidiaries is to serve as a marketing arm for their parents.

Besides the choice between FDI and exporting, both of which are strongly dependent on SMEs' financial resources, contractual agreements are alternative and attractive ways to internationalise. In the following section cooperation agreements are investigated by describing their advantages and disadvantages. Licensing agreements as a particular form of cooperation are analysed in more detail. Contractual agreements are emphasised as there are increasing tendencies to use these forms of internationalising SMEs' competitive advantages.

SME cooperation strategies

The restructuring of industries is a basic theme in analysing the strategic effects of the EMU. The consequences are increased competition, increased importance of scale-economic advantages and higher levels of innovation. Besides mergers and acquisitions, called 'hard' restructuring, to increase scale economies, the restructuring can also be reached through different types of cooperation agreements, called 'soft' restructuring.[29] SME cross-border cooperation agreements are a relatively recent phenomenon, but have gained increasing importance.

Reasons for the increasing conclusion of such cross-border, inter-firm agreements are the faster technological innovation, shorter product-development times and flexible manufacturing techniques. The objective is to reach the critical mass of resources for remaining competitive. Official data confirmed that from 1990 to 1995 the number of cross-border, inter-firm agreements increased world-wide from about 1,760 to about 4,600 (apart from strategic R&D partnerships). EU firms participated in 40 per cent of them, Japanese firms in 38 per cent and US firms in 80 per cent.[30]

Cooperation agreements are attractive if the performance of an activity with a partner is higher than performing it within one organisation or through an arm's length transaction. They can range from pure market relationships through traditional links between firms to complex groups and alliances that represent a fully and formally developed cooperation.[31] Moss Kanter[32] distinguished 'mutual service consortia', where similar firms in similar industries pool their resources to gain a higher benefit than they are able to do separately; joint ventures, where the partners need complementary skills to each other (technology with market access for example); and 'value-chain partnerships', where firms in different industries, but complementary in their skills, join their forces to create value (supplier–customer relationships for example). Commitment by the firms involved is high as changes and joint activities take place in many functions of the organisation. A disadvantage is that operations often overlap.

Mariti and Smiley[33] defined cooperation agreements as long-term, explicit and between two or more firms. A one-time purchase of goods and services is not a cooperative agreement. Cooperative agreements are voluntary, cooperative efforts to create or maximise the joint value of the participating firms.

A cooperation agreement requires that each partner contributes to it and receives benefits that exceed those of alternative forms.[34] Cooperation agreements may capture different kinds of benefits:

- First, there may be economies of scale by pooling the volume of one activity. This also leads to higher economies of learning compared to the situation if each firm operates separately.[35]
- Second, benefits through cooperation agreements emerge by acquiring, selling or pooling the access to a certain knowledge or ability of another firm. This may consist of a special know-how or technology, of an attractive distribution channel or of capital. Advantages are the reduction of costs and time that would be necessary to achieve the necessary competence in the activity on their own.[36]

  Within those cooperative ventures one partner provides upstream competencies, such as R&D, manufacturing, etc., while the other contributes with its downstream resources, such as distribution channels, marketing and service activities. By joining their forces it may be possible to avoid expensive duplication of effort.[37] Gammelsaeter and Guvag[38] argued that for SMEs the alliance with an international partner is seen as a way of bringing in expansion capital and acquiring access to international markets. They also emphasised the importance of mutual learning within those partnerships.

  Cooperative agreements, leading to similar kinds of benefits, are favoured by special EU support measures. European cross-border cooperation in research and technological development encourages SME participation to increase their specialisation, their technological externalities and to decrease their costs.[39] These programmes are a consequence of the Single Market Programme as initially stated by the 1987 European Commission White Paper, stressing the importance of SMEs for the economic development of the EU.
- Third, cooperation agreements permit the firm to spread its risk among the different partners.[40] The risk-spreading argument is especially important in industries that are capital and investment intensive.

  SMEs, which are often characterised by a lack of financial resources and international experience, can overcome these shortcomings for a potential internationalisation by spreading the risk among different partners. In addition, the conclusion of a cooperation agreement permits them to preserve their independence.
- Fourth, with the conclusion of a cooperation agreement some influence on the behaviour of a competitor becomes possible.[41] It may be a means to influence its technological development and its cost and price structure. This argument holds, however, only in the case of strategic alliances which are concluded between competing firms.[42]
- Fifth, the competitive position of SMEs that participate within a cooperation agreement can be improved. Potential long-term arrangements

among firms allow them to 'gain or sustain competitive advantage vis-à-vis their competitors outside the network'.[43] Duijnhouwer examined the advantages of such SME business relationships in eight European countries and found that the firms improved their competitive position as a result of entering into such relationships.[44] The SMEs performed better in terms of employment and turnover than their colleagues who had not entered into such agreements.

For a firm, cooperation agreements also involve costs that must be offset against the benefits:

- First, there are the costs of selecting an appropriate partner(s). Bronder and Pritzl and Moss Kanter emphasised this partner selection process.[45] The participating firms have to know their own firm and their industry well. There should be a good personal rapport between the executives of the firms and there should be a certain compatibility between their historical and philosophical background, common experiences, values, principles and hopes for the future. Differing cultures, nationalities and languages render the partner selection process difficult.[46]

  As SMEs suffer from shortages in management time, money and international experience, the screening of a potential foreign partner is difficult compared to a large firm. Special EU support measures promote cross-border cooperation agreements among SMEs. Programmes such as 'Business Cooperation Network (BC-NET)', 'Business Communication Centre (BCC)', 'Europartenariat' and 'Euro-Info-Centres (EIC)'[47] facilitate the partner selection process.
- Second, there are the costs of coordinating the cooperation agreement as it is expensive in time and money.[48] Coordination costs may be less if there is a high degree of similarity between the cooperation partners. However, coordination costs depend strongly on the activity where the cooperation takes place. A standardised product needs less interaction between the partners than the creation of common knowledge in a research centre.

  Also, the number of participating partners can affect coordination costs.[49] If the number of partners in a cooperation agreement is growing, the whole organisation must be restructured and the means of coordination must be increased. The role that each partner plays in a cooperation agreement reflects not only the legal form of the cooperation agreement, but also the quantity and similarity of skills and resources that each partner brings into the alliance.
- Third, cooperation agreements may evoke the risk of creating a competitor through the transfer of expertise or market access to a cooperation partner.[50] This is a high risk for SMEs that are often highly specialised in one or two product lines. Cooperation agreements between competitors with similar core businesses, with similar skills

and covering the same markets risk failing as one partner tries to compete with the other.

In this sense, Bleeke and Ernst[51] emphasised cooperation agreements between complementary equals. These cooperation agreements are long-term and based on real cooperation in which both partners trust in the maximisation of each other's qualities. Within the EU, however, only 16 per cent of the alliances can be considered as complementary.[52] Siecor, for example, an independent joint venture between Siemens and Corning, has been in existence for more than twenty-one years and brings together complementary skills in telecommunications and glass technology to become specialised in the fiber-optic-cable business.

Also, Gomes-Casseres[53] emphasised that cooperation agreements work best when the participating firms complement one another. Related to the dimension of specialisation or diversification, one possibility of cooperation can be that a SME specialises with respect to its product range and looks for partners with a complementary product line.[54]

Despite these findings, some authors, such as Lorenzoni and Baden-Fuller or Hamel *et al.*,[55] pointed out that a certain competition or rivalry in cooperation agreements leads to higher outcomes for the cooperation partners. Hamel *et al.* pointed out that one condition for such a successful rivalry is that the size and the market power of the partners should be modest compared with industry leaders. An example is the Italian packaging machinery sector, where producers borrow the design of a new machine from specialist designers. SME partners improve the prototype afterwards in a unique way and the focal firm repurchases and exploits the new design by licensing it to producers for the final development and marketing phase. For the final phase, national or international producers are involved.

- Fourth, another cost factor in cooperation agreements is the resource generation and distribution issue.[56] From the beginning, the partners can demonstrate their stakes in the relationship and each other by investing in each other. These constitute a tangible sign in long-term commitment.[57]

Benefits have to be divided among the cooperation partners. These are not always easy to calculate, especially regarding intangible assets. Therefore a cooperation contract has to clearly expose all questions surrounding resource generation and distribution.

The 1997 ENSR enterprise survey previously mentioned examined transnational SME cooperation related to the opportunities offered by the European Single Market.[58] SMEs working together with a foreign partner mention a larger selling market as a major opportunity (27 per cent compared with 10 per cent of those not working together with a foreign partner). In addition, SMEs working together with a foreign partner are

Table 3.1 Transnational cooperation related to opportunities offered by the European Single Market as perceived by entrepreneurs in 1997

	Working together with a foreign partner	
Opportunities	*Yes*	*No*
Larger selling market	27%	10%
Simplified collaboration with international enterprises	29%	10%
Lower production costs	11%	6%
Other opportunities	24%	12%
No opportunity	30%	59%

Source: European Commission (1997), 'The European Observatory for SMEs', p. 114.

more aware of other opportunities arising from the Single Market Programme (24 per cent compared with 12 per cent of those not working together with a foreign partner). Lower production costs and a simplified collaboration with international enterprises are also important opportunities for SMEs working together with a foreign partner. 30 per cent of the SMEs working together with a foreign partner perceive no opportunity at all and this figure rises to 59 per cent in the case of those SMEs not working together with a foreign partner. Therefore, it is obvious that SMEs with a foreign cooperation partner are more aware of the opportunities and threats of the Single Market Programme.

Even if FDI and exporting are still important means of internationalisation, formal and informal cooperation agreements have become attractive. For SMEs, these agreements are an intermediary form enabling them to benefit from their competitive advantages abroad or to gain new ones due to their cooperation with an appropriate partner.

A special form of cooperation agreements is licensing. Through the illustration of this cooperation form, problems with patents can be analysed as licensing agreements are connected in a majority of cases with a patent. For highly specialised SMEs, investing a lot of money in the development of new and sophisticated products, patents provide some protection for the national and international exploitation of their competitive advantage.

The example of licensing[59]

Licensing combines the technology and skills of the licensing firm and the local knowledge of the licensee.[60] Licensing may be useful to extend the life of an idea or technology and to reach small or difficult markets. A major advantage of licensing is that it is a means of limiting the need for capital and exposure to risk where local manufacture is required.[61] To the client it offers a ready-made business for which the learning curve with its attendant costs is much less than for the normal process of developing a business. The aspect of low commitment is especially attractive to SMEs.

Licensing would always be more attractive than FDI if the licensor could extract the licensee's entire rent,[62] but this is not feasible in reality. One can consider licensing and FDI as alternatives and the choice of one or the other mode is dependent on the following factors:

- First, a licensing agreement is preferred to a FDI if the rents to an intangible asset are short-lived. This happens in cases where the industry's technology changes often. In this context, Telesio[63] found that licensing agreements increase even more with the importance of R&D than FDI does.
- Second, licensing may be chosen if the licensor lacks some assets that are needed for FDI. These assets can be necessary human resources, management skills, capital or international experience. For this reason licensing may be a preferred entry mode for SMEs as they often lack the assets necessary for FDI.[64]
- Third, the question of risk may affect the choice between FDI and licensing. The licensor has little control over the marketing policies of the licensee and there is the possibility of an opportunity cost where the licensee does not exploit the market fully.[65] But, on the other hand, the licensor does not expose a large amount of fixed assets as in the case of a FDI, which reduces its risk.

  Another risk may be that a licensor's technological advantage is in the hands of a licensee who is a future competitor. In this case exporting should be favoured to licensing so that core technologies can be protected.[66] The loss of control over a firm's technological knowledge and its foreign exploitation is accentuated for the smaller firm which has limited capacity to develop marketing activities on a broad scale.[67]
- Fourth, a licensing agreement should be avoided if it is too costly to arrange. These costs include the determination of the licensee's profile, sourcing the licensce's prospects, evaluation and comparison of the licensee's prospects and finally the selection of the most appropriate licensee candidate. Average licensee negotiations last six months to one year.[68] Once negotiated, its main difficulties lie in the costs of maintaining the contractual arrangement. These transaction costs focus on the identification of the advantage, policing costs and the danger of creating a competitor. Within the EU, negotiations between nationals of the different countries are exposed to all the perils of cross-cultural communication.

Welch[69] tried to quantify the costs of licensing and by doing so captured the importance of transaction costs. He investigated the role of patents, know-how and other forms of proprietary knowledge and the difficulties of firms in appropriating benefits from the international exploitation of those technological advantages. The SMEs of the sample appeared to enter licensing as a separate internationalisation strategy rather than as an element of a foreign investment strategy. International experience in its various forms had a positive effect on licensing through the development of relevant skills and knowledge which enhanced the process of risk reduction.

A firm can only use licensing to enter a foreign market if it can secure the legal protection of its industrial property rights in the target country. Otherwise it must keep its patentable knowledge as a trade secret.[70] By keeping a patent as a trade secret a firm acquires protection against potential imitators, but also prevents its use by potential buyers. A patent system, established by the public authorities, gives the owner of the knowledge a monopoly in its use and therefore leads to increasing efficiency in the market of knowledge.[71] Without suitable protection the owner of an invention tries to exploit it himself by internalising the market. The length of a patent grant and the level of penalties for possible infringements are factors on which the number of licensing agreements depend.

Within the EU industrial property rights are guaranteed. The European Patent Convention came into force in 1977 for the countries of the European Economic Community, Switzerland and Sweden. Patent applications are administered by the European Patent Office, located in Munich. If search and examination procedures are satisfactory, the patent is published in the European Patent Bulletin eighteen months after the date of application. The public has nine months to file an opposition. After this time a patent is issued which is effective in all the member countries for twenty years from the filing date.[72]

The number of patent applications has increased from 10,000 in 1980 to 25,000 in 1990. The highest share (about 47 per cent in 1990) refers to inventors located in Germany, followed by France (19 per cent) and the United Kingdom (14 per cent).[73]

Despite the existing laws, SMEs are anxious about losing their competitive advantage to a potential competitor. A small firm tends to be more susceptible to dependence on the licensee and its only form of control is the one which it is able to build into the licensing agreement. The licensing agreement has to cover territorial rights, performance requirements and the settlement of potential disputes.

In addition, smaller firms rarely protect their products and innovations even in cases where these are remarkable technological improvements. Among the reasons for this are the expenses and the time required for the patenting process. Also, protection through marketing activities is often considered too expensive.[74]

The number of licensing agreements varies across countries and industries. In the UK year, for example, the share of licensed sales in total foreign production was only 5 per cent in the textile, leather, clothing and footwear industry, 21.5 per cent in mechanical and instrument engineering, but 71.1 per cent in the shipbuilding industry.[75]

As with licensing agreements, one can also classify subcontracting under cooperative forms. There may be some additional insights, however, as SMEs use this form not only nationally and internationally, but also on a local level. In this sense, the following section on subcontracting provides the connection between cooperation agreements and the mechanisms of location, described in chapter 4, where the functioning and the effects of SME agglomerations are analysed.

Subcontracting:[76] a strategy favoured by SMEs

Subcontracting is usually visualised as a pyramidal model based on cooperation among parties at several levels, each of which is responsible for the completion of an assembly, a sub-assembly, a part or a component of the finished product.[77]

In most sectors of industrial activity, from the traditional ones such as textiles and automobiles to the high technology industries such as telecommunications, subcontracting to SMEs and also subcontracting by SMEs became a reality. Subcontracting allows prime contractors to focus and specialise in those activities that are crucial to the performance of their firms. But also the vast network of supplying firms can become highly specialised and increase their competitive stance. The importance of these networks has been demonstrated in many countries, as described by Porter.[78]

Subcontracting firms are increasingly becoming an important consideration in prime contractors' decisions regarding where to locate, and the subcontracting firms have to continuously develop a wide range of capabilities in response to the demand for better quality, flexibility, price and delivery times.[79] In addition to the national and international level, SME subcontracting is used on a local level. Even if its major characteristics resemble those of other contractual forms, some additional findings have to be taken into consideration:

A first advantage may be that subcontracting offers a way to reduce costs. Thus, a firm can subcontract an activity because it cannot achieve enough volume to do it efficiently in-house or because the firm is too large to match the costs of smaller operators.[80] The subcontractor can obtain even lower costs by a further specialisation.

Taking the decision to subcontract some activities can be a difficult task for a firm. The problem is to find the critical size beyond which costs are going up. This critical size is not only industry-dependent, but is also dependent on the activity of the value-chain. The opportunity of reducing costs by means of subcontracting can be attractive in the case of production and service activities. Service activities may consist of distribution and after-sales service or of internal administrative costs.[81]

A second advantage is to be found in the superior motivation and increased flexibility of a SME subcontractor. In most cases the director of the SME is also the owner, who works within his firm and knows that extra profits are due to his efforts and innovativeness.[82]

A third advantage is the increased specialisation of the subcontracting firm in just one activity of the business system. Due to this specialisation they are able to produce at lower costs, even at the same volume, than an integrated firm. Through the increased specialisation the firms get the opportunity of working with full-capacity utilisation.[83] Economies of scale and, within an agglomeration of SME subcontractors, economies of scope, may result.

This can best be illustrated by SME agglomerations in Northern Italy where the biggest SME (very often the assembler) subcontracts the production to smaller SMEs in his region. There are about sixty-five geographic zones and in each zone SMEs are specialised in one product.[84]

A fourth advantage of subcontracting activities is the development of ideas, with feedback exchanges between subcontractors and subcontracting firms on manufacturing processes, quality and production organisation. In many cases relationships tend to be long-standing and assistance is provided in the case of difficulties between the partners (such as advance payments, extension of credits, etc.).[85]

A fifth advantage is the opportunity for the subcontractor to acquire or learn something new about the technology of the subcontracting firm. However, in cases of technical advances firms often internalise their key processes in order to ensure strict quality control and limit the leakage of valuable technical know-how.[86] Otherwise they risk transferring their competitive advantage to a subcontractor, who then becomes a successful competitor, or the subcontracting firm diffuses the competitive advantage over to competitors.[87]

It is always difficult to exclude opportunistic behaviour within cooperation agreements, as has already been described for licensing agreements. Both parties are involved: the subcontractor can become a competitor of the subcontracting firm and the subcontractor is often highly dependent on just one or a couple of important customers who buy the majority of their production.[88]

The increasing use of subcontracting is a recent phenomenon due to increased specialisation and disintegration tendencies. As is the case with all inter-firm cooperation forms, these have been favoured foreign-market entry strategies since the 1980s. Despite this favourable development of cooperation forms, FDI and exporting continue to be attractive modes of internationalisation. A United Nations survey of 1997[89] predicted that SMEs would pursue their internationalisation strategies under the form of exporting, FDI and other contractual cooperation forms.

The abolition of NTBs within the EU certainly sustains the increased use of all foreign-market entry strategies. The enlarged market access and the reduction of transaction costs function as push-factors. The different internationalisation models and foreign-market entry strategies emphasised the importance of location-specific factors and in particular firm-specific advantages.

> *Hypothesis 2*: Each SME's internationalisation is based on the exploitation of its firm-specific competitive advantage in the host countries. Because of the existence of different competitive advantages there are different models of internationalisation.

To complete the research on SMEs' internationalisation strategies, a firm's choice of location has to be taken into consideration. The 1992 market opening led to an increased optimum size of SMEs. This influences SMEs' strategies of internationalisation because they have to stay competitive in an enlarged market. If their strategies of internationalisation are affected through the Single Market Programme, this also has repercussions on their choices of location. Among different approaches of location choice the attractiveness of SME agglomerations plays a primary role.

4 Mechanisms of location

Country- and firm-specific factors determine a firm's choice of location. Country-specific factors include home- and foreign-market size, the existence of a particular infrastructure, demand, costs, and home- and foreign-market structure. Firm-specific factors include a firm's business know-how, its technological capabilities, the degree of product differentiation and the following of a niche strategy. The enlarged market access with its decreasing NTBs influence these country- and firm-specific factors.

A firm can be located within an agglomeration of enterprises (or industrial district) at home and abroad or outside such an agglomeration. In some industries there are highly specialised industrial districts even if the majority of all enterprises in the industry are located outside such districts. A firm's choice of location and in what manner this choice became affected through the abolition of NTBs was investigated in chapters 2 and 3 on internationalisation models and market entry strategies. It is therefore interesting to analyse the case of SMEs located in industrial districts. As argued in chapter 1, the establishment of the EMU influences enterprises in these districts and the districts as a whole entity. Because of the diminishing transaction costs within the EU the relations between SMEs of a district might have changed. The difficulties involved in the different approaches regarding location choice are described below.

Different approaches for location choice

A firm's choice in favour of a certain location can be analysed:

- as the result of a decisional process *or*
- as the result of a convergence between firm and territory *or*
- by the attractiveness of a geographic concentration of enterprises.[1]

If the owner or manager is confronted with the problem of information being limited and expensive, then the choice of a firm's location is the result of a decisional process. Aharoni distinguished different phases of the decision process.

The first stage is doubt about a future location. The decision-maker is confronted with an unsettled or incoherent situation. The second stage is the inquiry or investigation of facts to which the analysis of the problems leads. In the third stage alternatives are suggested and the fourth stage is that of verification. The fifth stage is the selection of the most convenient location among the alternatives, in accordance with the firm's primary goal.[2]

According to Mucchielli, the choice of a firm's location can also be based on considering the combination of advantages of the host country and firm-specific advantages.[3] Country-specific comparative advantages include relative advantages regarding costs, country size and the dynamic of demand at home and abroad. Firm-specific advantages exist due to a reduction in production costs (because of technological innovations, new production factors, skilled labour) and product differentiation (situation of competition, label, promotion).[4] Environmental changes also resulted from the fact that the establishment of the EMU changed some country- and firm-specific variables. The result is that the firm has to adapt its strategies to a 'new' convergence between firm and territory.

The case of geographic concentration or agglomeration of enterprises is interesting for SMEs. Meijboom and Rongen distinguish agglomeration or clustering effects according to geographical, organisational and strategic concepts.[5]

Economic geography concepts relate the existence of clustering to history and accident. In this case, the presence of one firm creates agglomeration effects. Whole firm clusters grow by interaction of increasing returns, the minimisation of transportation costs and the existence of a large local demand. Sometimes there can be geographical advantages initiating the creation of firm clusters.[6] Organisational concepts relate clustering to vertical disintegration. Existing clusters of small firms grow into clusters of very specialised firms that facilitate personal contacts and maximise trust. Strategic concepts evoke the stimulation of innovation among highly competitive firms within clusters.[7] Agglomerations or clusters of firms are also called industrial districts.

Industrial districts

Industrial districts or clusters of enterprises are defined as 'a sectoral and geographical concentration of enterprises' by Humphrey and Schmitz.[8] Porter[9] defines them as 'geographic concentrations of interconnected companies and institutions in a particular field'.

Once such a concentration exists, external economies[10] are likely to emerge. Alfred Marshall introduced the concept of external economies[11] in order to explain '(a) why and how the location of industry matters, and (b) why and how small enterprises can be efficient and competitive'.[12] In addition, Marshall[13] argued that external economy gains lower factor prices, generate economies of scale and scope, affect profits positively, and, through knowledge flows, enhance technical progress. But already Lösch has argued that with 'at least one center' the maximum number of purchases can be made locally and therefore the sum of the minimum distances between industrial locations is lowest. In consequence, transport lines are reduced to a minimum.[14]

By following the ideas of Marshall, Krugman[15] and Venables[16] described the idea of industrial clustering in economics. They identified three reasons for localisation:

1 Labour market pooling: The sectoral and geographical concentration of firms creates a pool of specialised and skilled workers. First, this concentration of firms attracts workers, and second, the turnover of workers from one firm to another within the industrial district is facilitated. In this sense, firms want to locate near other firms to benefit from the shared pool of labour with industry-specific skills.
2 Intermediate inputs: Through clustering, firms can support more specialised local suppliers of input and services. For example, different firms can use a pool of occasional machines. Another characteristic is the existence of a pool of subcontractors.[17] The creation of firms in an upstream industry happens through the demand in the downstream industry. Because of transport costs the firms will locate in proximity to the firms in the downstream industry.
3 Technological spill-overs: Clustering facilitates the rapid diffusion of know-how and ideas. These technological externalities are in many cases an informal exchange of ideas.

   This last reason for localisation became essential because of the increasing importance of knowledge-based economic activity. Since knowledge is created and transmitted more efficiently by firms characterised by a high local proximity, there is a high propensity for economic activity based on new knowledge to cluster in a geographic area.[18]

Porter also emphasised these three reasons.[19] He argued that firms that are part of a cluster operate more productively through better access to employees and suppliers, better access to specialised information, complementarities and good access to public institutions and public goods. Proximity improves communication and close informal relationships between the firm owners is common. There are low search and transaction costs in recruiting due to an existing pool of experienced and specialised employees. Complementarities exist under the form of product complements or coordination of activities across different firms. Sourcing locally instead of from a distant supplier lowers transaction costs. The number of potential input and output linkages between firms within those industrial districts are enormous and make them extremely flexible.[20] Industrial clustering in a particular locality permits firms to gain useful infrastructures, an appropriate specialisation and diversification facilitating the provision of specific goods and services, 'more convenient relative prices and qualities of the labour force and of primary and intermediary goods'.[21] Proximity is important for the transfer of information, knowledge and expertise.

Clusters often extend downstream to channels and customers and laterally to manufacturers of complementary products and to firms related by skills, technologies or common inputs. Finally, they may include governmental and other institutions such as trade associations, universities and research centres.[22] In this sense, clustering is an alternative approach, midway between arm's length markets and vertical integration, to organise the value-chain.

Schmitz and Nadvi[23] emphasised the notion of 'joint action' in industrial districts. This joint action is reached through the cooperation of individual enterprises (for example by sharing their equipment for developing a new product) and through business associations and producer consortia where groups of firms join their forces. These business associations can be very successful in supporting their members' export activities, as for example in Italy where 350 consortia have been created by SME federations or local communities.[24] This lobbying is extremely successful in representing their members' international interests. The consortium which represents the textile industry opened a permanent showroom in Singapore, for example.[25]

But proximity, important for cooperation, is also important for rivalry in those industrial districts. As Porter notes, '[D]omestic rivalry, like any rivalry, creates pressures on companies to innovate and improve. Local rivals push each other to lower costs, improve quality and service, and create new products and processes'.[26] First, there is competition in

Table 4.1 Forms of joint action in clusters

	Bilateral	*Multilateral*
Horizontal	e.g. sharing equipment, joint marketing, joint purchase of inputs, sharing of know-how	e.g. sectoral association, trade fairs, technology and producer service centres
Vertical	e.g. producer and user improving components, quality control, labour training	e.g. alliance across value-added chain between various associations: strategic approach *vis-à-vis* external competitors

Source: Schmitz, H. (1998), 'Collective efficiency and increasing returns', p. 7.

factor markets for inputs, and second, firms compete for sales in the product market.[27] In many cases this domestic rivalry can become personal, compared to national or international rivalry. They compete not only for market shares, but also for people and technical excellence.

Rivalry is especially important in pressuring firms to cut costs, improve quality and to innovate.[28] This concentration of rivals, customers and suppliers promotes efficiencies and specialisation.[29] The influence of geographic concentration on improvement and innovation is enormous. If the speed of information flows and the diffusion rate of innovation are increased, rivalry is intensified. In addition to the increased productivity and innovation, clustering affects competition by stimulating the formation of new businesses.[30] An employee with a certain amount of experience sees more financial and personal advantages in founding his own firm than in staying dependent. Within the cluster, barriers to entry are lower than elsewhere and the potential entrepreneur can benefit from established relationships.

Corò and Grandinetti[31] found traces of cooperation, communication and competition in the following processes:

1 the specialisation of production
2 learning and innovation
3 the emulation of successful behaviours (catching-up processes)
4 the diffusion of innovation by means of inter-firm relations and local spill-overs.

It is therefore up to the firm to evaluate the advantages of agglomeration or cooperation against the disadvantages of higher competition.[32]

The relationship between SMEs within agglomerations can be capital-intensive networks such as in Germany, or labour-intensive networks such as in Italy. One reason for this is that the international specialisation of the Italian economy is strongly oriented towards traditional goods,[33] compared to the German economy. Higher-quality products can be associated with a higher content of skilled labour.

A good example is the Italian ceramic tile industry, concentrated around the small town of Sassuolo in Emilia-Romagna. In 1987, Italian producers accounted for about 30 per cent of world production and almost 60 per cent of world exports.[34] The relationship between Italian tile and equipment manufacturers is a very close one and they are often located next door to each other. Italian equipment manufacturers compete for local business and Italian tile manufacturers often receive better equipment prices than foreign firms. An increasing number of highly specialised workers and technicians accompanied the growth of the industry. Service firms, such as transportation firms, consulting firms, etc., became established around Sassuolo.

Competitiveness of firms in industrial districts is achieved by high quality, know-how or design intensity, as well as by flexibility. In many cases there is a customisation of products and therefore frequent changes in both products and processes.[35] In common with their German neighbours, Italian entrepreneurs admit that 60 per cent of their investments are destined to improve the product quality and only 30 per cent to increase their production.[36]

Despite some national differences, one factor that clusters have in common is that they evolve continually as new firms and industries emerge or decline and local institutions change. Clusters are very sensitive to internal rigidities and external threats. Such rigidities intervene if firms persist in old behaviour without adapting to a new environment. Cooperation and rivalry have to remain sufficiently vigorous in the district to compensate for environmental changes that diminish the cluster's competitiveness.[37]

The theoretical basis of the functioning of cooperation and rivalry are transaction costs and game theory. The establishment of the EMU increased SMEs' international transactions. This influenced not only the relationships of firms in industrial districts to other EU firms, but also the traditional inter-firm relationships in the district. The following section describes the influences of transaction costs and game theory on inter-firm cooperation.

The basis of each cooperation

All kinds of inter-firm cooperation have been explained from both an economic and sociological perspective. Contributing literatures from the economic perspective include transaction-cost economics and game theory. From the sociological perspective, relevant contributions come from the social-exchange theory and the norm of reciprocity.[38] But the attention in the literature on industrial agglomerations has increasingly turned from economic reasons for the growth of new industrial agglomerations, such as product specialisation and vertical disintegration,[39] to social and cultural reasons.[40] To explain the existence and functioning of industrial agglomerations the different approaches are, however, rather complementary.

According to Williamson, the avoidance of the costs of repeated transactions on the marketplace is the primary motivation for undertaking cooperative agreements. Transaction costs arise through the people's inability to analyse everything in advance, through an uncertain business future, through the presence of few players for a given kind of transaction, and through the possibility that some players may be opportunistic.[41] Williamson distinguished transaction costs of *ex ante* and *ex post* types. The first are the costs of drafting, negotiating and safeguarding an agreement. Ex post costs of contracting include

> (1) the maladaptation costs, incurred when transactions drift out of alignment . . . , (2) the haggling costs incurred if bilateral efforts are made to correct ex post misalignments, (3) the setup and running costs associated with the government structures . . . to which disputes are referred, and (4) the bonding costs of effecting secure commitments.
>
> (Williamson 1985: 20–21)

In a majority of cases, these costs are interdependent and difficult to quantify.

Generations of trust can reduce transaction costs between cooperation partners to prevent or correct opportunistic behaviour. With a sufficient level of trust between the partners they can avoid internalisation even in situations with higher transaction costs. Bidault and Jarillo[42] argued that internalisation is a means to reduce uncertainty from the transaction and therefore is supposed to result from a lack of trust. The authors described two sources of trust. The first source is the similarity of ethical values (it is more difficult to trust someone from another country) of the participating parties, and the second source is time or experience, demonstrated by game theory (by repeating a game an unlimited number of times). However, it is important to note that the problem of trust is not overcome through internalisation. This problem exists also within one firm.

In this sense it is possible to claim that in industrial districts transaction costs are low through the similarity of ethical values. For the theoreticians on industrial districts, the existing trust between firms is a consequence of their common culture and experiences. Mutual trust persists through repeated and regular interpersonal contacts between delivering firms and their customers in one region.[43]

A good example is the Benetton franchising system, which is based on a system of mutual trust. About 90 per cent of Benetton's franchising partners are located in the Venezia region. In Europe, Benetton does not rely on legal contracts, but rather on unwritten agreements. Mutual expectations are clearly expressed, which saves time and money. Even if firms other than Benetton rely strongly on trust relationships, they utilise contracts and formal controls as a complement to trust relationships.[44]

The prisoner's dilemma illustrates best the game-theory model. In the basic scenario the prisoner's dilemma is applied to bilateral exchange relationships that require significant investments in specialised assets. The two participating players have the choice of either cooperating and trusting each other or of acting opportunistically. However, a player can get a higher payoff if he acts opportunistically whatever the other player does.

Table 4.2 The prisoner's dilemma

		Column player	
		Cooperate	*Defect*
Row Player	Cooperate	$R=3$, $R=3$ Reward for mutual cooperation	$S=0$, $T=5$ Sucker's payoff, and temptation to defect
	Defect	$T=5$, $S=0$ Temptation to defect, and sucker's payoff	$P=1$, $P=1$ Punishment for mutual defection

Source: Axelrod, R. (1984), *The Evolution of Cooperation*, p. 8.

Table 4.3 A second configuration of the prisoner's dilemma

		Column player	
		Cooperate	*Defect*
Row Player	Cooperate	$R=5$, $R=5$ Reward for mutual cooperation	$S=0$, $T=3$ Sucker's payoff, and temptation to defect
	Defect	$T=3$, $S=0$ Temptation to defect, and sucker's payoff	$P=1$, $P=1$ Punishment for mutual defection

Source: Based on Gulati, R. *et al.*, *Expansion Management Review*, winter: p. 12.

The prisoner's dilemma in its original and simple form is a good illustration regarding the lack of trust. The conclusion that it is best to act opportunistically continues to hold for a repeated game. Cooperation in this basic scenario is never possible.

There is, however, another form of the prisoner's dilemma which explains cooperation. There are two possible equilibria: both players cooperate or both players do not cooperate. But the payoff for cooperation is higher than the payoff for acting opportunistically.[45] Motivations to cooperate are the sharing of costs and risk, technological advantages through common R&D, fast market access, increasing market share, etc.

This alternative form of the prisoner's dilemma explains the conclusion of alliances, but also the cooperation within industrial districts. However, this form is based on the hypothesis that decisions are taken simultaneously and only for one time.

Axelrod[46] extended the concept of the prisoner's dilemma to situations where firms could cooperate on a long-term basis. This form introduced the hypothesis that the game is played an infinite number of times. The decision rule in this infinitely repeated game is 'tit for tat', or the strategy of cooperating on the first move and thereafter doing whatever the other player did on the previous move. The players have the choice of cooperation or defection. The scenario always starts with cooperation by the first player as he knows that this strategy leads to a maximisation of his benefits. If the second player reacts opportunistically the first player does the same and his gain will be below the gain of the second player. But also the second player has a lower gain as in the case of cooperation. If the second player starts cooperating because he realises that he can gain more by doing so, the first player also reacts by cooperating.

Axelrod examined rules to achieve better outcomes for a population of players in the long run when the future is important and the number of future interactions between the players is unknown. The success of 'tit for tat' is related to the players being nice, retaliatory, forgiving and clear.[47] Players with opportunistic behaviour always fare poorly in the long run. Axelrod concluded that players who did not use the combination of this rule consistently would underestimate the value of forgiving the opportunism of the other player. Actors whose decision-rules stress cooperation and trust dominate the population of players in the long run. This domination of players acting according to 'tit for tat' is particularly strong in industrial districts. Otherwise the equilibrium between cooperation and competition would not function.

Tables 4.4, 4.5 and 4.6 demonstrate some possibilities of how two players could act according to the rules of 'tit for tat'. In case 1 (Table 4.4), player A cooperates whereas player B defects from the beginning. The result of this strategy ('all D's') is that player B has a higher payoff than player A. But his payoff is still lower than in the case of cooperation.

In case 2 (Table 4.5) both players cooperate in the beginning. Player B acts opportunistically from the fourth interaction on and player A follows in the fifth interaction. Player B returns to a strategy of cooperation in

Table 4.4 Case 1: Player A cooperates but player B defects

Game	*1*	*2*	*3*	*4*	*5*	*6*	*7*	*8*	*9*
A	C	D	D	D	D	D	D	D	D
B	D	D	D	D	D	D	D	D	D

Table 4.5 Case 2: Both players alternate between cooperation and opportunistic behaviour

Game	*1*	*2*	*3*	*4*	*5*	*6*	*7*	*8*	*9*
A	C	C	C	C	D	C	C	D	D
B	C	C	C	D	C	C	D	D	C

Table 4.6 Case 3: Player B defects and cooperation ceases

Game	*1*	*2*	*3*	*4*	*5*	*6*	*7*	*8*	*9*
A	C	C	C	C	D	D	D	D	D
B	C	C	C	D	D	D	D	D	D

the fifth interaction and player A follows. This is repeated in the seventh interaction where player B again tries to defect. Case 3 (Table 4.6) is similar to case 2. But the players do not return to cooperation after the defection of player B in the fourth interaction.

Granovetter[48] stated that there are three reasons why individual economic actors will trust one another and act in trustworthy ways: first, it is in their social or economic interest to do so; second, they believe it is morally right; and third, the actors are doing so as part of the regularised expectations that characterise their personal relations with their transaction partner(s).

Also, Jarillo and Ricart[49] emphasise the importance of generating trust in business relationships. They point out that repetition permits cooperation and that threats must be credible. They illustrate their framework by a subcontractor relationship where the creation of a potential competitor is always possible.

To the creation of trust Buckley and Casson[50] added the notion of 'forbearance'. Forbearance arises when one party refrains from cheating another party. One can consider a cooperation as efficient when a given amount of mutual forbearance generates the largest possible amount of mutual trust. These elements bring in the concept of altruism or the sacrifice of short-term opportunistic gains for longer-term gains, which the Williamson framework lacks.

In social-exchange theory the cooperative behaviour is based on the general consensus that individuals who reward others force them to return that favour. By doing so, a social functioning is possible in the future. Blau and Alba expected that the nature of the return would be similar to that of the original reward.[51] These exchanges are voluntary and motivated by the expected returns. Of course, the exchanges take place in formal and informal cooperation agreements. The majority of cooperation agreements concluded between foreign partners are, however, formal. But in industrial districts this cooperation is often informal.

Based on Axelrod's theory, Hill emphasised the concept of reputation between the cooperating partners.[52] As reputation has a huge economic value when setting up relationships, opportunistic behaviour can quickly destroy that reputation. It is beneficial to have a reputation of 'tit for tat' behaviour because it beats aggressive behaviour in the long run and it is a 'non-zero-sum approach'.[53]

In cases of geographical dispersion it may be difficult to obtain complete information on a potential partner's reputation. In addition to geographical dispersion, cultural distance renders a firm's reputation as a 'tit for tat' player difficult. Trusting a national or even a local seems easier than trusting a foreigner. The removal of NTBs and the development of sophisticated information technology has improved communication between the cooperation partners of the different EU countries. Mutual understanding of the different cultural values will lead to a further reduction of transaction costs, and having a reputation as a 'tit for tat' player will become important for trans-border transactions.

In industrial districts the relationship between SMEs is characterised by a complex web of cooperation and competition.[54] For the successful functioning of this strong interdependence a reputation as a 'tit for tat' business plays a major role. The removal of NTBs affected not only those SMEs outside such industrial districts, but also those located inside. It is possible that SMEs inside industrial districts may be more affected as their degree of internationalisation is higher.[55] One can therefore suppose that these inter-firm relationships become intensified because of the strong cooperation inside these districts. This leads to an increased specialisation of the firms. But firms exist because producing for others is efficient compared to self-efficiency. This efficiency is due to economies of scale, to specialised activity and to the prevalence of low transaction costs.[56] New firm foundations in industrial districts may be a consequence.

Hypothesis 3: Decreasing NTBs lead to increased international transactions of SMEs. This leads to an increasing specialisation and consequently to more cooperation between the firms in industrial districts.

5 Conclusions

Numerous theoretical lenses have been employed to increase the understanding of SMEs' international strategies. There are an increasing number of books and articles dealing with this issue. There are, however, only a limited number of articles that deal with SMEs' internationalisation strategies related to the European integration. In this sense, this literature survey delivers some useful insights. In order to answer the three hypotheses an empirical survey becomes necessary.

It is obvious that the Single Market Programme, with its removal of NTBs, facilitated SMEs' international transactions despite some persistent problems. Through the reduction of border delays and red tape, and the harmonisation of technical standards, EU trade became cheaper. It is important to note that the internal market delivered proportionally greater benefits to SMEs than to larger firms, especially in sectors where there was a high incidence of NTBs.[1] In these sectors SMEs had to respond to the enlarged market through an increase in their international transactions. If the firm was able to exploit its competitive advantage efficiently on a national level before the removal of NTBs, the firm had to exploit this same competitive advantage in other EU countries after the establishment of the EMU in order to stay competitive. SMEs that were already highly internationalised felt some incentives to increase their internationalisation activities or to change their foreign-market entry strategies. In some cases, extra-EU transactions were replaced by intra-EU transactions.

Like SMEs outside industrial districts, the removal of NTBs affected SMEs located within such districts. Due to their higher degree of internationalisation, firms located in industrial districts[2] might have been even more affected through the 1992 market opening than firms located outside the districts. One of the main characteristics of an industrial district is its high degree of inter-firm cooperation. In order to meet increased market demand they have to intensify the cooperation with the partner firms in their industrial district.

One can consider the removal of NTBs within the EU as a push-factor for SMEs located both inside and outside industrial districts. However, the changes regarding industrial districts are interesting. First, inter-firm relationships in industrial districts may be affected by the 1992 market opening, and second – which can be considered as a consequence – the international competitiveness of the whole industrial district may change. Perhaps only the 'fittest' industrial district in each industry may survive within the EU in the long term.

In order to answer these open questions, in particular the three hypotheses based on the literature survey, empirical research is necessary. Part II of this book therefore begins with a short description of the empirical approach.

Part II

Empirical research

The empirical research consists of two major parts. First, there is an industry description of the MSE sector in order to provide some idea of recent developments in the EU. Important aspects of the description are a short industry profile, the trans-border flows in the three countries under investigation, existing regulations and persisting market forces which include demand, supply, production process and competition.

The second chapter contains the field research. There are two approaches: first, a questionnaire research, and second, case studies. The description of the questionnaire research is preceded by short country descriptions in order to provide an idea of the SME sector in France, Germany and Italy. An anonymous questionnaire was sent to 300 SMEs: 100 to France, 100 to Germany and 100 to Italy. All 300 SMEs were located outside industrial districts. The returned questionnaires permit an answer to hypotheses 1 and 2.

The case studies are preceded by a short description of each industrial district. There are seven case studies, written in cooperation with five SMEs located in the industrial district of Tuttlingen (Germany) and two SMEs located in the industrial district of Nogent (France). The case studies permit us to answer all hypotheses, but in particular hypothesis 3.

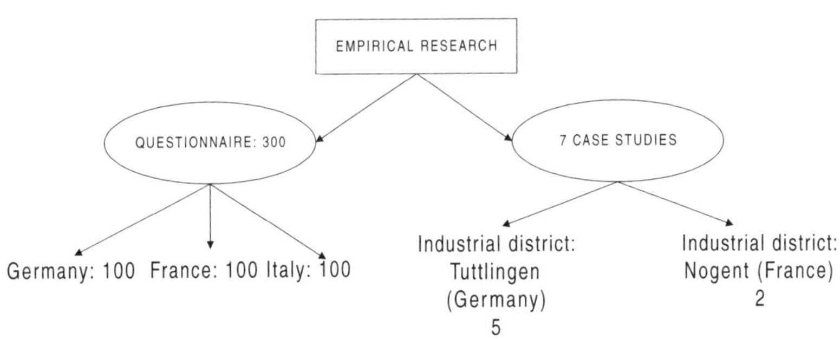

Figure 6.1 Framework of the empirical research.

6 The European medical and surgical equipment (MSE) and orthopaedic appliances industry

During the past ten years there has been a strong growth in EU production and consumption in this industry. An ageing of the EU population, rising income levels, a higher level of health awareness, increasing technological innovation and harmonisation of regulations within the EU have acted as drivers of demand. Globally the USA dominates the industry, accounting for 60 per cent of the Triad production, compared to the EU's share of about 25 per cent in 1994.

Industry profile

Sector description

According to the EU classification, the sector consists of the following seven product areas:

- manufacture of medical apparatus for diagnostic work
- manufacture of medical, surgical and veterinary equipment and instruments
- manufacture of dental instruments and apparatus
- manufacture of orthopaedic appliances and artificial limbs
- manufacture of electro-medical equipment
- production of hand-made orthopaedic footwear
- manufacture of medical and dental appliances.

In 1994, Germany was the leading EU producer of MSE with 54 per cent of total value added. Other major producer countries were France (20 per cent), the United Kingdom (14 per cent) and Italy (8 per cent). These four countries generated 96 per cent of the EU value added in this sector. Figure 6.2 shows the value added for each Member State of the EU.

Recent trends

Table 6.1 illustrates that consumption and production have grown strongly in each year. Employment in the sector increased slowly and

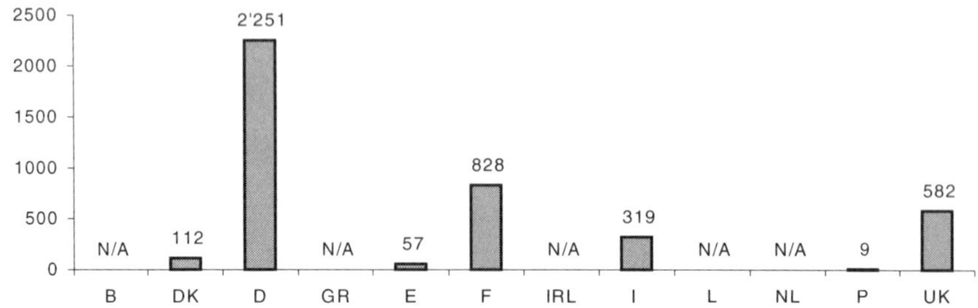

Figure 6.2 Value added by EU Member States in the MSE industry in 1994 (in million euros). Source: DEBA GEIE.

reached a peak in 1992 at 108,000. The stagnation of employment can be connected to the slow growth in the sector in 1992 and 1993. From 1995 on, employment rates grew again to reach another peak in 1996.

The EU had a trade surplus in this sector from 1985 and 1990, reaching its peak in 1986. But consumption has grown faster than production, which caused extra-EU imports to grow faster than extra-EU exports. There has therefore been a deterioration of the EU trade balance between 1986 and 1991. This trend was reversed in 1994 when the deficit became less. In addition, extra-EU exports and imports fell sharply. In 1995 the trade balance deficit reached another peak and started to fall from 1996 on. Both extra-EU imports and exports again started to grow from 1995 on. One can therefore see a steady improvement of the export competitiveness from 1996 onwards.

The EU, Japan and the USA all experienced strong increases in production and consumption from 1985 to 1994. However, production shares remained almost constant with the USA reaching about 60 per cent, Japan about 15 per cent and the EU increasing slightly from 20.7 per cent in 1985 to 24.1 per cent in 1994.

In 1994, the USA and the EFTA states were the major destinations for EU exports. But their export share declined from 45 per cent in 1989 to 41 per cent in 1994. The reason for this may be partly due to regulatory factors in the USA (the 1990 Safe Medical Devices Act) and partly due to the enlarged European Single Market. The inclusion of Austria, Finland and Sweden reduced the total extra-EU export figure by 100 million euros. The EU-12 exports to these three countries used to be greater than the extra-EU exports of the three new Member States. As extra-EU imports remained almost the same, a widening of the EU's trade deficit in the sector was a consequence. In 1994, the USA, Switzerland and Japan accounted for 76 per cent of EU imports whereas the USA was the largest source with 44 per cent.

Table 6.1 MSE: main indicators in million euros

	1985	*1990*	*1991*	*1992*	*1994*	*1995*	*1996*	*1997*	*1998*
Apparent consumption	3,952	6,497	7,605	8,158	8,802	9,902	10,620	11,260	11,950
Production	4,410	6,579	7,394	7,902	8,675	9,342	10,070	10,820	11,650
Employment (thousands)	92	101	106	108	108	114	120	120	120
Extra-EU exports	1,657	2,151	2,335	2,460	1,887	2,850	3,020	3,180	3,350
Extra-EU imports	1,198	2,069	2,546	2,715	2,014	3,409	3,570	3,620	3,650
Trade balance	458	81.2	−211	−255.7	−126.8	−559.4	−550	−440	−300
Ratio exports/imports	1.38	1.04	0.92	0.91	0.94	0.84	0.85	0.88	0.92

Source: own estimate (based on EUROSTAT), from 1995 on EUROSTAT estimates for EUR15.

Flows in the three main countries

The investigation of trans-border flows in France, Germany and Italy confirms these general results. These three countries were the major actors within the EU, in addition to the United Kingdom.

Intra- and extra-European imports and exports in these three countries are analysed in Tables 6.2, 6.3, 6.4 and 6.5 to compare the development of the flows. The development of the flows was dependent on country- and firm-specific factors, on the world-wide economic cycle and on EU policies. However, it was difficult to relate the development of those flows to dominant factors and influences. Certainly, the Single Market Programme with its removal of NTBs and harmonisation of technical standards had a strong influence on the development of trade flows, but the 1995 enlargement of the EU also played an important role.[1] It is therefore difficult to separate the influences of the different political measures on the development of these flows in the three countries under consideration.

In all three countries there was a significant increase in intra-European imports of MSE from 1988 to 1996. In France, this signified an increase of 64 per cent, in Germany an increase of 65 per cent and in Italy it was 55 per cent. In the same period, extra-European imports increased by 57 per cent in France, 67 per cent in Germany but only 5 per cent in Italy. In this context it is interesting to divide the data into two periods (1988 to 1993 and 1993 to 1996) to find out if there has been a '1992 effect'. Tables 6.2 and 6.3 illustrate the results.

It is clear that from 1988 to 1993 intra-European import growth rates were much lower than extra-European import growth rates, with the

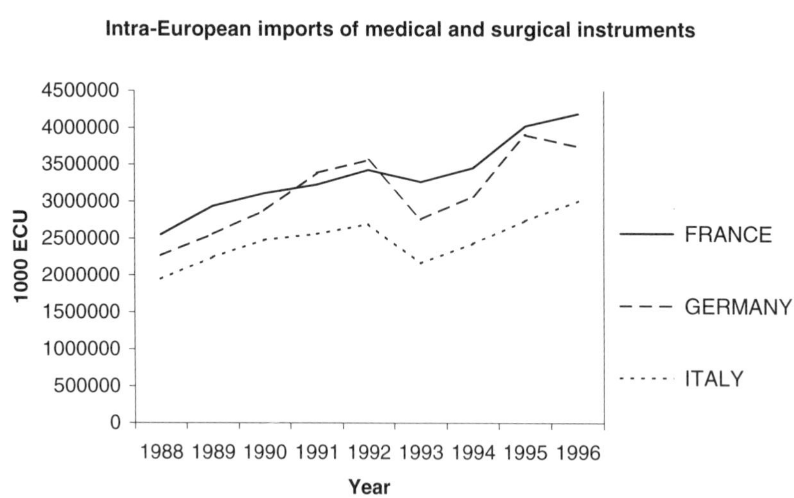

Figure 6.3 Intra-European imports. Source: EUROSTAT, 1997.

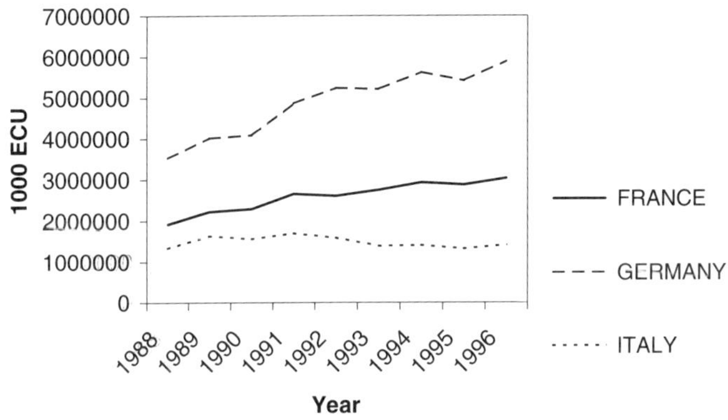

Figure 6.4 Extra-European imports of medical and surgical instruments. Source: EUROSTAT, 1997.

Table 6.2 Average annual growth rates of intra- and extra-European imports in the MSE industry (%)

	Intra-import 1988–96	*Extra-import 1988–96*
France	64	57
Germany	65	67
Italy	55	5

Source: own estimate.

Table 6.3 Average annual growth rates of intra- and extra-European imports in the MSE industry (%)

	Intra-import 1988–93	*Extra-import 1988–93*	*Intra-import 1993–96*	*Extra-import 1993–96*
France	28	43	28 (32)	10
Germany	21	48	35 (49)	13
Italy	11	4	39 (39)	2

Source: own estimate.

exception of Italy. The contrast with Italy is striking – either Italy was very protectionist before the Single Market, or it was very efficient. From 1993 on, this development was reversed and intra-European import growth rates were higher than extra-European import growth rates. This development is even more pronounced if the 1995 EU enlargement is not taken into consideration (percentage in parentheses).[2] Extra-European

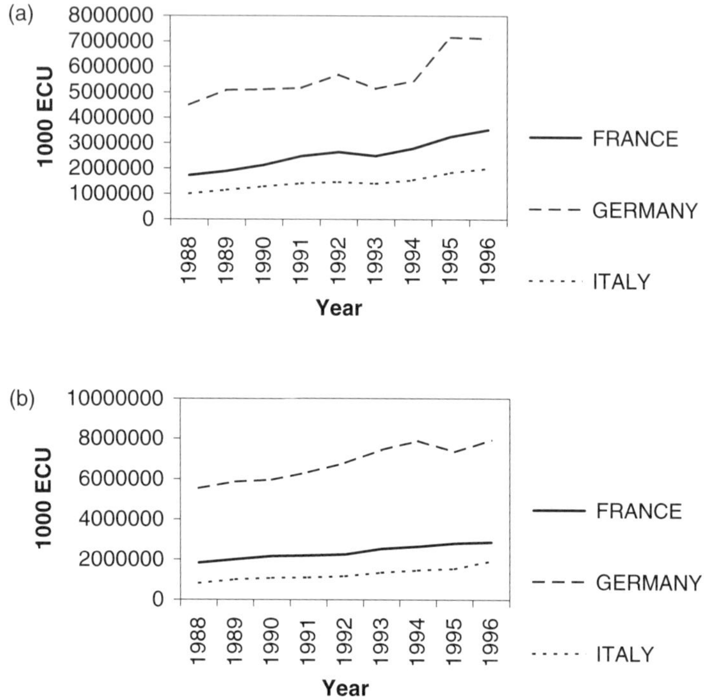

Figure 6.5 (a) Intra- and (b) extra-European exports of medical and surgical instruments. Source: EUROSTAT, 1997.

imports have been replaced by intra-European imports. Therefore, trade creation or trade diversion has taken place. This development could have been related to the facilitation of EU trade and the harmonisation of technical standards due to the Single Market Programme.

Intra-European exports increased from 1988 to 1996 by 104 per cent in France, 58 per cent in Germany and 101 per cent in Italy. At the same time, extra-European exports increased 57 per cent in France, 44 per cent in Germany and 136 per cent in Italy.

France had an intra-European export growth rate nearly twice as high as the extra-European export growth rate. But well before 1993, France concentrated mainly on intra-European exports. From 1993 on, this development was reinforced. Table 6.5 illustrates the development of export flows from 1988 to 1993 and from 1993 to 1996 (in %).

As in the case of intra- and extra-European imports, extra-European exports have been replaced by intra-European exports (again trade creation or trade diversion). This development is even more pronounced if

Table 6.4 Average annual growth rates of intra- and extra-European exports in the MSE industry (%)

	Intra-export 1988–96	*Extra-export 1988–96*
France	104	57
Germany	58	44
Italy	101	136

Source: own estimate.

Table 6.5 Average annual growth rates of intra- and extra-European exports in the MSE industry (%)

	Intra-export 1988–93	*Extra-export 1988–93*	*Intra-export 1993–96*	*Extra-export 1993–96*
France	44	38	41 (41)	13
Germany	14	35	38 (46)	7
Italy	41	64	43 (44)	43

Source: own estimate.

one does not take into account the EU enlargement as illustrated by the percentages in parentheses. Therefore, one can talk of a clear '1992 effect'.

German producers of MSE were the strongest actors compared to other countries of the EU. Within the EU, the German MSE industry enjoyed a growing trade surplus. This trade surplus in intra-European trade became strong from 1992 on and again from 1994/95 on. But extra-European trade also showed a strong surplus from 1992 on. From 1992 on, the whole MSE industry expanded and the growing trade surplus can be interpreted in this sense. But the growing intra-European trade surplus from 1994/95 on was clearly a consequence of the Single Market Programme. At the same time the increase in the extra-European trade balance surplus ceased. Both France and Italy had deficits at this time, whereas Italy had a clear trade surplus in extra-European trade from 1993/94 on.

Regulations

EU and international regulations have changed the competitive environment of the sector within the EU. The quality assurance models of ISO[3] 9001, 9002 and 9003 represent three distinct forms of quality system requirements suitable for the purpose of a supplier demonstrating its capability, and for the assessment of the capability of a supplier by external parties. These standards are generic and independent of any specific industry or economic sector.

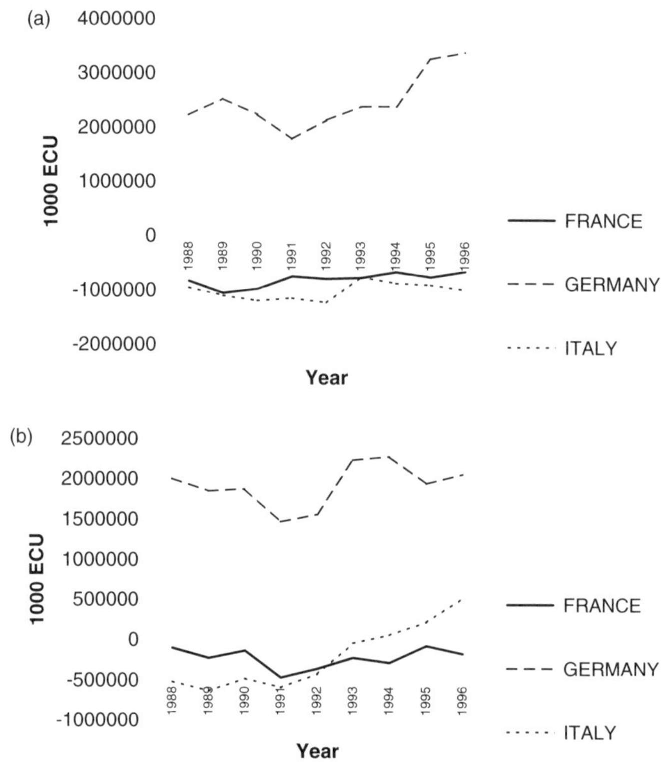

Figure 6.6 (a) Intra- and (b) extra-European balance – medical and surgical instruments. Source: EUROSTAT, 1997.

The EN[4] 46001 of 1996 is applied only in connection with ISO 9001. This norm takes the general standard as a basis and adds some regulations concerning medical and surgical devices.[5] Supplying firms that produce active implantable medical devices, medical devices and in vitro diagnostics have to fulfil certain quality obligations before bearing the stamp of approval.

In addition to ISO 9001 and EN 46001 there are at least three EU directives that have affected the movement of medical and surgical devices in the EU:

1 The Active Implantable Medical Devices directive, effective since 1993, concerns the manufacture and sale of pacemakers and other implantables.
2 The Medical Devices directive became effective in 1995 and covers medical devices generally.

3 The In Vitro Diagnostics directive became effective from 1998 and concerns areas such as endoscopic technology.

An important requirement of these directives is that any device sold in the EU has to comply with a set of harmonised rules and bear the stamp of approval (the EC mark[6]) in order to enjoy free movement in the EU Member States.

Market forces

Demand

EU demand for MSE has increased strongly since 1985. There are five reasons for this development.

The first reason is demographic trends. The average lifespan of each EU citizen is increasing, therefore there is a general ageing of the population. Improved healthcare creates a demand for further improvements. This means that people live longer and demand improved healthcare.

The second reason is the gradual increase in the income levels of EU citizens. As people become richer they spend a greater part of their income on healthcare. As people get older and richer, they get more and more interested in health matters. Manifestations of this increased awareness are the growing number of television programmes on this topic and publications about health matters.

The third reason is technological innovation. The MSE sector is highly research-intensive and there has been a wide range of technological innovations. For example, through technological advances, video diagnostic methodologies, including improved data transmission and picture storage become possible. Another important area is minimally invasive surgery which is one of the fastest growing product areas in the sector. This specific product area includes endoscopes (viewing of organs by the use of narrow, lighted tubes), laparascopies (systems relying on punctures) and products such as light sources and imaging devices. Advances in the accuracy of corneal-measurement methods permit the development of an array of surgical techniques to correct eyesight. In addition, improvements in data-processing systems have transformed many applications such as anaesthetic processes, and improvements in materials technology have benefited prosthetic and orthopaedic devices.[7] It is important that many of those technological innovations are cost-saving. To the extent that hospitals and doctors are price-sensitive, this increases the quantity demanded.

The fourth reason is that MSE has become more consumer-friendly and disposable. This has supported greater self-administration and out-patient therapy. Compared to past demand, which was mainly driven by hospitals and traditional care-givers, this recent process allows hospitals to save money on MSE. Whether greater involvement of the patient in this process pushed demand forward is debatable.

Supply

The USA is the leading global producer of MSE, accounting for 52 per cent of EU imports in 1989 and for 45 per cent in 1994. But it accounted for only 24 per cent of EU exports in 1989 and for 17 per cent in 1994. This is attributed to a large homebase, a highly developed healthcare market and strong R&D investments.

Japan and Switzerland hold the second place in the sector. Japan accounted for 15 per cent of EU imports in 1989 and for 14 per cent in 1995. For Switzerland, it was 15 per cent in 1989 and 18 per cent in 1994. Japan covered 9 per cent of EU exports in 1989 and 8 per cent in 1994. The EFTA countries (with Switzerland included) accounted for 25 per cent of EU exports in 1989 and for 24 per cent in 1994.

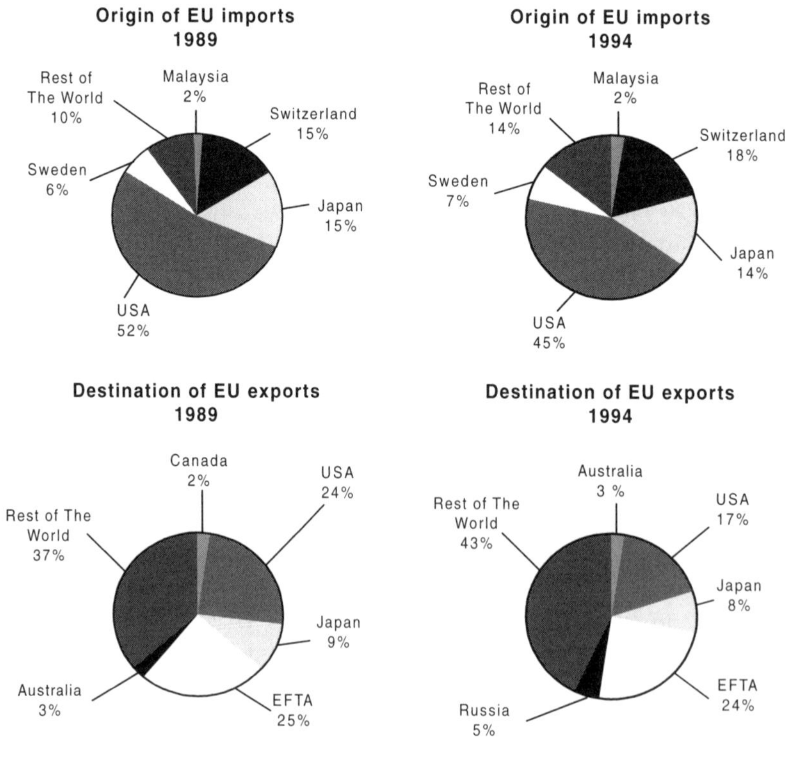

Figure 6.7 Destination and origin of EU imports and exports of MSE (in %; 1989, 1994). Source: EUROSTAT, 1997.

Other countries that gained importance as EU suppliers and destination countries were Malaysia, Pakistan and the Pacific Rim countries. An important part of the EU's lower price segment sales was already captured by these markets. Malaysia accounted for 2 per cent of EU imports in 1989 and for 2 per cent in 1994. The 'rest of the world' covered 10 per cent of EU imports in 1989 and 14 per cent in 1994. In 1989 the EU directed 37 per cent of its exports to the 'rest of the world' and by 1994 this had increased to 43 per cent.

Production process

Even if historically this sector did not require sophisticated production processes, this has changed dramatically. Today, the technical complexity of the sector requires advanced production processes. A consequence is that an increasing number of firms in this sector outsource certain production steps, creating a large network of subcontractors that are highly specialised in particular product areas. This development is assumed to be accentuated through the further adoption of electronic communication links between firms. Process innovation is extremely important in the MSE sector.

On one side there are technologically sophisticated medical instruments such as endoscopes and on the other side there are standardised surgical instruments such as knives, forceps and tweezers. To illustrate the production process of a standardised surgical instrument, the different production steps are described in Appendix 5.

Within the EU, labour and non-labour costs have risen more or less in line with productivity. However, costs rose much faster than productivity during 1991 and 1992, whereas in 1993 and 1994 they grew at the same rate.[8]

Competition and main actors

The MSE sector consists of many SMEs, which often act as subcontractors, and a few large enterprises. A majority of SMEs are in highly specialised niches. Despite their small size they are able to compete with larger firms in their specific sector of activity.

Major global actors in MSE are those specialising in healthcare, such as Baxter (USA) or Gambro (Sweden), and conglomerates that have different manufacturing activities, such as Siemens (Germany) or Philips (The Netherlands). In addition, large defence firms have examined the feasibility of transferring some of their skills into the MSE sector. Other important Swedish producers are Arjo (hygiene systems and patient-handling products), Getinge (sterilisation and disinfection systems) and Moelnlcyke (disposables). In addition to Baxter, which is the world's largest producer of healthcare products, producing in almost all areas of

Table 6.6 MSE production of major producers in the world market in million euros (1985–1993)

	1985	*1990*	*1993*
EUR12	3,881	5,204	6,217
USA	8,285	6,787	9,189
Japan	3,125	3,878	5,362
Canada	271	315	417
Israel	311	216	333
Taiwan	97	149	220
South Korea	62	134	208
Brazil	307	165	192
Hong Kong	78	85	106

Source: Elsevier Advanced Technology, Oxford, UK. *Yearbook of World Electronics Data 1995.*

medical equipment, other American producers are 3M, Becton Dickinson, Bristol Myers Squibb, GE, Johnson and Johnson and Pfizer. Important Japanese firms are Olympus and Toshiba.

Draeger Werke (Germany), l'Air Liquide (France), Ohmeda (United Kingdom) and British Oxygen (United Kingdom) are all specialised in the production of anaesthetic apparatus and equipment. Important EU firms in orthopaedic appliances are Smith and Nephew (United Kingdom), Dow Corning (France), Otto Bock (Germany), Waldemar Link (Germany) and Gebrüder Martin (Germany).

Some EU leaders in particular product applications are Karl Storz (Germany) and Richard Wolf (Germany), both specialising in the manufacture of fixed endoscopic devices, where each of them held about 35 per cent of the world market (1995). This leadership was possible despite the relatively small size of the firms. German firms with fewer than 100 employees produced about half of the world's output of MSE in 1995. Aesculab in Tuttlingen (Germany) is one of the few large firms in this area (Table 6.6).

Regional distribution

A specific characteristic of the regions involved with the production of MSE is their high development in terms of engineering knowledge. In the EU one can find those regions or industrial districts in the UK Midlands and the so-called 'banana', which covers the South-East of England, via the Paris region and Eastern France, down through Germany and into Northern Italy.

The MSE industry is often concentrated in clusters[9] of highly specialised SMEs. In this traditional craft sector, which was only recently transformed into a high-technology industry, the specialised know-how of the participating firms reinforces clustering and firms learn to take

Figure 6.8 The famous 'banana'.

advantage of cooperation. Economies deriving from the concentration of business services, the existence of a pool of specialised workers and technological spill-overs constitute positive agglomeration effects in industrial districts specialising in MSE. Examples are the region of Tuttlingen in Southern Germany, the region of Nogent in France and the region of Lecce in Italy.

Due to rapid technological changes in the industry, closeness to R&D centres and universities is important in all regions. Technological spill-overs are not only reinforced through inter-firm cooperation, but also through the cooperation between firms and research centres.

Outlook

The ageing population and an increased awareness of health matters act as stimulating factors on the demand side. In addition to increasing incomes, these factors lead to strong growth tendencies in the MSE industry.

The technological sophistication of the products has grown further. Harmonised EU standards within the sector benefit both EU and foreign producers. Once the product conforms to EU standards it circulates without hindrance in all countries of the EU, compared to the situation before the Single Market Programme when producers had to satisfy the purchaser country's standards. Therefore, small niche producers can continue their strategy of product specialisation and access much wider markets than before.

For low end products, asset migration to developing countries such as Pakistan, Thailand, Malaysia and China is a common practice, either via fully owned operations or by joint ventures with local firms. But the future success of EU firms in the MSE industry depends on their ability to achieve technological equivalence with US producers in high end areas and to cope with increased competition from developing countries in low end products. Focused R&D investment, product differentiation and constant improvements in marketing and distribution are important success factors.

Our investigation of intra- and extra-EU imports and exports for France, Germany and Italy has shown that there was a pronounced '1992 effect' in the MSE industry. It is obvious that EU firms investing in 'new' products benefited from the removal of border controls and the harmonisation of technical standards.

7 Field research

The information in this chapter is given in the following way: first, the questionnaire research is introduced by briefly outlining the different questions and describing the role of SMEs in the three countries under investigation. Second, the conduct of the case-study research is introduced. Both industrial districts are presented with reference to their historical background and actual situation. Each SME is described by a case study.

Conduct of the questionnaire research

The objective of the questionnaire research was to find out if the 1992 removal of NTBs affected SMEs located outside industrial districts. It may also be possible to reveal country-specific differences.

The first versions of the questionnaire were based on the literature survey of Part I. Other versions followed in cooperation with the CEOs and other leading managers of the firms that are presented below. The questionnaire was further improved by the suggestions received during the interviews with French and German SMEs. Altogether, the formulation of the questionnaire took about four months.

Aimed at SMEs, the questionnaire had to be short but very precise. Altogether, there were eleven questions on three pages, some of them 'multiple choice', some of them fixed-alternative, some of them open-ended; the majority, however, were closed.

The firms were first asked if they were distributors or producers of new products or standardised products or both. Then they had to indicate which activities of their value-chain took place at home or abroad. Other questions concerned their foreign-market entry strategies and the reasons for their international operations. In order to find out if the EMU influenced their international strategies, they were asked if the abolition of different NTBs provided an advantage or a drawback for their firm.

The questionnaire was translated into French, German and Italian. The final version of the questionnaire is in Appendix 2. The addresses of the

SMEs originated from *Europages*. The choice of the 300 addresses in France, Germany and Italy was random. It was difficult to exclude all cases in which the SME belonged to a larger firm.

Each country's history, institutions and policy have a considerable influence on the location of the enterprises, on R&D activities and therefore on SMEs' internationalisation strategies. Therefore, the following section contains a short description of the SME sector in the respective countries.

The countries selected

Germany

German industry is highly clustered. Porter identifies important clusters in chemistry and in the area of metals, metalworking and associated machinery. Some of the most important metal-processing industries grew out of Germany's historical position in iron and steel production. But there has been a parallel growth of suppliers and buyers, both of whom have reinforced each other.[1]

One main characteristic of the German SME sector is its heterogeneity. At one end are innovative SMEs with a strong market position, which employ highly qualified personnel to produce high-quality products. At the other end are SMEs which mass-produce a relatively simple, substitutable product, which operate in markets with sharp fluctuations of demand and in which the jobs require few qualifications.[2] These two strategies can be found within one industry.

Depending on these different strategies, firms compete either on the basis of differentiation or on the basis of costs at an international level. In many specialised industries, such as the MSE industry, an international orientation is necessary to achieve critical volume to reap economies of scale. In most cases selling is technical and less based on advertising.[3] Due to the technical and scientific backgrounds of most German SME owners, there is a desire to achieve technical perfection and high quality. Often, the owner is involved in all aspects of the business, especially in technical ones, and establishes close relationships with his employees. In many cases, the firm structure is hierarchical and patriarchal.[4]

Compared to most European and Asian countries the German government is weakly involved in industrial policy. There is no foreign-trade ministry in Germany as foreign trade is principally seen as the role of firms and not of government. Export financing takes place on a commercial basis and not through a government agency.[5] However, one important area of policy measures aimed at the SME sector is that of research and technology policy. About 25 to 30 per cent of total federal expenditure on civil R&D is channelled to SMEs with fewer than 500 employees. But SMEs contribute only 13 to 16 per cent of total research expenditures to the economy as a whole, which means that SMEs are supported at a level that far exceeds their importance to the research process in the economy.[6]

France

France is a special case as the long-term trend towards concentration in French industry appears irreversible. But a general trend towards regionalisation was given by the *loi de décentralisation* in 1982, when the regions acquired more decision-making power over R&D expenditures which was beneficial for the development of high-technology clusters among SMEs.[7] SMEs account for about 99 per cent of all enterprises in France; they employ around 69.4 per cent of its working force; they realise 63 per cent of the turnover and 60 per cent of the value-added by French enterprises.[8]

According to estimates, about 30 to 40 per cent of SMEs in the industrial sector develop international operations. Among exporting SMEs within the manufacturing sector, 15 per cent of them realise 72 per cent of all exports, even if they represent only 22 per cent of employment and 26 per cent of turnover.[9] French SMEs' internationalisation is often encouraged by large enterprises through subcontracting.

Italy

The Italian production system is characterised by relatively small enterprises and establishments. SMEs with less than ten employees represented 94.2 per cent of the total number of Italian firms in 1992.[10]

The Italian industry is highly concentrated geographically as the majority of SMEs are in Northern and Central Italy (91.1 per cent).[11] Geographical concentration in industrial districts is prevalent in Northern Italy. Many industries are centred in one or two towns, such as the food industry in Parma, the packaging machinery industry in Bologna and the steel industry in Brescia.[12] There are about sixty-five geographic zones of highly specialised SMEs. Italian SMEs have a strong family orientation and there is a strong tendency for the family to live in one area.[13]

The two major areas of SMEs' specialisation are all kind of mechanical industries and the manufacturing of traditional consumer goods. The typical Italian SME is a highly specialised producer of a limited range of goods, organised very flexibly in order to meet customer needs. Innovation efforts are continuous and even the traditional craft firm introduces new technology and up-to-date equipment.[14] Customised production in small batches goes hand-in-hand with a highly fragmented market where firms must be able to respond quickly to fashion and demand changes.[15] Italian SMEs have to provide rapid service to their customers at home which provokes an intense home-market competition and rivalry that is extremely beneficial in an international context.[16]

From 1992 until 1994, the number of sales abroad from the Northern Italian region increased by 30 per cent. Exports doubled between 1986 and 1994, sustained by the devaluation of the Italian lira.[17] Among Italian enterprises with 51 to 100 employees, 68 per cent are exporters; among enterprises with 101 to 300 employees, 80 per cent are exporters; and among those with 301 to 500 employees, 83 per cent are exporters.[18]

The industries in which Italian firms are internationally successful are highly segmented, specialised or fragmented. These industries are characterised by low standardisation, low investment in fundamental research and low capital-intensity.[19] Even if Italy is relatively weak in formal research, due to the lack of formation and funding in universities and government laboratories, Italian firms are strong in adapting foreign technologies and applying them to particular end-use applications. Modern flexible manufacturing technologies are applied to traditional products.

Further upgrading of Italian industry is constrained by relatively high costs of capital. SMEs suffer because of high interest rates for extended periods and the absence of venture capital. The public equity market is relatively new, few firms are listed and the proportion of shares traded is small.[20]

In Italy, the Ministry of Foreign Trade is responsible for the policy relating to exports. Their export policy includes the promotion of information on export consortia of small firms by offering financial support in the areas of export promotion and marketing and schemes for insuring and financing export activities and guarantees.[21] It is, however, important to note that government support for Italian enterprises was especially directed at the developing countries.[22]

Conduct of the case studies

The objective of the case-study research was to find out if SMEs located in industrial districts felt affected by the EMU. An interesting question was if there were major differences between the SMEs located in industrial districts and the SMEs located outside with respect to their degree of internationalisation and international strategies.

The case studies were conducted with five SMEs in the industrial district of Tuttlingen (Germany) and two SMEs in the industrial district of Nogent (France). The selection of the firms was random as their addresses were obtained through the Chamber of Commerce and *Europages*. Initially, three case studies were planned in each industrial district. However, interest and feasibility dictated our choice in practice.

In Tuttlingen, seven out of thirty-two contacted SMEs responded. One answer was, however, negative and one interview was of no use because of the owner's anxiety regarding local competition. In particular, the smaller firms (up to twenty employees) that participated in the case-study research preferred to stay anonymous. In three out of the five firms strategic management is handled by the director and owner because of their small firm size (less than twenty employees). In these cases the owner was the contact person for the interviews. In the two larger firms we met the manager who had the responsibility for strategic issues regarding the internationalisation process.

In Nogent, one out of fifteen SMEs sent a positive answer. This relatively small firm (eight employees) put us in contact with a medium-sized firm that can be considered as the leader of the region. In the case of the small firm, the director was the contact person and in the medium-sized firm it was the manager who was responsible for international operations.

The questionnaire on which the interviews were based was semi-directed. The interviews lasted between one and two hours. They were taped with the permission of all respondents. Because they were taped, there was little danger of distortion. Afterwards the interviews were typed in the respective languages and summarised in a case study. At the same time we noted questions to fill in the few gaps that we found in our material. We phoned or faxed our contact persons to get answers to missing points. The missing points were included in the case study and sent to the contact persons for a final overview and to obtain their agreement. In some cases a second interview was granted to clarify some points.

A major problem for the elaboration of the case studies was the missing indirect information such as annual reports, articles or earlier research. The case studies of smaller firms therefore strongly reflect the attitudes and character of the owner.

Similar questions on their internationalisation strategies and the industrial district were asked in all firms.[23] We started with general questions about the manager and his role in the firm and went on to general questions about the firm. Since these firms are small, there is a

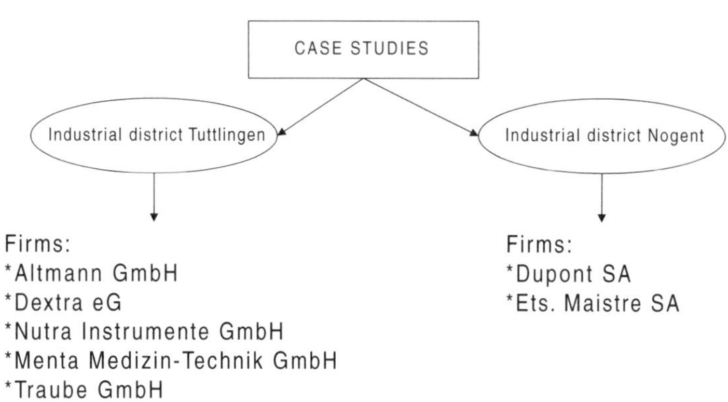

Figure 7.1 Case studies.

strong interdependence between the history and description of the individual and the firm. After the more descriptive questions we moved to questions on their internationalisation behaviour. We focused on how the firm acted in this arena and asked about the influence of the removal of NTBs on their internationalisation strategies. The final questions were on the firm's position in the industrial district.

The industrial district of Tuttlingen

In 1999, Tuttlingen had about 60,000 inhabitants and around 250 firms[24] with 4,500 employees who were specialised in the production or distribution of MSE. Tuttlingen is situated in Baden-Württemberg, well known for its high proportion of SMEs. In fact, the Baden-Württemberg area has the highest concentration of research institutes in Europe and accounts for 30 per cent of Germany's R&D efforts.[25]

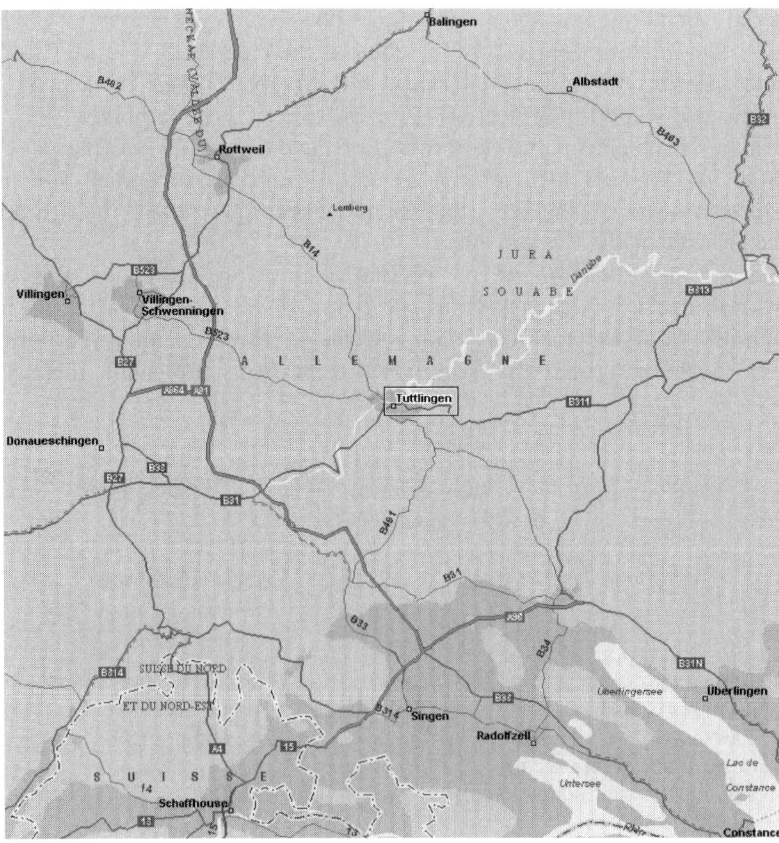

Figure 7.2 Location of Tuttlingen (map).

There are historical reasons for the concentration of the MSE industry in Tuttlingen.[26] As far back as the sixteenth-century mining companies were located in the region around Tuttlingen. Easy open-cast working was done by the farmers in their fields. The ores were brought to the mining companies. There were iron-foundries that produced nails in high quantities. In addition to nails, they started to produce knives that were sold on the Swiss market in particular. The production of surgical knives began around 1840. But until the middle of the nineteenth century, the production of surgical knives was in the hands of craft firms producing all kinds of knives. In the middle of the nineteenth century there was increased competition from firms located in Solingen in the centre of Germany. The firms in Solingen had the advantage of being located close to heavy industry and raw materials. These advantages facilitated the craft firms' changeover to mass production. In this sense, the future looked rather dark for the firms in Tuttlingen.

This situation changed with one man. The break-through was the foundation of Aesculap by the cuttler Gottfried Jetter in Tuttlingen in 1867. Gottfried Jetter used to travel as a journeyman around Europe and learnt the production techniques of surgical instruments in Paris, Geneva, Strasbourg and Marburg. Back in Tuttlingen, he put together all existing instruments in a catalogue and started to produce in large quantities. The large-scale production of stock was new in the middle of the nineteenth century as instruments used to be produced on special order. For Tuttlingen, this company's creation was important because of the competition from the cutlery sector in Solingen. Inventions such as X-rays, chloroform and asepsis pushed the development in the surgical instrumentation industry forward. In 1998, Aesculap was the leader in this area of production, not only in the region of Tuttlingen, but also world-wide. It had about 2,800 employees, exported to 140 countries and had production plants in Poland, Malaysia and the UK.[27]

Within the region, the company birth rate was traditionally high. Employees used to be trained in enterprises such as Aesculap before starting their own business. The wave of business creations was particularly high after World War I when manpower was relatively abundant. During this hard time exporting was very difficult because of inflation. Some craft firms had already combined their distribution activities and were therefore able to operate internationally despite the hard time. These interesting firm constellations survived. An example are the Gebrüder Martin-Medizin-Technik. After World War II, Medicon was founded as a cooperative with similar objectives. Other firms with a world-wide reputation and a high market share are Karl Storz and Hencke-Sass, Wolf, both specialised in endoscopes and highly internationalised.

A second wave of business creations occurred in the 1960s and 1970s. Later, in the 1990s, some fifteen to twenty businesses per annum were founded.[28] By imitating and following Aesculap's and other leading firms' strategies, the firms in this sector were characterised by a high degree of internationalisation.

Leading firms in Tuttlingen started their delocalisation of labour-intensive production steps relatively early in the 1960s and 1970s. Destinations were Malaysia and Pakistan in particular and, in the 1990s, China and Eastern European countries. As can be seen in the following case studies, this leads to interesting firm constellations and cooperation agreements.

It is important to mention that before 1960 there were at least ten swage forges in Tuttlingen, while in 1999 only two of these had survived because of strict environmental legislation in Germany.

ALTMANN GmbH

> About 30% of our products have been introduced less than 3 years ago. In 1993, ALTMANN presented the world's first ever fully autoclavable endoscope on which all possible leakage routes are laser-welded or soldered. In this sense, one of our most important reasons to internationalise is the access to new technologies and business know-how.
>
> (Mr Hoppe, Vice President Sales and Marketing)

COMPANY BACKGROUND

The firm was founded in 1923 by Georg Andreas Altmann who started his career in the area of medical instruments as an apprentice at Aesculap in Tuttlingen. After this apprenticeship his work as a travelling apprentice took him across Germany and also to Berlin. In 1923 G.A. Altmann returned to his home town of Tuttlingen where he founded his own manufacturing company for medical technological products, together with an apprentice in a basement. Reusable syringes and cannulae, which were synonymous with the founder's name (he was known under the name of 'Spritzen-Altmann'), were the most profitable source of income for the company for decades. The world's first calibrated syringes with glass cylinders originated there. Both World War II and the German 'economic miracle' led to an increasing demand for syringes and cannulae. G.A. Altmann limited his products to just a few lines, which he continuously improved. In 1957 the number of staff reached 344, 48 of them apprentices, and an old factory building in the centre of Tuttlingen was bought.

In the 1960s, the first steps towards minimal-invasive diagnostics and therapy presaged major breakthroughs in medicine. G.A. Altmann recognised these developments and acquired the Berlin endoscope manufacturer Wittge in 1960 with the aim of securing the company's future via diversification.

The founder, G.A. Altmann, was a real character. A man who knew everyone in the company personally by name, '[A] man who during the boom years, would take his leave of people who had just done a twelve-hour day with a curt "Bye", but say "Thank you!" to those who stayed fourteen hours.'[29] He was an archetypal Swabian entrepreneurial legend, highly economical, good at business, starting modestly yet going far.

In 1965, G.A. Altmann was forced to sell his company due to age and family reasons to Huber Industries, an American conglomerate, which planned to expand into the medical technology market with the purchase. There were, however, a few collisions between American and Swabian managerial methods and several abrupt changes of management damaged ALTMANN. The fast-growing disposable-syringe and cannulae sector, already added to the product range in 1966, was shifted to a new factory in Leibertingen, near Tuttlingen, in 1972. In 1973, the Berlin Wittge company was dissolved and shifted to Tuttlingen.

RECENT DEVELOPMENTS

In 1976, ALTMANN was sold by Huber Industries to the Windisch family. Stability returned under the company's new ownership and its new managing director, Werner Müller. The Windisch era began, however, with some painful restructuring measures. Around 30 per cent of the staff were made redundant. Through high investments and tough development work the endoscope sector was made into the mainstay of ALTMANN'S business. Steady sales growth in this sector from 1982 onwards made clear that this decision was far-sighted.

A second component was the reorganisation of the reusable-syringe product range by concentrating on application and injection systems for veterinary and dental medicine. In 1998, ALTMANN was one of the world's leading manufacturers of these products.

The third component concerned the international activities of the company. ALTMANN had been a successful exporter since the 1950s, but consistent orientation towards the world market, and the securing of export activities through its own subsidiaries and production facilities in the most important international markets, were further strategies followed by the Windisch family.

In addition to these three main aspects of restructuring, ALTMANN changed its organisational structure entirely. In 1985, Mr Hoppe replaced area management by product management. The whole organisation was separated into clearly defined strategic business units to achieve transparency, efficient planning and control. Efficiency of the whole organisation structure increased because of the growing specialisation of each product manager and each team.

In 1984, the disposable-syringe business was sold to the Almo group, the largest European manufacturer in that sector. ALTMANN retained a share of 18 per cent and was still directly responsible for the product. The company distributed about 20 per cent of Almo's output of disposable syringes. The sale of this traditional sector became necessary as neither company could reach separately the critical mass necessary to remain internationally competitive. Through the merger of both production plants, ALTMANN was able to achieve important economies of scale.

Another milestone was the take-over of the leading microlens manufacturer Trautmann, Germany, in 1997. ALTMANN was thus enabled to perfect its core competence in the endoscope sector. The objective was long-term control over this essential technology. In January 1999, ALTMANN'S share in Trautmann increased to 75 per cent, to grow further to 100 per cent from January 2000 on. ALTMANN used to buy around 60 per cent of its microlens components from Trautmann and 40 per cent from another highly specialised firm located in Switzerland. Before the take-over ALTMANN negotiated with both firms, each of which was confronted with changes due to the age of their directors. Both firms were highly interested in a take-over, but ALTMANN favoured the German partner. Compared to Germany, Switzerland was considered an extremely expensive location for the production of microlens components. Wages were much higher in Switzerland than in Germany, and the production of those highly specialised components consisted of around 10 per cent material costs, while the rest were wage costs. In addition to cost reasons, Germany's membership of the EU influenced the choice in favour of Trautmann. In this context Mr Hoppe emphasised:

> The non-participation of Switzerland in the EU influenced strongly our decision against our Swiss partner. A problem with which we are permanently confronted is the development of the Swiss franc. The Swiss franc is up since a certain time which makes the acquisition of Swiss components expensive. And the future is uncertain....

Trautmann realised about 90 per cent of its turnover on the German market. Despite the take-over by ALTMANN, Trautmann continued to distribute microlens components to competitors of ALTMANN. The parent company clearly supported this strategy. In 1998, ALTMANN employed about sixty people at Trautmann in Göttingen.

THE PRODUCTS

During the seventy-five years of the firm's existence its product range changed through the take-over of other firms and through the firm's own discoveries, inventions and product improvements. Some important milestones were the invention of the calibrated metal/glass cylindrical syringe by G.A. Altmann, the simplification of the disposable syringe and the improvements of the lenses in the firm's endoscopic devices. In 1998, the product range consisted of the following articles:

- medical endoscopes and accessories
- reusable injection and application systems for dental and veterinary medicine
- technical endoscopes and accessories
- flowmeters and flow controllers
- disposable syringes and disposable cannulae.

In 1998, the whole endoscope sector created more than 50 per cent of the firm's turnover, whereas it used to be only 15 per cent in 1983. Through important investments in R&D in the 1980s, endoscopes gradually became the firm's main sector of growth and profit. Technical endoscopes had already reached a certain turnover level in the 1980s which later stagnated, whereas the sector of medical endoscopes continued growing. The exception was 1992/93 when an international crisis struck the sector of minimal-invasive surgery.[30] 1998 constituted the most successful year in the firm's history.

All R&D activities are located in the headquarters in Tuttlingen to optimise invention and improvements of the product range. Good contacts with research and medical practice are seen as key factors for success. In this sense, the advantage of close cooperation with universities and Fraunhofer Institutes was emphasised. The restructuring of the firm's organisation in strategic business units promoted this cooperation between the firm and research institutes by defining and assuming clear responsibilities. The instruments are assembled from start to finish by self-directed, interlinked teams. This cooperation between the firm and research institutes has always taken place in close coordination with the firm's customers who are in a central position between the firm and the end user.

ALTMANN'S INTERNATIONAL ACTIVITIES

ALTMANN has been a successful exporter since the 1950s, but the securing of export activities via its own subsidiaries and production facilities in the most important international markets constituted a new challenge following the Windisch era, even though the firm had traditionally earned a large part of its turnover abroad. In 1998, about 75 per cent of the firm's annual turnover was due to its international operations. But, out of the remaining 25 per cent earned on the home market, a part was certainly destined for international customers due to indirect exporting activities.

Out of the 75 per cent, a growing share (30 per cent) went to EU countries. Despite these rather positive EU results, ALTMANN'S major market was the USA (45 per cent). The huge US market is clearly considered as a key for the future success of the firm in the area of medical endoscopes and accessories. Success on the US market is viewed as a precondition for success in Europe.

Exports and imports ALTMANN'S export strategies are based on exclusive representatives and commercial agents. However, the firm's exclusive representatives are not based on contracts, but on gentlemen's agreements. The constellation of these distribution mechanisms is strongly dependent on both the product and the respective cooperation partner. In Spain, for example, the firm has an exclusive representative for its medical endoscopes and two or three commercial agents for the distribution of its reusable syringes, whereas in Italy ALTMANN has an exclusive representative in the area of gynaecology and, in different regions, commercial agents for the other products.

The firm buys the majority of its raw materials, such as steel and glass, in Germany. It buys only some highly specialised articles such as precision tubes in Switzerland. Apart from some specialised basic inputs, ALTMANN still buys 40 per cent of its microlens components from its Swiss partner despite the acquisition of Trautmann in 1997.

Contacts abroad are made through congresses, fairs, direct mailing, marketing reports and advertising in special magazines. The firm's major customers are its representatives and commercial agents on the one hand and, on the other, large multinational corporations that need ALTMANN'S products to complete incoming tenders. The growing importance of the endoscope sector reinforces the firm's competitive position. The only sector where ALTMANN is still forced to compete for tenders is in reusable syringes. The firm's endoscopes are always present in the tenders of their large multinational customers. According to estimates, 80 per cent of the firm's annual turnover is due to about thirty important customers and the rest is spread among 500 smaller ones.

The firm's preference for own subsidiaries and production plants The Windisch era and its restructuring led to a new approach regarding ALTMANN'S foreign-market entry strategies. The firm deepened its orientation towards the world market and further secured the firm's export activities via its own subsidiaries and production facilities.

A first step in this direction was the foundation of ALTMANN UK in 1987, responsible for distribution activities in the UK. The decision in favour of its own subsidiary in the UK was, however, more an opportunistic than a strategic decision. Over a period of several years, ALTMANN had been forced to change their exclusive representative at least three times. After the bankruptcy of their last partner, the company decided to avoid future situations which involved starting from scratch. The initial decision to invest directly in the UK was therefore provoked by the wish to avoid future uncertainties with potential cooperation partners. The main advantages resulting from this direct investment was a strong and controllable market presence in the important English market.[31] It became much easier for ALTMANN to operate in this relatively isolated market than before. But it was also an opportunity to determine for themselves the prices for the end-user. By 1998, the UK subsidiary employed ten people.

The direct investment in Massachusetts, USA, was strategically planned. In 1991, ALTMANN founded its own subsidiary with production and service facilities in this important market. The US market was one that the firm knew well. In 1982, ALTMANN had made its breakthrough on the US endoscope market with a new distribution partner. The minimal-invasive therapy and diagnostic sector flourished and the company committed itself to the development of new endoscopes. Due to these prior experiences on the US market ALTMANN knew about the importance of after-sales service. In this context Mr Hoppe emphasised: 'Hospitals in the USA want to have machines or instruments replaced in the case of problems within 24 hours. This is impossible for a firm located only in the German market. Market presence was therefore a necessity.'

After having reached the critical size for an own subsidiary, the firm did not hesitate in becoming established. In the beginning, the US subsidiary fulfilled only service activities. The second step on the US market was the transfer of some final assembling activities in the sector of endoscopes from the German to the US market. By doing this, the firm became more independent from US protectionism (FDA)[32] and strong DM/$ exchange-rate fluctuations. ALTMANN planned to transfer further activities of the product's value-chain to increase their presence where important market growth was expected to take place. In addition, it was very helpful to emphasise *vis-à-vis* US customers that major parts of the production process were taking place in the USA. The value creation in the USA was about 50 per cent for repair activities and 30 per cent for the new instruments in 1998. But the USA was also an interesting testing ground for new products because of the more innovative attitudes of US doctors compared with their European colleagues.

Despite the planned transfer of further activities to the US subsidiary, ALTMANN favours the German location for the production of mechanical and microlens components. In the two production plants in Tuttlingen, highly specialised personnel, the German 'Facharbeiter', are trained to work with high-tech machines. They are at the top of the world scale regarding their profession. To reach this high degree of sophistication and persistent international competitiveness, ALTMANN'S apprenticeship quota is always superior to 10 per cent of the work force, which mean 30 apprentices out of 240 employees in 1998.

The Polish subsidiary started its operations in 1994. The main reason for the establishment of a production plant in Poland was lower labour costs. At the beginning of the 1990s the choice of a country with relatively low labour costs had become necessary for the production of labour-intensive products such as reusable injection and application systems. Different countries were investigated in detail. Initially, the firm held discussions with companies in Pakistan and Malaysia. Malaysia was preferred because it was recommended by a German firm that maintained close and regular contacts with ALTMANN. The fall of the Berlin Wall facilitated the decision process of ALTMANN. In this context Mr Hoppe pointed out:

> Suddenly we had Pakistan before our doors, which constituted an enormous advantage for our firm. The decision in favour of a particular location became easy. In Poland, we are able to have the same advantages as in Pakistan or Malaysia regarding labour costs, but the distance is much shorter.

In 1998, ALTMANN already employed forty people in the ex-combinat for medical instruments. One advantage was the relatively high level of technical training of Polish employees. Even if the training of employees, the organisational structure and the spatial conditions did not permit the production of high-tech products up to 1998, future plans foresaw the production of medical endoscopes thereafter. The majority of reusable injection and application systems produced in Poland are used in the veterinary area rather than in the area of human medicine. The German headquarters prepared the entire production processes, then transferred the appropriate machines and training programmes for all the employees to Poland.

INFLUENCES OF THE EUROPEAN ECONOMIC AND MONETARY UNION

ALTMANN considered the different currencies in the EU to be the strongest hurdle. Despite the removal of border controls and red tape since 1992, ALTMANN criticised the emergence of new administrative paperwork.

The introduction of the single currency The introduction of the euro from January 1999 constituted a challenge for the firm and was therefore prepared for conscientiously. Regarding the changeover, ALTMANN introduced two programmes, one for the year 2000 and the other for the arrival of the single currency in 2002. Since January 1999, the firm has been able to send out its invoices in euros, but only to customers who desired this. In the middle of 1998, ALTMANN sent a letter to their customers asking them if they preferred the national currency or the euro during the transition period. At the same time ALTMANN received letters from their large multinational customers informing them that invoices were to be expressed in euros from January 1999.

The major advantage expected from the introduction of the single currency was the end of exchange-rate risks within the EU countries. ALTMANN was often forced to bear the entire exchange-rate risk, especially when cooperating with smaller firms. Exchange-rate losses were common since the firm did not hedge the risk.

According to Mr Hoppe, the introduction of the single currency will lead to more competition within the EU. Increased price transparency will lead to major adjustments between the EU countries because of important price differences between one country and another. Scandinavia is, for example, very expensive in the endoscope sector compared to Germany. Because of the introduction of the single currency, Scandinavian competitors will be obliged to decrease their price level in order to stay competitive.

Harmonisation of technical standards The quality of ALTMANN'S medical instruments is tangible and in conformity with ISO 9001 and EN 46001. All ALTMANN products therefore come with fully documented production, so that the life-cycle of any product can be completely traced in the event of any maintenance or repair becoming necessary.

ALTMANN felt the harmonisation of technical standards to be a challenge. With 380 employees world-wide, it is a large firm for the Tuttlingen region. The establishment of quality management was less of an administrative burden or a cost problem for ALTMANN than it would have been for a smaller firm. In addition, this was an opportunity for the firm to differentiate itself at an early stage from its smaller competitors in the Tuttlingen region. The firm introduced ISO 9001 in 1994, and EN 46001 and the CE certification years before it became a legal necessity. Despite the initial administrative burden ALTMANN recognised the long-term benefits of this early introduction *vis-à-vis* its competitors, but also with regard to its own organisation structure.

> The introduction of quality management led to some important reorganisations in the firm. The change of some processes and structures was obvious, but it is always difficult to change things that have been done in the same way for years.
>
> (Mr Hoppe)

The initial administrative costs were entirely compensated by fewer defective products and increased customer satisfaction.

In addition to quality management, ALTMANN declared the protection of the environment to be a central corporate aim for its seventy-fifth anniversary year in 1998. With the first environment declaration and certification according to EC directive No. 1836/93, an important step had been taken. Over 130 documented environmental projects were under way at ALTMANN in 1998.

Despite the harmonisation of technical standards in the EU, Mr Hoppe criticised the attitude of France in this matter. According to a common EU standard for the sterilisation of endoscopes, operating temperatures had to be 134°C for seven minutes. The only country world-wide insisting on 134°C for 18 minutes was France. As a result, French producers encountered many problems with their endoscopes. Because of the failure of the French to adopt harmonised technical standards, and also because business has to be conducted in French, ALTMANN considers France the most difficult market within the EU. Only a few of the large multinationals are good French customers.

INDUSTRIAL COMPETITORS

ALTMANN feels competition from different actors on a world-wide basis, but also at a national and local level. Low-tech products, such as reusable injection and application systems, are strongly affected by the competition from countries with relatively low labour costs, such as Pakistan, China and Malaysia. The opening of a production plant in Poland was a necessary step to meet the competition from these cheap-labour countries.

Competition in the endoscope sector comes from other middle-sized firms and large multinationals that have the money to invest continually in innovation. In this sector, competitors are located in developed countries such as the USA and Europe.

Tuttlingen, where ALTMANN has its traditional headquarters, offers a special infrastructure for the firm. This industrial district contains about 250 other SMEs, but also some large firms that produce and distribute MSE. Nearly all firms are highly internationalised despite their small size. Joint ventures or production plants in countries with relatively low labour costs to produce low-tech products efficiently, and also the invention and production of high-tech products, are common strategies. According to Mr Hoppe, the resulting competition acts as a strong stimulant for further innovative activities and improves day-to-day business.

Despite competition ALTMANN benefits strongly from cooperation with other local firms producing medical instruments. It maintains regular contacts, based on informal agreements, with about twenty firms in the Tuttlingen region. Even if ALTMANN'S purchases from these firms are relatively low in volume, these contacts, based on the mutual trust of all participants, are considered as very important. This informal cooperation includes the mutual recommendation of potential customers.

> If you've been in Tuttlingen for decades you know the infrastructure here. Some call it the 'Medical Mafia'.... It is important to know

> who works together with whom and from where the firms receive their goods. Such information can be very useful.
>
> (Mr Hoppe)

Mr Hoppe pointed out that ALTMANN benefits strongly from the international reputation of Tuttlingen. A potential customer knows that he is able to find everything concerning MSE in this relatively restricted agglomeration of highly specialised firms. To facilitate the customers' orientation, about 200 SMEs, ALTMANN among them, published a medical guide that each hotel in Tuttlingen offers at the reception desk. Firms' addresses and their products are described in the guide. Of course, large firms in Tuttlingen do not favour this project as they are not interested in their smaller counterparts becoming too internationally independent.

DEXTRA eG[33]

Mr Schneider, director of the sales department, pointed out: 'DEXTRA is an association of 18 SMEs in the medical and surgical instrumentation sector. The association was founded with the objective of distributing the products of its member firms on a national and international level.'

COMPANY BACKGROUND

In 1941, six workshops of the MSE industry, all of them located in Tuttlingen, founded the DEXTRA cooperative. The period of World War II rendered distribution difficult in this traditionally highly internationalised industry. The firms therefore combined their efforts and founded a distribution centre under a special legal form. From 1941 to 1998, new production firms joined the cooperative and some left it. In 1998 eighteen SMEs were members of the association. These eighteen producing firms employed some 300 people and DEXTRA another 70 directly.

The main task of DEXTRA changed in the 1980s and became more sophisticated. Growing competition forced DEXTRA to function as a real distribution centre, by organising all the marketing. Customers had to be found and DEXTRA instruments had to be promoted all over the world. This was closely related to the development of a more sophisticated product range.

> Once upon a time, when we had a pair of scissors or a needle, everybody knew what it was. We did not need a specialist to tell us if a product was useful and extraordinary by its quality. Today, with the more complicated product range, special knowledge and individual advice became a necessity for selling the products.
>
> (Mr Schneider)

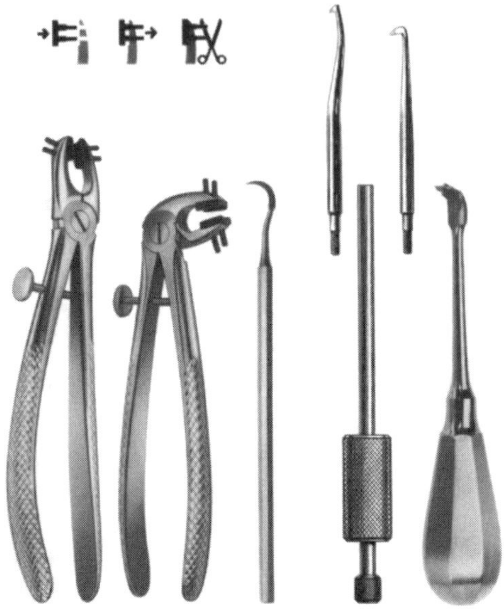

Figure 7.3 Surgical instruments 1.

PRODUCTS

DEXTRA member firms produced about 17,000 different instruments, all of them illustrated in a large catalogue. The complete DEXTRA range includes a relatively full line of instruments for general surgery as well as for some major specialities. Five major product areas can be distinguished: first, there are surgical instruments used for operations in hospitals; second, there are dental instruments for use by dentists or in the dental departments of hospitals; third, there are titanium implants for neuro- and hand surgery, oral and maxillofacial surgery, and plastic and ENT[34] surgery; fourth, there are container systems for the sterilisation and storage of instruments; and fifth, there are micromotor systems, needed to drive and operate attachments such as hand pieces, saws, etc.

Of the whole product range distributed by DEXTRA, 80 per cent is permanently available from stock, which implies strong financing and production capabilities.

THE INTERMEDIARY FUNCTION OF DEXTRA

Membership of DEXTRA is possible only under certain conditions, as admission must be of interest for the whole cooperative. Since 1979, no new member has been admitted.[35] The main reason for a manufacturing firm to request admission is the assurance of efficient distribution. After buying steel forgings, firms are able to concentrate on the design, production and finishing process. Increased specialisation is the result. Increased specialisation on the production side and large product diversification on the marketing side means that DEXTRA is able to compete successfully for incoming tenders.

While the functions of DEXTRA have become more sophisticated, its principal role of intermediary between manufacturing firms and customers has not changed. In accordance with the contract concluded between member firms and DEXTRA, DEXTRA is obliged to sell what is produced. This is, however, only valid regarding exports. The eighteen manufacturing firms are allowed to sell a certain percentage of their production under their own name, but only on a national level. In this context, Mr Schneider emphasised the importance of the DEXTRA brand. The quality standard of DEXTRA products is safeguarded by additional quality control in the distribution centre, after having been checked already by the manufacturer.

The intermediary function of DEXTRA between its member firms and customers is important in the area of research and development of new instruments or the improvement of old ones. Mr Schneider described the role of DEXTRA as a practical one. The manufacturing firms offer their products to DEXTRA, becoming informed in this way if their products fit in the product range of the distribution centre. DEXTRA, on the other hand, provides the market feedback. They are in contact with doctors all over the world and receive their ideas concerning product development and potential improvements.

> On the supply side, we have the firms, asking us to take this or that in our product range…on the other side, we have the doctors, telling us their experiences with our instruments during an operation. In this case, we have to inform our manufacturing firms about the propositions. The question is always if they are realisable.
>
> (Mr Schneider)

The manufacturing firms have to test the improvement or development of instruments for technical and financial viability. The price is determined in part by the potential quantity that is expected to be sold.

One of the main tasks of DEXTRA is therefore the coordination of information between manufacturing firms and customers, but also between the manufacturing firms themselves. The manufacturers have to be pushed in a direction that leads to the production of complementary products. Despite these efforts a certain overlapping of products is inevitable, sometimes even desirable, in order to be able to cope with sudden extra demand.

DEXTRA'S member firms produce about 95 per cent of its product range offered to the final customer. The firm obtains the rest of its product range from various domestic and international manufacturers, depending on the product. For the sterilisation container, for example, silicon mats and seals to close the container are imported from the USA.

1 per cent of DEXTRA'S turnover comes from other firms located in Tuttlingen, who buy DEXTRA products and stamp their own label on them. In this context, DEXTRA has to make sure that the products do not compete with DEXTRA internationally. About 1.5 per cent of DEXTRA'S turnover – a few years ago it used to be between 10 and 15 per cent – comes from selling to foreign firms, most of them in the USA, who re-sell under their own brand. Some US firms have an office in Tuttlingen to facilitate the process.

RESEARCH AND DEVELOPMENT ACTIVITIES

Increasing demand for more sophisticated instruments confronted DEXTRA with a revision of its initial role. In addition to the products, the advice now has to be sold. It is therefore necessary to have employees and commercial representatives who know the instruments.

Regarding the development of new instruments, there is a rather irregular but increasing cooperation with technical schools. Mr Schneider emphasised that cooperation between research centres and DEXTRA has gained in importance:

> Actually we would like to modernise and update our container systems. Something has to be changed on the form, its handles, its ventilation possibilities, etc. We don't always have enough people at DEXTRA to resolve this task. We have to contact therefore for example a technical school to get some solutions for our problem.
>
> (Mr Schneider)

Because of the cost of outsourcing a research project, DEXTRA tries to resolve problems first 'in-house'. If they have not been able to find an adequate solution, they ask a technical school to help. DEXTRA favours cooperation with technical universities and Fraunhofer Institutes in the future.

THE INTERNATIONALISATION OF THE DISTRIBUTION CENTRE

DEXTRA was founded with the objective of promoting the international distribution of MSE of its member firms. In 1997, DEXTRA exported their product range to about eighty countries all over the world.

Until the middle of the 1980s, however, DEXTRA exported about 95 per cent of the product range and distributed only 5 per cent to the German market. This relatively low percentage destined for the German market gradually increased and reached 20.5 per cent in 1997. According to Mr Schneider this development has nothing to do with DEXTRA'S product development, but was mainly due to a natural re-balancing of DEXTRA'S activities.

There are three reasons for DEXTRA'S recent increased concentration on the German market. First, German reunification opened interesting opportunities in Eastern Germany. From 1990 on, DEXTRA was busy developing this underrepresented market. Second, foreign customers wanted to know something about DEXTRA'S activities in Germany to get an idea of their product range and their reputation. Being successful in Germany became a kind of precondition for being successful abroad. A third reason was that DEXTRA'S initial concentration abroad had been in countries other than Germany, due to the dominance of a large competitor, Aesculap, on the German market. As Aesculap did not cover all markets world-wide, it had been easier to distribute DEXTRA products on other foreign markets, rather than in Germany, but DEXTRA now needed to establish itself in the German market.

> I joined DEXTRA in 1985. From my accent you recognise that my origins are not in Tuttlingen, but in Hamburg, Northern Germany. From the beginning I couldn't get used to the sentence: But, we've always done it like that . . . why should we change. . .? Of course, if you want to change something it must make sense, there must be a reasoning behind it.
>
> (Mr Schneider)

In 1997, 50.7 per cent of DEXTRA'S turnover originated in Europe, the German market not included. Africa accounted for 4 per cent, Asia 12.5 per cent, South and Latin America 6.4 per cent, and only 6.1 per cent in the USA. European turnover referred, however, to the whole of Europe, Central and Eastern Europe included. But the markets with the highest turnover were still France, Italy, Spain and The Netherlands. The Scandinavian countries were not so highly represented. The markets where DEXTRA generated a high percentage of its turnover were all markets with relatively uncomplicated and easy access.

International market entry strategies Despite its size, DEXTRA has undertaken no FDI. Its concentration on exporting activities corresponds better to its corporate form as a cooperative. The one exception was a wholly owned distribution subsidiary, first in Detroit and later in Atlanta. This subsidiary was, however, closed on the death of its director, an American who had married a German.[36]

In 1998, the whole distribution process was organised through exports. In general, DEXTRA tries to find firms to distribute its products on an exclusive basis. They must be specialised in the medical sector to sell the products efficiently in their respective countries, especially since they are given exclusive distribution rights to sell DEXTRA products. This is essential when taking into account the increasingly high-tech level of the products. In some large EU countries such as Spain, France and Italy, DEXTRA has several commercial representatives in different regions, to cope with the market size. Some exceptions are Northern Italy where DEXTRA has its own employee – a national – and Austria and Switzerland where only one firm distributes DEXTRA instruments, despite the market size and the decentralised structure of these countries.

The distributors are allowed to offer complementary products in addition to the DEXTRA product range. In some cases, these firms are representatives for another firm in the MSE sector. DEXTRA makes sure that this happens only for products where they are absent or under-represented. A good example is the production of instruments used for heart surgery, where DEXTRA is not specialised.

The choice of appropriate distributors takes place at medical and surgical congresses or professional exhibitions. In this sector of activity, it is always necessary to know which firms are on the market, who the competitors are and which reputable firm has lost a distributorship and is looking for a new one. Personal contacts furnish another opportunity for finding an appropriate partner. Contacts with other firms, not directly involved in the same sector of production as DEXTRA, have proved to be useful. The knowledge of the market is an important factor.

In prospecting for a potential foreign partner, the firm size plays an essential role. DEXTRA preferrs cooperation with SMEs. Smaller firms concentrate their efforts to a higher degree than larger firms on the distribution of DEXTRA instruments. The majority of small firms distributing DEXTRA instruments abroad need to achieve a certain turnover with them in order to guarantee their own survival. A larger firm would be less dependent on DEXTRA.

In addition to these experiences, DEXTRA includes in each distribution contract a clause which specifies that the representation is not taken over by another firm in the case of an acquisition. This protection through an exclusive contract became necessary because some small partner firms have been bought by larger firms or financial institutions. After the acquisition these firms lost their identity and their interest in DEXTRA products.

Problems of the internationalisation process DEXTRA only indirectly encounters the problem of exchange-rate risks. During exporting, the exchange-rate risk in almost all cases benefits the foreign partner, who is invoiced in DM. On occasions, however, a customer has not been able to pay his invoice a few months later due to exchange-rate changes. In some cases DEXTRA took over these exchange-rate differences to help out a smaller firm.

A major problem for the DEXTRA distribution centre is still the certificates needed in addition to ISO and EN certification. These are time-consuming administrative procedures for the firm. Some countries ask for technical details concerning the fabrication of the instrument which constitute a secret that has to be kept inside the firm. Mr Schneider showed us a letter that illustrated this problem:

> This is coming from China and I don't know what will happen. For the registration of DEXTRA products in China we will need physical requirements, mechanical requirements, buyer compatibility requirements, packaging, etc. I don't know what is behind all that.

An additional problem in some countries, such as Indonesia, for example, is the impossibility of calculating prices. In these cases, the foreign distributor informs DEXTRA that higher prices are demanded. It is up to the respective representatives to handle the matter on their own, but DEXTRA sometimes extends financial help.

EFFECTS OF THE SINGLE MARKET PROGRAMME

The removal of border controls has an indirect effect on DEXTRA'S export strategies. The feedback coming from its partner firms abroad has been unanimously positive. Export activities are becoming faster and cheaper.

French protectionism, before and after the Single Market Programme, is criticised, however. Despite the official removal of border controls and the associated administrative barriers, the French continue to protect their home market by asking for instruction manuals in French or a particular product form.

The harmonisation of technical standards is advantageous for DEXTRA'S extra-EU export activities. Being ISO 9001 compliant and CE certified opens up interesting opportunities because these standards are known and recognised all over the world.

Mr Schneider pointed out that the existence of different standards in the low-tech standardised surgical instrumentation industry was not a problem before 1992. The problem lay rather in the different standards regarding high-tech medical instruments, such as micromotor systems. The firm therefore welcomed the Single Market Programme with its harmonisation of technical standards. DEXTRA had already included micromotor systems in its permanent product range at the beginning of the 1990s.

The Single Market Programme led to another advantage for DEXTRA. Receiving information regarding new tenders became easier since these are centralised by the Commission and published in the official Journal of the EU. Finally, new electronic media facilitate the information flow. Despite these improvements, information about EU aid programmes destined for Bosnia and Macedonia arrived too late for the distribution centre to act. This was because nobody at DEXTRA had time to spare, since everybody was entirely occupied with their usual tasks.

DEXTRA welcomed the introduction of the single currency, and the distribution centre started to prepare itself for the introduction of the euro in November 1998. The company has taken this opportunity to change its entire software system, and the price list has been published in both euros and DM since March 1999. Customers have therefore had the choice between a euro or a DM invoice. For DEXTRA, the main advantage of the introduction of the euro is the elimination of currency exchange-rate risks within the EU. Foreigners who buy DEXTRA products are no longer afraid of paying more when they finally receive the goods after months of waiting.

DEXTRA is not afraid of increased competition due to the introduction of the single currency. According to Mr Schneider, price transparency was already very high before the establishment of the monetary union. Firms had to compare and permanently adjust their prices anyway to stay competitive in their industry.

INDUSTRIAL COMPETITORS

DEXTRA feels competition from two sides: first, from enterprises located in Tuttlingen, and second, from enterprises located in countries with relatively low labour costs.

Competition in Tuttlingen One of DEXTRA'S major competitors in Tuttlingen is Aesculap. This firm is still the world's largest supplier of MSE and its brand is traditionally connected with high quality. They have various production plants in developed and developing countries and are represented world-wide through a relatively dense network of distributors. In addition, their product range is very large as they offer everything from standardised instruments to new products with a high R&D content.

On the other hand, competition is keen among the 250 SMEs in Tuttlingen. They compete fiercely on national and international markets. Competition between so many small firms in Tuttlingen, all of them specialised in the same industry, has a stimulating effect on DEXTRA, as they are permanently forced to innovate.

International competition DEXTRA strongly feels world-wide competition, particularly from countries with relatively low labour costs such as Pakistan, India, Poland and China. Among these, the most competitive are the enterprises of Sialkot in Pakistan. Enterprises in Tuttlingen supported these firms for years through money, machines and know-how. The quality of the Pakistani products has improved through the supervision of the production process by employees of firms in Tuttlingen. The instruments are produced cheaply in Sialkot and need only some final changes in Germany to fulfil the origin requirements to obtain the stamp 'Made in Germany'. Complicated steps in the production process, and high-tech products, are still fabricated in Tuttlingen. Besides Pakistan, China is expected to become an important cheap labour supplier in the surgical instrumentation sector.

Compared to these countries with relatively low labour costs, competition within the EU plays a less important role. DEXTRA has, for example, some French competitors that are highly specialised in dorsal surgery implants because they have good surgeons in this area. Another example is a firm in Switzerland specialising in microinstruments. But DEXTRA feels these firms to be a stimulant, rather than a disturbance.

Mr Schneider emphasised that international competition from emerging countries has a positive effect on the enterprises in the industrial district of Tuttlingen. For decades Tuttlingen was alone in the MSE industry. This situation has changed completely and has stimulated the firms in the whole area.

NUTRA INSTRUMENTE GmbH

Mr Müller, the director and one of the principal shareholders of the private limited company, showed us the three-floor storage building next to his firm. On the ground floor of the building, arriving surgical instruments were checked and stored, the NUTRA sign was stamped on them and they were sent away immediately, in response to incoming orders. Mr Müller emphasised:

> We don't have our own production or R&D facilities... we are a 'me-too' firm. We concentrate on the distribution of standardised surgical instruments on a world-wide basis. We are closely connected to a firm in Sialkot, Pakistan, that produces for us and they hold a stake in our firm.[37]

COMPANY BACKGROUND

NUTRA was founded in December 1975 by an experienced instruments specialist, Karl Stetter. NUTRA has since acquired further experience over a period of twenty years as a provider of services and supplier of surgical instruments.

In 1987, Ernst-Dieter Müller took over as the managing partner after the founder of the firm retired. He introduced modern computer-controlled logistic systems enabling the firm to handle complete instrument projects, including sterilisation trays and containers.

Mr Müller was also very experienced in the field of MSE. He was trained in the 1950s by Aesculap and continued his career with Karl Storz Endoscopes of Tuttlingen before becoming the general manager of Gebrüder Martin Medical Technology,[38] a large distributor. By 1972,

Mr Müller had acquired knowledge of the Pakistani market and gained experience in fabrication and assembling techniques in Sialkot.

Mr Müller himself does the quality control, the selection and purchase of hammer-forged instruments and all planning in his firm. He emphasised the difficulties in estimating in advance the quantities of hammer-forged instruments they needed for one year. Because of their high dependency on unique tenders, future planning was extremely difficult.

In 1997, the company capital was DM 1 million, fully paid up. NUTRA'S annual turnover was around DM 15 million. There are twenty full-time jobs.

THE PRODUCTION PROCESS

NUTRA was founded with the objective of distributing standardised surgical instruments such as scissors, thumb forceps, needles, handles, knives, etc. The instruments have to be stainless steel, as they are washed, disinfected, and sterilised frequently. To promote sales, a catalogue illustrates an enormous choice of surgical instruments, where each instrument is presented in three languages – English, French and German.

The basic material for the production of standardised surgical instruments is steel. German forging plants buy their steel from German producers or sometimes from France.[39] To guarantee the stainless character of the steel, it has to conform to the German DIN standard and in addition correspond to the right alloy. NUTRA buys the forgings, necessary for the production of surgical instruments, at forge plants on the basis of special catalogues that illustrate only forgings. There are two forge plants in the Tuttlingen area and four in Solingen that deliver NUTRA with hammer-forged instruments on a regular basis.

These hammer-forged instruments which are delivered to NUTRA are sometimes transformed by another firm in Tuttlingen, cooperating with NUTRA, and are finally sent away by air transport to Sialkot, Pakistan. The majority of the instruments which are returned from Pakistan are sent away without any further modifications. Each year NUTRA sends about DM 1 million of hammer-forged instruments to Sialkot for transformation. The transformation process in Sialkot lasts between six and nine months, which complicates forward planning. Since the early 1970s, the transformation and assembly of hammer-forged instruments has not been possible in Germany for cost reasons.

THE ROLE OF SIALKOT

Since its foundation in 1975, NUTRA has collaborated in a joint venture with a firm in Sialkot, employing about 600 people. From the beginning the Pakistani firm had a stake in NUTRA, but it does not work exclusively

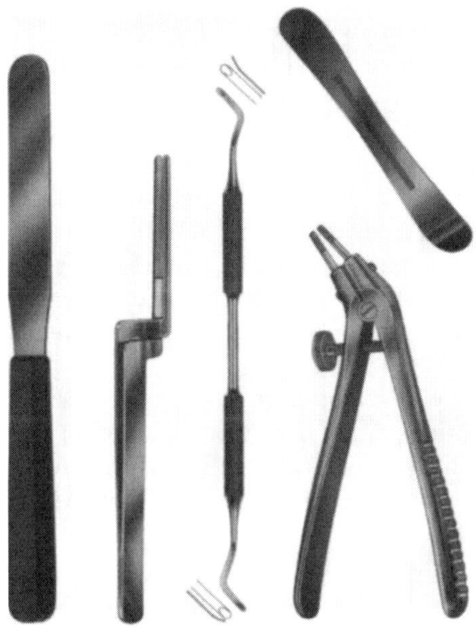

Figure 7.4 Surgical instruments 2.

for its partner. About 50 per cent of its value-added is due to transactions with NUTRA.

The relationship between NUTRA and its Pakistani partner is very close. NUTRA buys all the machines and hand tools that are used in the Sialkot firm. Sometimes the machines are second-hand from Germany, where they are no longer used, although in some cases they are new. Sometimes an employee of NUTRA is sent to their partner in Sialkot to train people; more frequently employees from Sialkot come to NUTRA to improve their know-how in the German firm. During our visit to the three-floor storage building there was a Pakistani employee, checking incoming surgical instruments.

DISTRIBUTION PROCESS

In 1997, NUTRA'S export activities contributed to about 55–60 per cent of its turnover. Of this, 15 per cent went to the EU, a relatively constant share for the decade. About 40–50 per cent was destined for the German market, and of this around 30 per cent went to other firms in the Tuttlingen area.

Adaptation to country conditions Depending on the country, NUTRA'S customers are specialised retail stores and firms or official health institutions that supply hospitals.

In Germany, for example, NUTRA'S main customers are specialised commercial retail stores. Direct service to hospitals is cost-intensive because the firm had to intensify their commercial network. In Switzerland and Austria, local commercial representatives distribute NUTRA products.

Corresponding to the country's social and political structure, distribution in Italy is rather regional, with one distributor for the Lombard region, one for the Piedmont, another for Latium and still another for Sicily. NUTRA cannot, however, supply the countries completely because of their small firm size. In France, everything is more centralised as there is only one commercial representative. In addition to this role as distributor, NUTRA functions as a supplier for some French firms that put their own label on NUTRA instruments.

In some cases, especially in the developing countries, direct service to health ministries or social institutions is possible. But, in addition to these direct contacts, NUTRA gives exclusive rights to local firms that distribute other complementary products. There is one firm each in Argentina, Columbia, Ecuador, Paraguay, Peru and Uruguay and two firms in Chile, whose mandate is to obtain public tenders for NUTRA.

Through the intermediary of these firms or from direct contacts, NUTRA has equipped a medical centre in the Kingdom of Saudi Arabia, a hospital in Malaysia, seven hospitals in Ecuador and four hospitals in Peru. In addition, the firm is a regular supplier to different health ministries in Saudi Arabia, Algeria and Indonesia, and to social security institutions in Mexico, Costa Rica and Peru. Mr Müller told us, 'We have collaborated with these firms for years... there is a certain confidence. We know each other and we phone each other almost every day.'

The majority of the firms with which NUTRA collaborates do not have their own production facilities. An exception is their distributor in Uruguay, which produces catheters, a complementary product. To compete efficiently for orders, distributors need to represent many suppliers of complementary products.

Each country has its political and social institutions and its culture to which NUTRA has to adapt its international strategies. A special case is Algeria, where NUTRA found a collaborator with excellent contacts in official institutions. Previously, Mr Müller had tried for a long time to distribute directly on the Algerian market. Because of political instabilities and risks this strategy was unsuccessful.

The quantity and quality of tenders depend strongly on the political and economic situation in the respective countries. Some countries' situations change rapidly, as, for example, in the case of Indonesia and Thailand, which were both stable markets for years, before becoming unstable in 1998.

NUTRA's customers in Tuttlingen NUTRA has about sixty regular customers in Tuttlingen, all of them small firms active in the same sector of activity, but specialised in different products and production processes. For these firms NUTRA functions as a Pakistani connection because they are too small to start their own joint venture with a firm in Sialkot. In addition, they do not have the capacity to wait between six and nine months for the transformation of the hammer-forged instruments.

During the first years of NUTRA'S existence these firms used to come to the back door by night to buy their surgical instruments. Nobody wanted to admit that it had become too costly to continue producing standard instruments in Tuttlingen. This attitude has changed. In 1998, the firms place their order, send a fax or make a phone call to NUTRA and collect the prepared instruments on the same day. On their firms' premises, they stamp their own brand on the instrument. In some cases they modify the product by polishing it to get another surface.

In return, NUTRA needs highly specialised precision instruments in the area of neurosurgery and heart surgery to complete their own orders. NUTRA buys these instruments in relatively low quantities from highly specialised small firms in Tuttlingen. They have tried to produce some of these high-precision instruments in Sialkot, but without success. The high quality of the instrument was not guaranteed.

INDUSTRIAL COMPETITORS

NUTRA feels competition from two sides: first, from other firms in Tuttlingen, working in the same sector of activity, and second, from firms in Sialkot, Pakistan.

Competition in Tuttlingen

> The town Tuttlingen is well known everywhere in the world for its surgical instruments. Hospitals all over the world connect this name to high quality instruments. Even if the name of the town is not protected, its inscription on a catalogue is valued as much as gold.... But in general, Tuttlingen is the competitor of Tuttlingen.
>
> (Mr Müller)

There are about 250 firms in Tuttlingen working in the same sector as NUTRA. Among these 250 firms are many small ones that are specialised in the production of only one instrument or in one step of one instrument's production process. Despite the cooperation between these small firms and NUTRA, there is strong competition for business.

In addition to these smaller firms, NUTRA has to compete with large firms such as Aesculap and Storz, both of Tuttlingen. Their brand is so well known and extended world-wide that it is difficult for other firms to compete. Because of their large size and production capacities, these firms are able to be represented everywhere. Their price level is similar to NUTRA'S. To stay competitive, these large firms are forced to transfer a large part of their production to Poland, Malaysia or some other country with relatively low labour costs.

Competition from Pakistan In developing countries in particular, demand for surgical instruments from Sialkot, Pakistan, increases constantly because of their low prices. Pakistani firms have learnt to improve their products and have become serious competitors of NUTRA on those markets.

However, most orders include not only standardised surgical instruments, but also sophisticated products that Pakistani firms cannot produce. For Pakistani firms it is therefore very difficult, indeed nearly impossible, to compete with Western firms for the so-called 'project business', especially in developed countries.

> A project consists, for example, of 4 kilos of standardised surgical instruments and of half a kilo of sophisticated articles. Sometimes there are projects where even we in Tuttlingen can't deliver everything. Some countries take as an example the instruments used in US hospitals. In this case, I am confronted with the problem that I can't ask a US producer to supply the missing article because he would like to have the whole project. Therefore, I have to ask if it is possible to leave out the missing products.
>
> (Mr Müller)

ANY OPPORTUNITIES THROUGH THE SINGLE MARKET PROGRAMME?

Mr Müller did not see increasing export tendencies within the EU for his firm. NUTRA has been highly international since its foundation. In 1998, the firm had regular sales in about sixty countries all over the world. The percentage of exports within the EU has been stable over the years.

NTBs The existence of NTBs did not disturb NUTRA'S trading activities in the EU. Standardised surgical instruments do not suffer from such barriers compared to sophisticated medical instruments that have to undergo various certification proceedings.

Euronorms are not needed to certify the quality of surgical instruments as they are classified under the 'product class 1' category.[40] NUTRA implemented a quality management system under DIN/ISO 9000 and was granted certification in January 1997. Subsequently, the use of the CE mark for NUTRA products has been authorised. The standards of DIN 100 on surgical instruments strictly rule production, testing methods and quality control. The Regierungspräsidium Freiburg, a division of the Government of the State of Baden-Württemberg, issues free sale certificates for NUTRA products. In addition, NUTRA is registered with the FDA[41] of the US as an accredited supplier to both government and private customers in the USA.

Even if these norms are needed to guarantee a certain quality of surgical instruments, the producers are often confronted with complaints from users who have not used the instruments the right way. Therefore, about fifteen firms in Tuttlingen, including NUTRA, had the idea of jointly publishing a brochure providing guidelines on how to handle surgical instruments correctly.

Introduction of the single currency By the end of 1998, NUTRA had not begun preparations for its changeover with the introduction of the new currency. It was in this context, Mr Müller pointed out, that he had to change the whole organisation of the firm in 1999. By doing so, the introduction of the new currency was taken as an opportunity to modernise the whole computer system of NUTRA.

Mr Müller criticised the introduction of the euro. To keep the stability of the new currency he would have preferred a certain harmonisation of the different social and fiscal systems before its introduction within the EU. In addition, he supposed that NUTRA does not experience many advantages from the introduction of the euro as its export activities are relatively low within the EU.

MENTA Medizin-Technik GmbH

Mr Schulze, director and shareholder of this small but highly specialised firm, emphasised: 'It becomes more important for us to concentrate on the European market due to the market opening of 1992. Our high-tech products are winners of the removal of non-tariff barriers.'

MENTA'S BACKGROUND

In 1988, Roland Schulze and his partner had the opportunity to buy a share in a small family business in Tuttlingen, producing standardised surgical instruments. In the same year, the firm was founded under the name of MENTA. Both of them were shareholders with equal parts in the private limited company. By 1998, there were three shareholders and the firm employed a total of thirteen people.

Roland Schulze and his partner both originated from Tuttlingen and started work directly after finishing school in the MSE industry. After a commercial apprenticeship in a company in Tuttlingen, Roland Schulze worked as a commercial agent in Spain for twelve years. Travelling around Spain about 180 days a year for his firm, he learnt to speak

Spanish fluently, to understand the Spanish market, to contact the right persons and to know with whom to cooperate. His partner did the same thing in France and the United Kingdom.

In the first year after the take-over they reached a turnover of DM 450,000. By 1998, this had grown to DM 4.5 million. They worked worldwide, in about sixty countries. As a relatively small firm, their main problem was how to supply large territories with enough commercial representatives.

THE PRODUCTS

Beginning as a small, traditional family business in 1988, by 1998 the firm had entirely changed its product range. The family business used to produce surgical instruments such as scissors, thumb forceps, needles, handles and knives. It was a costly and work-intensive process for the new owners to change the character of the product range. In this sense, Mr Schulze pointed out:

> It was our intention to leave the standard business and to specialise ourselves in the area of neurosurgery. In fact, there are too many producers of scissors, thumb forceps and knives. In addition, there is a second German capital in this area, called Sialkot in Pakistan... regarding prices we had no chance to be competitive.

Over the years, the firm became specialised in neurosurgical equipment, constantly increasing its degree of specialisation in the areas of the head and spinal column. They abandoned the initial production of surgical instruments and established their own research and development. The firm's major cooperation partners are the Frankfurt University Hospital, the Dortmund Nord Hospital and a hospital in Saragossa, Spain. In conjunction with the Frankfurt University Hospital MENTA developed new equipment for face surgery, and with Dortmund Nord and Saragossa it innovated in spinal surgery equipment.

Besides this long-term cooperation with the Spanish and German hospitals, the firm also has important projects with the Bruges University Hospital in Belgium and the Istanbul University Hospital in Turkey. With the Bruges University Hospital MENTA is developing transpalatal distraction devices destined for patients suffering from dentofacial deformities, whereas the project in cooperation with the Istanbul University Hospital covers the development of a fixation system for the spinal column.

Alongside these projects, the firm offers some 12,000 surgical instruments. MENTA uses them to complete incoming tenders. The firm no longer produces them in-house, but buys them from other firms located in Tuttlingen.

INTERNATIONAL OPERATIONS

Development MENTA was highly internationalised from its foundation on. During the first years after the take-over it earned 99 per cent of its turnover through exports with a standardised product range. In 1998 the firm generated 75 per cent of its turnover through export activities and the remainder from the German market.

It was a special challenge for MENTA to concentrate its activities on Germany because the market is large and not saturated by these products. Future strategies were devised to lead to an increase in the German share. Mr Schulze and his partner directly served their German customers with the exception of neurosurgery in Bavaria, where they had a commercial representative. For two persons it was, however, very difficult and time-intensive to serve the whole German market. This direct customer service on the home market was made possible only by offering a very specialised high-value product.

> We are too small for the run-of-the-mill business. It would be necessary to build up a whole network of commercial agents in Germany to profit from the day-to-day business. But this would signify too high investments for our small firm.
>
> (Mr Schulze)

As a small firm, they chose a step-by-step approach and tried to further develop their existing contacts abroad. The firm identified England, Spain and Italy as main markets with a high future potential. England is an important market for MENTA because of its high standard of operation techniques. Its percentage of EU turnover was between 15 and 20 per cent in 1997. Italy is a good market for the whole sector even if it fluctuates. In 1997, its percentage of EU turnover was about 8 per cent and MENTA expected high future growth for its products. In 1997, the Spanish market represented around 50 per cent of MENTA'S EU turnover. For some projects the Spanish market has only an intermediary function as they are destined for South American customers.

Of course, demand is always strongly dependent on MENTA'S partners in the respective markets. In this sense, Mr Schulze admitted that the French market is not very important for his firm as it lacks sufficient contacts there.

> I have to target markets where I see high potential. To serve the French market efficiently I would have to take off one year to travel around France to obtain the necessary contacts. Of course, I have neither the time nor the money to do so.
>
> (Mr Schulze)

For this reason, MENTA achieves a relatively low turnover on the French market despite its high potential. In Scandinavia they are confronted with similar problems. There is high potential, but it is costly and time-consuming to develop further.

MENTA considered South America as a whole to be an interesting market in terms of its size. But the major problem in this large market is its high political instability. There are years when a high turnover in Mexico is possible and the year after they might be bankrupt. Then there are years when the highest turnover is achieved in Brazil until the government introduces tariffs, and so on. MENTA takes into consideration the whole world for its international operations.

The value-chain MENTA earns 90 per cent of a project's value-chain in Germany, if the project is in cooperation with a German university. In this case the firm makes all necessary clinical tests in the home country. Mr Schulze explained this as follows:

> If I have a Spanish doctor working with me on a project, all risk analysis takes place in Spain while he is doing his surgery, whereas the whole production process takes place here in Tuttlingen. For our projects in Bruges and Istanbul, for example, tests have been made in the respective hospitals and we here in Tuttlingen take care of their results in our development and production phase.

In these cases the percentage of a product's value-chain made abroad is higher. Storage and distribution activities take place at the headquarters in Tuttlingen.

Import of components The basic material for the development of MENTA'S medical instruments is titanium. Most titanium is imported from Russia by specialised agents in the respective countries. MENTA is in regular contact with five agents in Germany who import their titanium from Russia, and one in Switzerland who imports it from the USA. The titanium has to be available in the appropriate quantity, and storage regarding both quantity and quality is important. But mainly the issue is how quickly and cheaply an agent can deliver the necessary titanium.

Apart from the titanium, MENTA imports certain parts from a Belgian producer and some final products from US manufacturers that are distributed within the EU.

MENTA's customers MENTA'S customers consist mainly of small firms. Sometimes they are only one-man-shows, located abroad. If they distribute other products in addition to MENTA's, complementarity is a condition. For MENTA it is essential to have commercial representatives who are able to discuss the sector of implants with the surgeon.

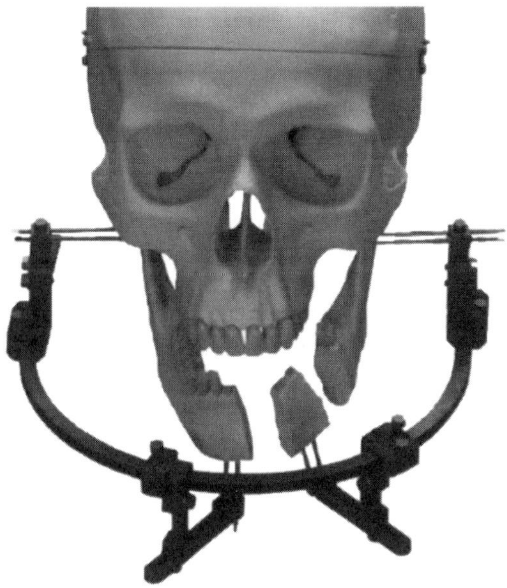

Figure 7.5 Titanium implants.

A commercial representative therefore has to know the product and the language, including special expressions, to cooperate successfully with hospitals.

> My own products cannot be promoted and sold with success if the commercial agent disposes of a whole supermarket of products. In this case he runs around with a huge catalogue of products without knowing the products in detail.
>
> (Mr Schulze)

In this sense, MENTA prefers relatively small commercial representatives. The firm once had a negative experience with a large distributor in Italy, which it had chosen to distribute its products. The result had been that their products were presented among many from other firms and the doctor went into the operating room to test them alongside these other products.

In a majority of cases MENTA selects appropriate foreign partners at international meetings and congresses. In this context Mr Schulze stressed the growing importance of congresses held in the USA. First, things happen some years earlier in the USA than in Europe, which is important for firms inventing and producing in the sector of implants. Second, congress participation is much higher in the USA than in Europe, which increases the choice for the partner selection process. In the USA there are about 7,000 participants and among them 500 to 800 Asians, whereas in Germany there are only around 350 participants and almost no Asians. But, increasingly, the selection of an appropriate partner now takes place through the intermediary of a doctor they already know. The search for an appropriate partner is easier in well-known markets, such as Spain, Italy or the UK. Therefore, the concentration on certain foreign markets is less influenced by proximity than by personal factors.

Distribution by Internet In 1996, MENTA put one of its product groups on the Internet in conjunction with the Universities of Frankfurt and Boston. As it was a relatively new product group, experiences were collected by putting interested persons directly in contact with the respective doctors.

However, Mr Schulze pointed out that he intended to give up selling by the Internet. As there were only a limited number of people interested in the product because of its high degree of specialisation, selling by the Internet was not profitable. To exploit distribution by the Internet it would have been necessary to put all articles in the form of a catalogue on the server. But the Internet did not provide enough security for this to be viable.

MENTA AND THE SINGLE MARKET PROGRAMME

MENTA indicated an increasing tendency to concentrate their product distribution on the EU market. It expected that this tendency will be reinforced in future years. Two factors are responsible for this development. First, the 1992 market opening makes it easier to sell and distribute products across borders and to travel within the EU. Second, MENTA changed its product range by concentrating more on high-tech projects and left the production of traditional standardised instruments in the hands of other firms in Tuttlingen.

MENTA strongly felt the removal of border controls and administrative burdens when exporting within the EU. Before the 1992 market opening it took about three weeks to export a product to Spain, but after 1992 a product arrived the day after it was sent from the German headquarters. All procedures of endless trans-border checks and the preparation of the permission to cross the borders in the form of special carnets were abolished. All these procedures had been time-consuming and costly for the firm. However, Mr Schulze pointed out that transit through Switzerland was still a problem.

Harmonisation of technical standards Within the whole sector MENTA felt strongly the harmonisation of technical standards. ISO 9001 and EN 46001 are less important for standardised surgical instruments because self-certification is sufficient in this case. Certification is necessary for instruments of product class 2, used in open heart surgery and the circulation system. Within this product class we find non-active implants, the main product of MENTA. For non-active implants, the EU conformity under the form of EN 46001 is a legal necessity.

Mr Schulze recognised the importance of these norms in his sector of activity and admitted that his firm had benefited from their introduction during the first years of their implementation. But he criticised the handling of these norms:

> In my opinion these norms are important for each firm because they avoid a degradation of quality within the firm. Very often, the entrepreneur and his employees do not have enough distance... the norms work against a certain blindness. But I criticise strongly the handling of these norms because they become an important source of revenue for the bureaucracy.

The introduction of the euro MENTA undertook various steps in preparation for the introduction of the single currency in 1999. The firm had welcomed its introduction because it was expected that transactions would become easier. But the euro has to be a stable currency.

MENTA had already implemented the change-over of its software by the middle of 1998. This permitted them to invoice in both currencies. The firm estimated the costs of this change-over to be about DM 5,000. These costs are seen as unique and are expected to be repaid by savings in the future.

In order to find out if their European customers were in favour of a change-over to euros or if they preferred to continue receiving their invoice in German marks, MENTA sent out a questionnaire mailing in 1998. As the rate of return of this mailing was very low, they supposed that the majority of firms were in a wait-and-see position. The final change-over to euro balance sheets was not supposed to take place later than the year 2000.

Even if MENTA expected easier transactions within the EU due to the introduction of the single currency, it did not expect to benefit from the emergence of new and easier financial opportunities. One of the main problems regarding access to EU and KfW[42] facilities is the lack of information concerning existing opportunities and appropriate contact persons.

EU research programmes MENTA tried to participate in a EU research programme in 1994 regarding a project in collaboration with the Frankfurt University Hospital. As investments were high they submitted their application to the European Commission. As partners, MENTA proposed themselves and the Frankfurt University Hospital. The project was rejected by the Commission because there needed to be three partners and among them at least one foreign partner. Mr Schulze criticised the decision of the European Commission by pointing out that they had a good project and the right partners. Why look in addition for a foreign partner if the right people are available on home ground?

INDUSTRIAL COMPETITORS

MENTA did not experience any increase in foreign competition after the 1992 market opening. However, the firm was aware of competition in the industrial district of Tuttlingen. MENTA cooperates with only three enterprises in Tuttlingen regarding marketing and distribution. The cooperation takes place on a mutual basis to fulfil the obligations of incoming public tenders. As MENTA had stopped the production of standardised surgical instruments, they were forced to buy them regularly from their three partner firms. In return, MENTA sold its own high-tech products to those three firms, who distributed them under their own brand.

> I don't want to sell my products to other firms than these three. Between these firms and MENTA there exists a high degree of confidence. I have known the owners of these firms for many years, their philosophy of distribution corresponds to ours. I don't share the philosophy in Tuttlingen: What is this one doing... maybe I can copy it? This is nothing for me.
>
> (Mr Schulze)

In the case of an incoming tender MENTA has to know first if the complete order must be delivered. If permitted, they deliver parts of the tender. If not, they contact their three partner firms in Tuttlingen.

STRATEGIES AND FUTURE OUTLOOK

Political and economic risks play an important role in MENTA'S foreign-market entry strategies and in the long-term choice of its partner countries. Exchange-rate risks have been important as many firms want to be invoiced in dollars. The dollar fluctuates strongly and Mr Schulze did not expect that the introduction of the euro would change this. Some countries have hard border checks and administrative formalities that hinder uncomplicated and fast export activities. Other countries, such as Taiwan, for example, do not accept international standards and want to add different norms. As Taiwan continues to ask for a free-sale certificate, it is important to convince the German bureaucrats of its necessity even if it is no longer delivered. An almost insoluble problem is also the rivalry between ISO and FDA, especially if both of them make their check at the same time.

Within the EU, however, these political and economic risks are now reduced to a minimum compared to other countries. MENTA considers the EU market as stable and willing to accept a high product quality. They are not able to sell a product with a value of about DM 10,000 to India if the patient has to bear most of thc costs. Even if, in relative terms, the degree of internationalisation of MENTA has diminished due to the growing importance of the German market, the increasing concentration on the EU market is essential.

An important step in this direction were two cooperation agreements which MENTA planned for the end of 1998, one with a Spanish partner and the other with an Italian.

TRAUBE GmbH

Petra Traube, director and owner of this small firm, pointed out: 'We produce the whole instrument and stamp the customer's brand on it before sending it out. The majority of them are big distributors and it happens that the same instrument competes under different brands world-wide.'

COMPANY BACKGROUND

Pertra Traube's grandfather founded the firm in 1948. Before World War II Mr Traube senior started his career in the MSE industry at Chiron,[43] a big company located in Tuttlingen.

In 1994, Petra Traube took over the family business from her father. Even as a child she had worked in the firm, helping out during her holidays. As a business student she spent weekends in her father's firm installing the computer system. This was in 1985, which was early for such a small firm. To begin with, Petra Traube's parents did not encourage her to take over the firm because of the responsibility and the risk connected with its high dependence on exports to the USA. Even in the 1970s there was a high risk of damages being awarded by US courts. After her studies Petra Traube started her professional career in the sector of financial services. Just before she took over the firm she established a German subsidiary for an Italian manufacturer of machine-tools.

In 1998, the firm employed seventeen people. Because of the high risk Petra Traube insisted on being the only member of the family involved in the firm.

The products and the production process In 1998, the firm produced some 600 mechanical surgical instruments, not including variants. As they do not sell the instruments under their own brand the firm does not illustrate them in a catalogue. Preparations are, however, being undertaken to create a brochure.

Changes in the product range took place at the beginning of the 1990s when minimal-invasive surgery was developed. Like many other firms, TRAUBE was forced to develop new instruments and to further improve existing ones. But, unlike other firms, it did not give up its traditional instruments. The development of the whole endoscope sector produced a need for appropriate mechanical surgical instruments. The firm was therefore able to respond to this new demand. As a result margins, which used to be low for traditional surgical instruments, improved.

The specialities among TRAUBE'S product range are:

- biopsy forceps
- rotating biopsy forceps
- self-retaining retractors
- laminectory rongeurs.

The firm is among the leaders world-wide in the area of biopsy forceps.

Even if most of the production process can be done by machines, TRAUBE prefers to retain a relatively high percentage of manual production, especially during the final stages. This manual work is only profitable because of small production runs.

Research and development activities The development of new instruments or the further improvement of existing ones takes place during the production process. The majority of cases are improvements to existing instruments; resources for research and development are rare. In addition, the manual workers employed by the firm are not able to develop new instruments because of their lack of scientific education.

The firm receives many ideas for further improvements from customers, who are in permanent contact with surgeons. The growing demand for endoscopes has led to increased cooperation between firms and universities. Thanks to such contacts, relatively small firms can undertake research and development activities. Petra Traube would like to undertake some cooperation projects in the future. But they are very time- and cost-intensive.

Cooperation with firms in Tuttlingen TRAUBE works with about ten firms in the Tuttlingen region, and the firm maintains daily contact with the majority of them. On the one hand, TRAUBE buys certain components from specialised suppliers, such as screws for biopsy forceps or hammer-forged instruments. On the other hand, the firm outsources parts of the production process that are too expensive to be done in-house. For example, a firm with specialised machines does the whole process of hardening. A few years ago TRAUBE did the process of hardening in-house, but it became impossible to make these expensive machines profitable with low production volumes.

Petra Traube explained, 'We have everything that we need in Tuttlingen. Here, all firms work with the same quality of steel. I don't need to pack and send it away . . . this proximity is a real advantage.'

INTERNATIONAL ACTIVITIES

From the beginning, a high percentage of turnover came from exports. In 1998, TRAUBE exported 80 per cent of its production to large distributors, most of them in the USA. Only 20 per cent was destined for the home market and out of this percentage about 15 per cent was absorbed by firms in Tuttlingen. These firms added TRAUBE'S instruments to their own range to compete with a whole product range for incoming public tenders.

Cooperation between TRAUBE and its suppliers/customers is informal, not based on contracts. Even if the firm adds new customers every year, the majority of the relationships are long-standing. Large distributors mean easy and uncomplicated handling of operations, but also increased dependency. In this sense, Petra Traube sees a need for a large number of small customers, even if the risk is high that these small firms might be bought up by larger ones or might go bankrupt.

As TRAUBE does not sell instruments under its own brand, an active promotion of the products at fairs, attendance at congresses and the elaboration of a brochure were not considered necessary until recently. Customers come to Tuttlingen anyway, as it is well known as a world-wide centre for medical and surgical instruments. Uncertain whether this will continue in the future, Petra Traube has decided to produce a brochure to attract customers.

Even if the US market provides the strongest potential for TRAUBE, it is a very difficult market. Despite the high sales volume, price pressure and changes are enormous. An appropriate distributor has to know exactly the relevant sector of surgical instruments, with all the possible variants. Fast changing distributors on the US side constitute a problem for TRAUBE.

Additional problems on the US market are exchange-rate fluctuations. Even if TRAUBE invoices in DM, they are indirectly affected by the problem through prices. The firm cannot sell instruments more expensively even if national suppliers increase their prices. Petra Traube criticises in particular the pressure on prices that results from mergers and acquisitions among their customers in the USA and the EU. Competition is based more on prices than on quality. However, the prices of low-quality instruments are still too high to compete with surgical instruments coming from countries with relatively low labour costs.

With the exception of France, TRAUBE encounters no problems regarding day-to-day business within the EU. French customers' actions and reactions are criticised as being unpredictable.

THE ECONOMIC AND MONETARY UNION

TRAUBE'S exports have become much easier as a result of the removal of NTBs within the EU. In particular, the firm considered the administrative burden to be a strong hindrance to exporting efficiently.

> I don't think that we're going to increase our international operations within the EU. There aren't so many customers world-wide interested in mechanical surgical instruments. The people who used to buy such instruments will do so also in future. Our relationships are decades old.
> (Petra Traube)

Technical standards In March 1995, TRAUBE became ISO 9001 and EN 46001 certified. The firm has taken part in a pilot project of the TÜV[44] and was one of the first small enterprises in Tuttlingen to become certified. This changeover involved much work and was facilitated by the early establishment of the firm's computer system.

In addition, the firm's own quality and security system facilitated the task. Petra Traube's father had already introduced it in 1977. Large parts of the ISO and EN certification corresponded to the firm's own quality system. The reason for the early introduction of this quality system was the high responsibility a manufacturer encountered when exporting to the USA.

This early ISO and EN certification led to an improvement of the firm's image *vis-à-vis* their customers. In particular, when large distributors insisted on quality management, TRAUBE was able to confirm that they had already established such a system decades ago.

Introduction of the single currency TRAUBE welcomed the introduction of the euro because of lower exchange-rate risks on intra-EU sales. In this context, Petra Traube criticised the effects induced by high lira fluctuations in the past. However, the firm does not expect an increase in its operations within the EU. Business relations are long-standing and the abolition of national currencies is not expected to change anything in this respect.

It became necessary to introduce a new software system not only because of the euro, but because the old software, introduced in 1985, needed renewing. The cost- and time-consuming changeover was expected to be completed by 2000. TRAUBE'S customers had not insisted on an earlier changeover. Some of them had informed the firm that they would continue to accept invoices in DM.

INDUSTRIAL COMPETITORS

TRAUBE'S main competitors are located in the Tuttlingen region and in countries with relatively low labour costs.

Competition from countries with relatively low labour costs Even if the majority of instruments coming from cheap-labour countries, such as Pakistan and China, are produced in high series and low quality, manufacturers in these countries improve their instruments continuously. They are able to imitate instruments despite their lack of technical and mechanical understanding. Petra Traube argues that manufacturers in countries with relatively low labour costs learn and adapt fast. They are the main competitors of TRAUBE.

In addition to this direct competition from cheap-labour countries, there are an increasing number of firms from the Tuttlingen region who established production plants or joint ventures in these countries. Big firms such as Aesculap had already delocalised their production in the 1970s. There are firms in Tuttlingen which buy hammer-forged instruments in Germany, send them to a country with relatively low labour costs to be processed, then mark 'Made in Germany' on the instrument when they are back in Germany. TRAUBE'S only advantage in competing with their practices is the superior quality of its instruments.

Competition in Tuttlingen The advantages of proximity in the region of Tuttlingen lead to easy information exchange among the actors. TRAUBE has the same supplier firms as other firms in Tuttlingen. Petra Traube points out that each time she employs someone new in her firm she has to check whether a relative works for a competing firm in the region. The danger of the firm's secrets leaking out is too high. But training as an electromedical technician exists only in this region. For this reason, the highly specialised workforce she needs in her firm does not exist elsewhere.

> Despite increased openness and internationalisation all over the world we stay rather concentrated on ourselves. This mentality to keep secrets may seem strange for someone who is not from the region and I had my problems when I arrived here after my studies and my work experience elsewhere. But we need it to survive. Today I understand that . . . I have become the same.
>
> (Petra Traube)

The industrial district of Nogent

Nogent is situated between Chaumont and Langres in the Haute-Marne region. Firms in the region are specialised in the production of knives, scissors, surgical instruments, forging and stamping.

In the fourteenth century the region of Langres became specialised in the production of knives. Mining companies emerged due to the existence of ores. The roots of this industrial district can therefore be traced to natural resources. In particular, during the nineteenth century the cutlery industry expanded from Langres all over the valley of Nogent. About

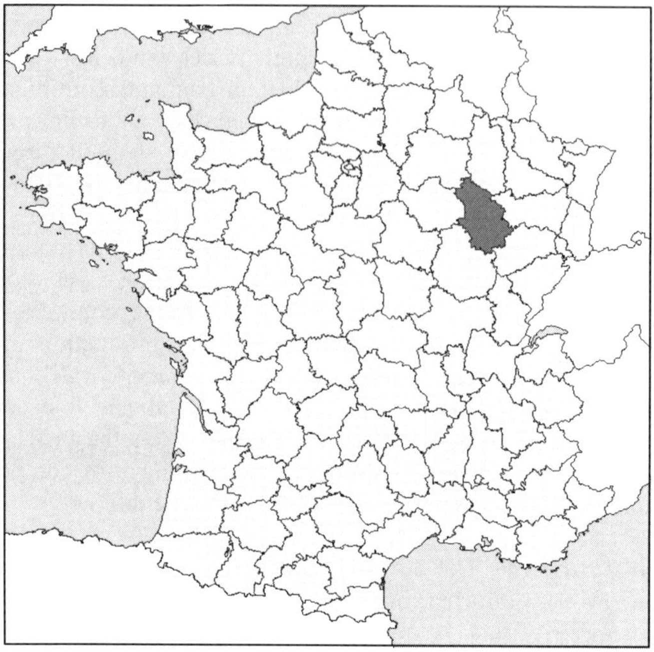

Figure 7.6 Location of Nogent.

6,000 people were employed in the industry. In the beginning of the twentieth century each village in the valley became specialised in a particular instrument or production process. There were a lot of very small craft firms (sometimes farmers) working for large distributing companies in Langres and Paris.

In the 1970s there was a diversification in the MSE industry. The use of titanium led to the production of artificial limbs and other prostheses. The majority of firms, however, still produce on a very small scale and are specialised in instruments demanding a lot of manual work.

In 1945, there were about thirty firms producing MSE in the industrial district of Nogent.[45] However, the number of firms and employees declined steadily until 1994. From 1994/95 on, the number of firms increased slightly from thirteen to eighteen in 1998 (see Table 7.1).

The number of employees decreased until 1994 when it reached its lowest level. In 1995, the existing firms (there was only one new foundation) more than doubled the jobs within their firms. This development can be connected to the fact that growth increased from 1993/94 on, after very slow growth rates in 1992/93.[46] In 1997 the number of employees diminished before growing again in 1998, whereas the number of firms increased slightly during the whole period.

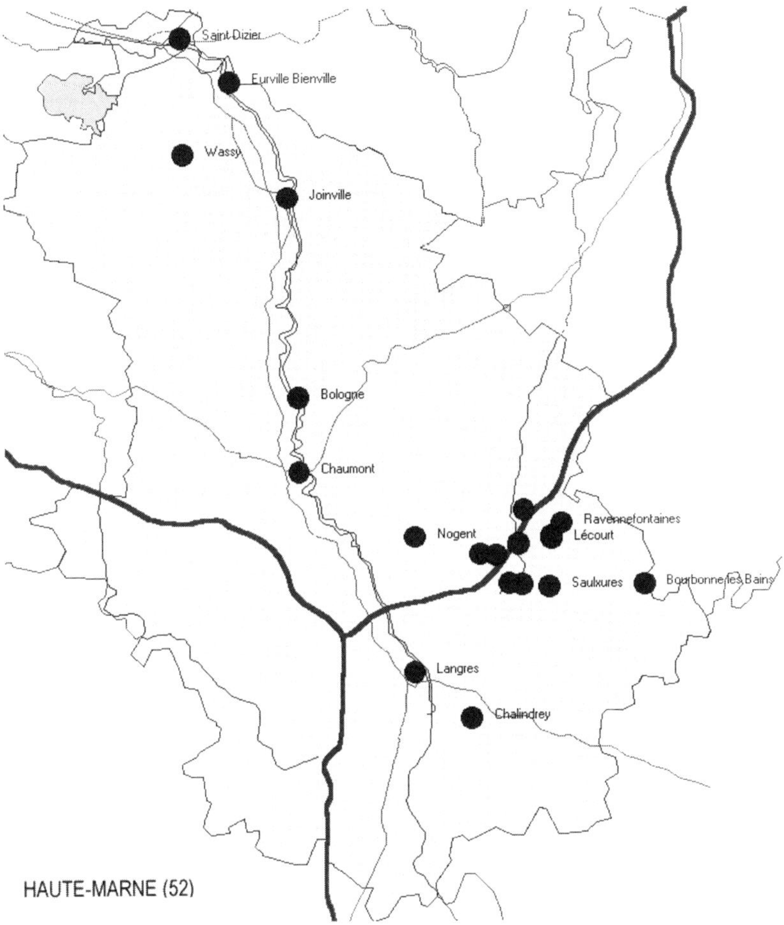

Figure 7.7 Location of Nogent.

Table 7.1 MSE industry in Haute-Marne

Year	*Number of enterprises*	*Number of employees*
1991	13	354
1994	13	192
1995	14	574
1996	16	572
1997	19	383
1998	18	465

Source: Chambre de commerce et d'industrie de Saint-Dizier et de la Haute-Marne (April 1999).

Table 7.2 Exports of the MSE industry in Nogent and France (% of total production)

	Bassin Nogentais		*France*	
	1989	*1990*	*1989*	*1990*
Exports (%)	26.9	24.7	21.6	17.1

Source: Banque de France (1991). *L'industrie dans le bassin Nogentais*, p. 24.

Although the data are available only for 1989 and 1990 (Table 7.2), some important results are shown. First, the rate of export is relatively low for an industry that is characterised by a high degree of internationalisation. In addition, the rate of export fell from 1989 and 1990. The rates in the industrial district of Nogent are, however, higher than the national rates. Second, the level of indebtedness is very high, both in absolute and relative terms, casting doubt on their ability to remain viable in the long run.[47]

DUPONT Sarl

The Director of Production, Mr Beau, stated, 'German producers of MSE are cheaper than the French. Compared to German producers we in France are not so highly internationalised and are concentrated on the French market.'

COMPANY BACKGROUND

Mr Dupont senior founded the firm in 1947, after World War II. After his training as a blacksmith he started to produce surgical instruments in the morning for delivery and sale the same afternoon by car. He was helped by his wife, who handled the commercial side of the business and developed a whole commercial system to efficiently distribute the instruments produced by her husband. When Mr Dupont visited the hospitals of the region there were an increasing number of surgeons asking him to repair instruments or develop new ones. Mr Dupont took on new workers and his small company grew rapidly in size.

The founder of the firm recognised early the potential of SMEs in the Nogent region that were specialised in the MSE industry. To meet growing demand, he started to cooperate with some of them by subcontracting some activities. Even during this early phase of the firm's existence, cooperation was not limited to firms in the Nogent region. Mr Dupont also cooperated with firms in Tuttlingen in Germany.

Before setting up his business in Nogent, DUPONT was located in a small village nearby. In 1974, a new 1,500 m^2 building was constructed in the industrial zone of Nogent.

> I joined the company some 20 years ago. The firm was specialised in the fabrication and reparation of surgical instruments and in their commercial distribution. In addition to these surgical instruments we distributed orthopaedic products that we bought in France.
>
> (Mr Beau)

In 1978, the firm had fifty-eight employees and eight sales representatives. The breakthrough for the small firm came in 1980 with its specialisation in artificial limbs, in the area of hips and knees. DUPONT established its own production plant in Nogent for surgical instruments, whereas DUPA produced and distributed artificial limbs. Growth in the orthopaedic sector led to an increasing number of employees and to the construction of new production plants of 6,000 m^2 in 1986.

From 1986 on, DUPONT/DUPA started to expand strongly in nearly all European countries by establishing distribution subsidiaries in Spain, Italy, Portugal, The Netherlands and the UK. An additional distribution subsidiary was located in the USA. These foreign distribution centres were owned outright or through majority by the company.

By 1996, DUPONT/DUPA employed about 600 people. The parent firm stayed located in Nogent, with 150 employees in the production plant and around 80 in the commercial and administrative departments. Other production plants and research centres were located all over France. Close collaboration with surgeons was a necessity. In 1995, the company's shares were introduced on the second market of Nancy in France.

In 1997, DUPA was sold to a US group by Patrick Dupont, son of Mr Dupont senior. He kept the smaller surgical instruments branch and founded DUPONT Sarl in 1997, after the sale of the orthopaedic sector. In addition, he took over the people employed in the surgical instrumentation sector. In 1998, there were about forty-five employees working for DUPONT Sarl. Today the firm is still a major producer and distributor of surgical instruments in the Nogent region.

The firm's backward cooperation In 1998, DUPONT Sarl offered an 800-page catalogue with about 4,000 instruments. However, the structure of the firm did not allow it to produce all the instruments on its own. Instruments representing about 40 per cent of the firm's annual turnover were produced by DUPONT, whereas 30 per cent were bought in from small firms in the Nogent region and the remainder came mostly from Tuttlingen in Germany. A few sterilisation containers came from Munich.

DUPONT works with six small firms in the Nogent region, each having its own specialisation. In addition, the company works with a few small firms in the Paris region, also producing very specific instruments.

Cooperation with firms in the Tuttlingen region is different. Links with medium-sized firms are preferred, even if prices are higher than

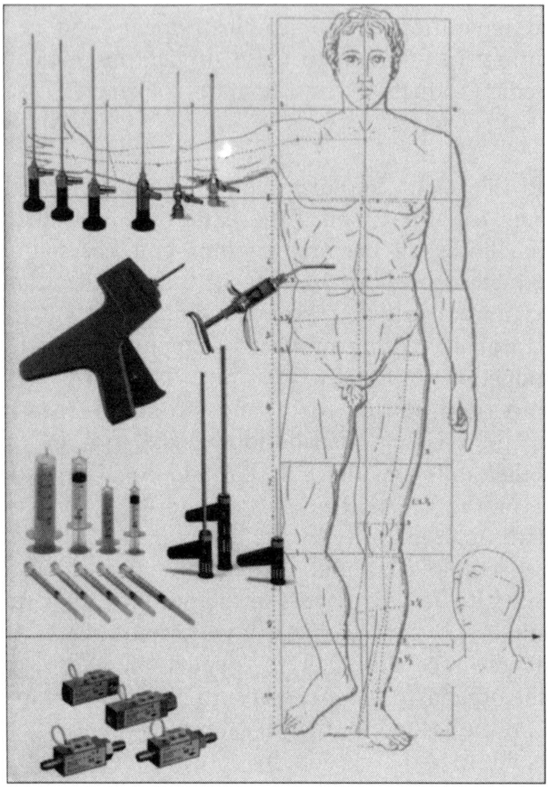

Figure 7.8 Surgical instruments 3.

those offered by small firms. The acquisition of a complete and homogeneous product range is important for DUPONT. The majority of the small craft firms in Tuttlingen are highly specialised in only one product that is distributed in a majority of cases by a larger firm. In addition, small craft firms need a relatively long delivery time because of low stocks.

> If DUPONT exists today on the French market it is due to its short delivery times. We have a permanent stock of instruments valued at about 8 million French francs. If a customer calls us today he gets the instruments tomorrow. As it is difficult for us to compete regarding prices we try to provide an excellent and fast service.
>
> (Mr Beau)

Contacts with the suppliers in the Nogent and Tuttlingen region date back twenty years.

INTERNATIONALISATION PROCESS

DUPONT established a partnership with a Pakistani firm in Sialkot in 1990, after a period of irregular contacts. The Pakistani partner firm employs about 200 people. The objective of the Pakistani firm is to have an exclusive partner in each country in order to avoid competition over similar product ranges. DUPONT allows their Pakistani partner to produce about 50,000 instruments a year to a value of $150,000.

The first step in the production process consists in the acquisition of hammer-forged instruments. DUPONT buys about 60 per cent of hammer-forged instruments in Tuttlingen because of available stocks and 40 per cent in France. Afterwards they send them directly to DUPONT's partner in Sialkot. The Pakistani firm does further manufacturing and assembling and returns the product semi-finished after about six months. Back at DUPONT, the product is submitted to thermal treatment to harden the steel and to polish it.

> It is our philosophy that the quality of a surgical instrument can only be guaranteed if a relatively high percentage of processing is controlled by DUPONT. Therefore, the hammer-forged instruments are bought in France or in Germany and the thermal treatment and polishing is done by DUPONT.
>
> (Mr Beau)

Buying a hammer-forged instrument in Germany and France corresponds to about 30 per cent of the product's value. The thermal treatment requires machines and special equipment, and polishing is a complicated manual process. These three steps are very expensive.

DUPONT's customers DUPONT possesses a commercial network that covers the whole of France. The sales force consists of ten commercial agents and a director of sales. The majority of clients visited by these commercial agents are French hospitals.

Only 4 per cent of DUPONT's turnover comes from exports and even these are indirect. DUPONT cooperates with large trading firms in France which need surgical instruments to compete for public tenders submitted to foreign governments, institutions or hospitals. These French trading companies are in general large, highly diversified multinationals.

Large multinationals are preferred by DUPONT because of their strong bargaining power abroad. Using this intermediary, the company is able to compete against strong German competition on an international level. In addition, these large firms guarantee immediate payment. This is an important factor for DUPONT, following some negative experiences in an Arab country, when the firm had to wait two years for payment.

> We deal with these large multinationals as we deal with hospitals. They make their proposal and choose the most appropriate firm regarding price and quality. Very often, the French government is involved in these foreign public tenders. They ask the French multinationals to do the job and the multinationals ask us.
>
> (Mr Beau)

THE CONSEQUENCES OF THE SINGLE MARKET PROGRAMME

DUPONT benefited from the removal of border controls and administrative burdens in 1992, and importing from Germany has become much easier. Hammer-forged instruments and sterilisation containers are now ordered one day and arrive the next.

DUPONT responds only to tenders published in the Official Journal of France. Mr Beau admitted that even if he asked the Community for information regarding outstanding tenders in other EU countries, DUPONT would not be able to present their instruments at the respective hospitals abroad because they do not possess an international distribution network. Hospitals never order from a catalogue. They want to see the instruments, and discuss them with the representatives. The creation of an international distribution network is considered too cost- and time-intensive.

Technical standards DUPONT's products are considered as instruments of the product class 1. They stay in general no longer than forty-five minutes in the human body compared to more sophisticated instruments. Instruments of the product class 1 need only an auto-certification CE, introduced by DUPONT on 14 July 1998. This date corresponds to the time that an auto-certification became a legal necessity for offering instruments for sale on the EU market. In addition, DUPONT expected to achieve ISO 9002 conformity in collaboration with the Chamber of Commerce Haute-Marne in the middle of 2000. Even if it was possible to have one norm without the other, successful sales of instruments belonging to this product class depend on dual certification and must be ISO 9002 and CE auto-certified. Regarding these technical norms, Mr Beau emphasised:

> We need these norms to sell our products. But the problem is that there are a lot of French producers that buy their steel in Pakistan, they manufacture their instruments there and finally put their CE certification on the instrument once it arrives in France. To obtain the CE auto-certification you have to submit your case at the French Ministry of Health.

Supplying firms from the Nogent and Tuttlingen regions have to attest that they are CE auto-certified. DUPONT sells the instruments with the CE auto-certification of the manufacturer and their own name as distributing firm. Instruments that have been subcontracted to cooperating firms receive only the CE auto-certification of DUPONT.

The introduction of the single currency DUPONT welcomed the introduction of the single currency, as exchange-rate fluctuations had affected the firm's profits in the past. Common practice was to allow for an average fluctuation that was modified every one or two years. The 1999 introduction of the euro signified an end to the uncertainties regarding currency changes and price differences.

Because of the software change in September 1998, the changeover to the single currency was no problem for DUPONT. The firm established the price-list in euros and French francs, then sent out invoices and offers in both currencies from 1999 onwards.

Despite the changes DUPONT is not afraid of growing competition. Mr Beau argued that each firm in the sector already had its part of the market. The firm's main competitors have been established in the French market for many years and DUPONT trusted the performance of its own comprehensive French distribution network.

DUPONT'S INDUSTRIAL COMPETITORS

From the foundation of DUPONT in the 1950s until the 1990s, competition changed from being purely national, or even local, to being international in character. Mr Beau criticised the strategies of small firms in the Nogent region that wanted to be producers and distributors without having the necessary capacities. By avoiding cooperation with other firms in the region, a lot of them were ruined in the 1970s and their number diminished rapidly. As a result local competition declined within the Nogent region. DUPONT now encounters competition from the following quarters:

First, there are competing French firms, selling surgical instruments at much lower prices than DUPONT. These firms are able to compete with very low prices as they have delocalised all steps of the production process to countries with relatively low labour costs, such as Pakistan, India or China. DUPONT continues to add a relatively high percentage of product value in France for quality reasons and therefore commands a higher price for the finished product.

Second, competition from German firms is strongly felt, in particular from firms in the Tuttlingen region. These firms started their delocalisation very early in the 1970s for cost reasons. Their instruments are highly competitive and the firms possess well-established international distribution networks. In this context, Mr Beau pointed out:

> French firms in the industry of surgical instruments understood the importance of delocalising their production 10 years too late.

German firms had the time to obtain important market shares on an international level. They speak an average of three foreign languages and encounter no communication problems with their foreign counterparts. In addition, German firms were intelligent and kept their own high-tech products at home. DUPONT is not able to compete with them regarding prices and market presence. And our foreign language abilities are not excellent.

DUPONT therefore concentrated its efforts on the French market with the objective of maintaining its market share.

Ets. MAISTRE SA

Mr Maistre, the Director, said 'The European Community did not bring any advantages in the past and is not expected to lead to any advantages in the future. We have higher costs and no protection.'

COMPANY BACKGROUND

Mr Maistre founded his little craft firm in Nogent in 1976. Before becoming his own boss he worked for nineteen years in another craft firm in Nogent where he learnt enough about the business to start his own production of surgical instruments. In 1998, he had between six and eight employees. Even if the commercial activities have become more important, Mr Maistre emphasised the manual character of the production process.

MAISTRE offers about 3,000 surgical instruments, illustrated in a small catalogue. These rather standardised surgical instruments represent a growing 30 per cent of the firm's annual turnover. The majority of products are, however, special instruments to insert implants, in which manual labour represents about 85 per cent of the value. The production of a relatively simple instrument takes about one working hour, whereas the production of a complicated and sophisticated instrument takes between ten and twenty hours.

MAISTRE buys around 5 per cent of its surgical instruments from other highly specialised producers in the Nogent region. These informal cooperation agreements with other small firms are based on personal contacts that have existed for decades.

MAISTRE's customers Until 1998, MAISTRE's concentrated its distribution activities on the French market. The firm did not work directly with the end user and passed via larger firms to distribute their instruments. Direct contact with the surgeon takes place only if some technical problems have to be resolved.

MAISTRE's exports accounted for about 1 per cent of its annual turnover. This low international involvement is, however, no exception as other small firms in the Nogent region show a similar percentage. The firm conducted its exports through one Swiss and three Belgian distributors.

The setting up of a commercial structure to increase the firm's international operations is seen as too time- and cost-intensive. MAISTRE works with about 160 distributors in France. 80 per cent of MAISTRE's annual turnover was due to around ten national customers.

CONSEQUENCES OF THE SINGLE MARKET PROGRAMME

According to Mr Maistre, the firm's exports to Belgium are complicated by border controls and missing parcels. This cross-border transport was time-intensive before and this was still the case after 1992. The market opening had not changed this annoying situation. On average, parcels took three days to arrive in Belgium. Administrative burdens were still high and discouraged MAISTRE from increasing its exports.

MAISTRE has offered products with the CE auto-certification since 1995. This opportunity has reinforced the position of small firms *vis-à-vis* larger distributors. Mr Maistre emphasised that before 1992 distributors wanted to promote only their own name on surgical instruments, ignoring the manufacturer's stamp, despite the producer's responsibility for the surgical instrument. Since 1992, the manufacturer has had the opportunity to promote his own label. The disadvantage is that too many labels are stamped on one instrument. Mr Maistre pointed out that the CE auto-certification has led to more administrative burdens in his firm without increasing the sales volume.

International certifications such as ISO were seen as a means of marketing without guaranteeing the quality of the surgical instrument. According to Mr Maistre these norms provided no protection from foreign competition. He considered patents too time- and cost-intensive.

Since 1999, MAISTRE has offered its products in both francs and euros. Mr Maistre expected no advantages from the single currency.

INDUSTRIAL COMPETITORS

Competition comes from three main actors. First, there is some regional and local competition which has declined constantly since the end of World War II. In 1945, there were about thirty small firms producing surgical instruments in Nogent, whereas in 1998 there were only about ten firms, cooperating closely with larger firms in the region. MAISTRE cooperates with five firms in the region which offer complementary products and services.

Second, MAISTRE competes with German firms that are considered as 'good and loyal competitors'. German firms have their production plants or representatives in France and realise high market shares. In addition, their products are of high quality. Mr Maistre, who attends exhibitions in Germany, considers the German market highly protected and successful market entry is described as 'impossible'.

Third, Pakistani competition is strongly felt by the small manufacturer. The lower end of the Pakistani price range for surgical instruments is only a tenth of MAISTRE's. As there are French distributors who have a production plant or a joint venture in Pakistan, or in another country with relatively low labour costs, they are able to lower their production costs. Not only large trading firms in France but also French government institutions are increasingly turning to these instruments from cheap-labour countries.

> I consider the Pakistani instruments as a disloyal competition. If you compare their wages with ours we cannot catch up with them. In addition, the Pakistanis improve their quality each year. I pay my social charges in France and the French civil servants buy Pakistani instruments... I consider this as disloyal.
>
> (Mr Maistre)

For these reasons, MAISTRE saw its only chance of survival in concentration on highly specialised surgical instruments, requiring a high percentage of skilled manual labour. These instruments are produced in relatively low quantities. Because of high precision, time and transport costs, these instruments are not less expensive to produce in a cheap-labour country than in France. MAISTRE is price-competitive only in this narrow sector.

In 1997, Mr Maistre sold his enterprise to a British financial holding. He stayed on, however, as director to train a young colleague to replace him in the near future.

Part III

Conclusions

This part contains the results of the field research and conclusions. Chapter 8 deals with the results of the questionnaire and the interpretation of the case studies. Chapter 9 answers to the three hypotheses by trying to approach economic and business concepts of internationalisation.

8 Results and interpretations

In the first section of this chapter the results of the questionnaire are described. It will be possible to see some important results regarding how SMEs outside industrial districts reacted to the EMU. The second section contains the interpretation of the case studies. In addition, the ways in which an industrial district can become internationally successful are described. In this chapter some initial conclusions are reached.

Discussion of the questionnaire research

Out of the 300 questionnaires sent to SMEs in Germany, France and Italy, only 47 were returned. Finally, 37 questionnaires were used to find out if the EMU affected SMEs' international strategies. The other ten letters contained negative answers or uncompleted questionnaires because of the firms' non-involvement in international activities or recent bankruptcies.

According to the Chamber of Commerce of Saint-Dizier and Haute-Marne, there were 3,483 enterprises in the MSE industry in France.[1] Out of the 100 SMEs to which the questionnaire was sent, twelve responses were finally used. In Germany the rate was 15 per cent whereas in Italy it was 10 per cent. As the rates did not differ too much from one country to another it is possible to make comparisons between SMEs' approaches towards internationalisation and the influence of the EMU.

The third question in the questionnaire investigated if the SMEs produced and/or distributed standardised or new products or both. The majority of the firms in the sample followed a double strategy regarding their product range. Besides the standardised products, they were specialised in one or two products requiring permanent innovation and adaptation. To facilitate the interpretation, the firms were asked to briefly describe their product range. German and Italian SMEs showed a higher concentration on new products than French SMEs. An explanation may be that Italian firms are characterised by low investments in fundamental research compared to German firms. However, they are very quick in adapting foreign technologies to their traditional product range.[2]

Table 8.1 SMEs' product range (% of enterprises)

Question 3	*Germany*	*France*	*Italy*	*Total*
New products	66.67	58.33	100.00	72.97
Standard products	73.33	66.67	70.00	70.27

Source: own estimates.

In question 4 the SMEs indicated whether the different activities of their value-chain take place at home or abroad or both. SMEs in all three countries have in common that their R&D activities are concentrated to a very large degree in their respective home countries. 80 per cent of the German SMEs, 75 per cent of the French and 70 per cent of the Italians located their R&D activities at home. Only some medium-sized firms that are highly internationalised located parts of their R&D activities abroad.

In all three countries nearly 57 per cent of the SMEs procured parts of their inputs abroad. The rate was pronounced for German SMEs in particular, where 80 per cent of the firms under investigation imported parts of their inputs, followed by 50 per cent of the Italian SMEs. A relatively low percentage of French SMEs procured parts of their inputs abroad, which can be connected to the higher concentration of the French industry. French SMEs were generally less international than their German and Italian counterparts.

In a majority of cases assembly and storage activities were concentrated in the home countries. In all three countries at least 80 per cent of the SMEs assembled and stored their products in the home country. Only some medium-sized German SMEs with large capacities maintained storage possibilities abroad.

About 51 per cent of all SMEs had distribution activities abroad and 32 per cent of them their service activities. The percentage was particularly high for German SMEs, followed by the Italians, which shows once again their high international involvement.[3] About 60 per cent of the firm's whole value-chain is produced locally in German SMEs, compared to about 64 per cent in France and 81 per cent in Italy.[4]

The seventh question analysed SMEs' foreign-market entry strategies. Even if 43 per cent of all SMEs realised or planned cooperation agreements or FDI in the EU or elsewhere, the majority of them intended to continue exporting despite high sales volume abroad and a relatively large firm size. Founded in the 1970s and 1980s, the majority of the SMEs had, however, the time to acquire experience through their export activities. But they continued their initial strategy. This attitude confirms the different empirical findings in the literature survey where SMEs often stay at the 'experimental level' of the internationalisation process.[5] SMEs that concluded cooperation agreements with foreign partners

Table 8.2 Location of the firms' activities (% of enterprises)

Question 4		*Germany*	*France*	*Italy*	*Total*
Design/R&D	At home	80.00	75.00	70.00	75.68
	Abroad	13.33	16.67	10.00	13.51
Procurement of inputs	At home	80.00	75.00	100.00	83.78
	Abroad	80.00	33.33	50.00	56.76
Production and assembly	At home	80.00	83.33	80.00	81.08
	Abroad	20.00	8.33	20.00	16.22
Storage	At home	100.00	83.33	90.00	91.89
	Abroad	20.00	0.00	0.00	8.11
Distribution	At home	100.00	91.67	100.00	97.30
	Abroad	60.00	41.67	50.00	51.35
Service	At home	93.33	75.00	90.00	86.49
	Abroad	40.00	16.67	40.00	32.43
Other	At home	0.00	0.00	0.00	0.00
	Abroad	0.00	0.00	0.00	0.00

Source: own estimates.

Note

As the majority of the SMEs procured parts of their inputs at home and abroad, the percentages of the rows can add up to more than 100%.

or established production plants abroad (or planned to do so) did not follow a progressive sequence as predicted by the Uppsala model. Intermediary stages of the internationalisation process were leapfrogged and the products were not sold first in the countries that had a similar culture.

All SMEs that realised or planned cooperation agreements or FDI had done so or intended to do so between 1992 and 2004. A majority of them intended, however, to do so from 1999 to 2001. A majority of SMEs planned joint ventures with other enterprises located in developed countries. Only one SME planned a joint venture with a firm in India for cost reasons. Less frequent strategies were acquisitions, the establishment of subsidiarics and licensing agreements. About 62 per cent of the recently realised or planned entry strategies were destined for EU countries. Surprisingly, 60 per cent of the Italian SMEs and 50 per cent of the French SMEs, but only 20 per cent of all German SMEs, realised or planned other foreign-market entry strategies in addition to exports. It was, however, impossible to establish a connection between the SMEs' willingness to expand their international entry strategies and their product range, the age of the firm or the number of employees.

SMEs' internationalisation strategies are strongly connected with the reasons for their internationalisation. Their reasons to internationalise were analysed in question 8. The most frequently cited reasons for going international were new market access, growth and the expectation of a higher turnover, which corresponded to the results of other empirical

Table 8.3 SMEs' reasons to internationalise (% of enterprises)

Question 8		*Germany*	*France*	*Italy*	*Total*
As subcontractor	1	6.67	0.00	0.00	2.70
	2	0.00	16.67	30.00	13.51
	3	46.67	33.33	40.00	40.54
Chance	1	46.67	16.67	20.00	29.73
	2	0.00	33.33	60.00	27.03
	3	33.33	25.00	0.00	21.62
New market access	1	86.67	75.00	70.00	78.38
	2	0.00	0.00	10.00	2.70
	3	0.00	0.00	0.00	0.00
Superior technology and business know-how	1	26.67	16.67	70.00	35.14
	2	33.33	33.33	10.00	27.03
	3	13.33	8.33	0.00	8.11
Cheaper inputs	1	13.33	25.00	40.00	24.32
	2	33.33	16.67	30.00	27.03
	3	20.00	16.67	10.00	16.22
Growth	1	86.67	66.67	70.00	75.68
	2	0.00	8.33	0.00	2.70
	3	0.00	0.00	10.00	2.70
Saturated home market	1	46.67	41.67	10.00	35.14
	2	6.67	16.67	70.00	27.03
	3	26.67	8.33	0.00	13.51
Follow customers	1	33.33	58.33	40.00	43.24
	2	20.00	8.33	10.00	13.51
	3	20.00	8.33	10.00	13.51
Risk spreading	1	33.33	41.67	50.00	40.54
	2	46.67	33.33	20.00	35.14
	3	6.67	0.00	20.00	8.11
Higher turnover	1	93.33	75.00	50.00	75.68
	2	0.00	0.00	30.00	8.11
	3	0.00	0.00	0.00	0.00
EU programmes	1	6.67	0.00	20.00	8.11
	2	26.67	25.00	20.00	24.32
	3	33.33	25.00	30.00	29.73
Other	1	0.00	8.33	0.00	2.70
	2	0.00	0.00	0.00	0.00
	3	0.00	0.00	0.00	0.00

Source: own estimates.

Note
1 = 'very important'; 2 = 'less important'; 3 = 'not important'.

investigations.[6] In this sense, 78 per cent of all SMEs indicated new market access as an important reason, while nearly 76 per cent of them indicated growth expectations and a higher turnover. These three reasons were considered as very important regardless of country differences. Another important consideration was the access to superior technology and business know-how (35 per cent of all SMEs), the ability to follow customers abroad (43 per cent), risk-spreading across different countries (41 per cent) and a saturated home market (35 per cent). Less important for the firms was the chance factor within their internationalisation process under the form of a fax or an offer from abroad (only 30 per cent) and the procurement of cheaper inputs (24 per cent). The former reason therefore received less importance compared to the findings of other empirical investigations.[7] The procurement of inputs is a 'resource and efficiency seeking' reason to internationalise that seems to have lost its traditional importance. It was replaced by the firms' competitive advantages under the form of new market access, technologies, business know-how, etc., which became important reasons to internationalise.[8]

Only three firms considered the participation in EU programmes as an important reason for their internationalisation process. All three firms, one of them located in Germany and the other two in Italy, were highly specialised in new products with a high R&D degree. For the majority of German, French and Italian SMEs, participation in EU programmes was less important or not important at all. One reason for the low interest may be that the majority of SMEs are not informed about the existing programmes and the possibilities to participate.

Surprisingly, only one firm considered subcontracting as an important reason for its internationalisation. The majority of SMEs did not think about subcontracting in an international context.

70 per cent of all Italian SMEs considered access to superior technology and business know-how as very important. This reason was considered as important as new market access and growth, reasons that also reached scores of 70 per cent. This confirms the argument that Italian SMEs are strong in adapting foreign technologies and applying them to their particular needs.[9] For Italian SMEs a higher turnover was less important compared to German and French SMEs. 87 per cent of German SMEs considered new market access and growth to be the most important reasons for their international strategies and 93 per cent considered a higher turnover to be most important. 75 per cent of the French SMEs cited new market access and a higher turnover as most important, and 66 per cent cited growth expectations.

47 per cent of the German SMEs and 42 per cent of the French SMEs considered a saturated home market as an important reason for their internationalisation compared to only 10 per cent of Italian SMEs. On the other hand, 58 per cent of the French SMEs indicated that following their customer abroad was an important reason for their internationalisation, compared to 40 per cent of the Italians and 33 per cent of the German SMEs. Many French SMEs internationalise through the intermediary of large multinationals. By doing so, many of them are forced to follow their larger customer abroad. For German SMEs, the chance factor was relatively important (47 per cent) compared to their French (20 per cent) and Italian counterparts (17 per cent). Italian SMEs considered

risk-spreading across different countries and the procurement of cheaper inputs abroad as an important factor in initiating internationalisation, contrary to the French and German counterparts. But Italian SMEs derive much benefit from government support of developing countries. Therefore a majority of them have strongly oriented their activities towards those countries, particularly before the establishment of the EMU. The relatively high percentage of Italian SMEs that indicated the procurement of cheaper inputs as a reason to internationalise must also be interpreted in this sense.

In question 9, SMEs were asked to estimate their sales volume in the EU before the 1992 abolition of NTBs, their sales volume in 1998 and their objectives for 2000. An important result was that sales had increased strongly up to 1998 and were expected to increase further thereafter.

Before 1992, 32 per cent of the SMEs destined less than 10 per cent of their sales to other EU countries and 30 per cent between 10 and 20 per cent. This meant that a total of 62 per cent of SMEs had exported less than 20 per cent of their output to other EU countries in 1992. Only 5 per cent of the enterprises of the sample had realised more than 50 per cent of their sales in other EU countries. In 1998, 52 per cent of the SMEs destined more than 21 per cent of their sales to other EU countries, whereas before 1992 this had been done by only about 21 per cent of the SMEs. Around 67 per cent of the SMEs in the sample planned to sell more than 21 per cent to other EU countries by 2000. In 1998, only 8 per cent of the SMEs realised more than 50 per cent of their sales with other EU countries, whereas 19 per cent of the enterprises planned to do so by 2000. The mode of SMEs by exports to other EU countries had therefore changed.

If one investigates the sales volume to other EU countries for the SMEs in the different countries, one finds out that 20 per cent of the German SMEs realised more than 31 per cent of their sales in other EU countries before 1992. 0 per cent of the French SMEs and 10 per cent of the Italians realised the same sales volume. In 1998, 33 per cent of the German SMEs had already sold over 31 per cent of their product to other EU countries. 8 per cent of the French SMEs and 20 per cent of the Italians realised the same sales volume. For the year 2000, 50 per cent of the Italian SMEs planned to sell over 31 per cent to other EU countries whereas 40 per cent of the German and 42 per cent of the French SMEs planned to do the same. Only 30 per cent of the Italians, 25 per cent of the French SMEs and 14 per cent of the German planned to sell 0 to 20 per cent to other EU countries in 2000.

It is therefore clear that the SMEs in all three countries increased their international operations in the EU. Before the 1992 abolition of NTBs, SMEs in all three countries showed a relatively low degree of exports within the EU. German and Italian SMEs exported, however, to a higher extent than their French counterparts. Up to 1998, German SMEs

Table 8.4 Estimated sales volume within the EU (in %)

Question 9		*Germany*	*France*	*Italy*	*Total*
Before 1992	< 10	26.67	41.67	30.00	32.43
	10 to 20	20.00	25.00	50.00	29.73
	21 to 30	20.00	8.33	0.00	10.81
	31 to 50	13.33	0.00	0.00	5.41
	> 50	6.67	0.00	10.00	5.41
1998	< 10	20.00	25.00	20.00	21.62
	10 to 20	20.00	16.67	20.00	18.92
	21 to 30	20.00	41.67	30.00	29.73
	31 to 50	26.67	0.00	10.00	13.51
	> 50	6.67	8.33	10.00	8.11
2000	< 10	6.67	8.33	10.00	8.11
	10 to 20	6.67	16.67	20.00	13.51
	21 to 30	33.33	25.00	10.00	24.32
	31 to 50	26.67	25.00	20.00	24.32
	> 50	13.33	16.67	30.00	18.92

Source: own estimates.

Note
The totals do not match 100% because some SMEs did not answer all questions but are included.

strongly increased their sales volume in the EU, followed by the Italians, and there was a relatively low growth rate for the French.

But, by the year 2000, French SMEs also planned to strongly increase their exports. The relatively low involvement of French SMEs during the early phases of the market opening can be connected to the high degree of concentration in the French sector that lasted up to the 1980s. A lot of French SMEs exported through the intermediary of large multinationals through subcontracting agreements. Compared with German and Italian firms, which benefited immediately from the 1992 market opening, French SMEs had a time lag in adapting to the new environment.

In question 10, SMEs of all three countries were further asked if the abolition of NTBs provided any advantages or drawbacks for their firms. One can say that the faster processing of exports was at the top of all perceived advantages with a total of about 76 per cent of all SMEs of the sample. 57 per cent of all SMEs strongly felt the harmonisation of technical standards, whereas 35 per cent perceived no effect at all. The effect was therefore clearly positive compared to the impact of adjustment of indirect taxes and the access to government procurement. 32 per cent of all SMEs felt positively affected by the adjustment of indirect taxes whereas 51 per cent perceived no effect at all; 27 per cent felt affected by the access to government procurement and 57 per cent perceived no effect. Even if there were no drawbacks in both cases it means that the majority of SMEs were indifferent to these advantages. Better access to imported components was an advantage for 43 per cent of all SMEs, for 41 per cent it had no effect at all and about 3 per cent felt some drawbacks. But even if a relatively high percentage of SME perceived no effect at all, there was also a high percentage that felt the advantages. About 41 per cent of all SMEs felt affected through the increased competition whereas 46 per cent perceived no effect at all. As a relatively high percentage of SMEs felt the drawbacks, the effect was rather negative.

These general results correspond to the results of the 1997 ENSR survey of the European Commission,[10] where it was shown that the removal of physical barriers and the harmonisation of technical standards had strongly affected manufacturing firms. For SMEs in the MSE industry, the adjustment of indirect tax payments was less of an advantage than for the benchmark enterprises in the ENSR survey. But the medium-sized enterprises in the sample perceived the adjustment of indirect tax payments as more advantageous than the smaller ones. Smaller firms considered the abolition of physical and technical barriers as most important for their international operations within the EU.

Returning to our own survey, SMEs in the different countries perceived the advantages and drawbacks of the abolition of NTBs in a different

Table 8.5 Advantages and drawbacks of the removal of NTBs (% of enterprises)

Question 10		*Germany*	*France*	*Italy*	*Total*
Technical standards	1	46.67	75.00	50.00	56.76
	2	6.67	0.00	0.00	2.70
	3	46.67	16.67	40.00	35.14
Indirect taxes	1	13.33	41.67	50.00	32.43
	2	0.00	0.00	0.00	0.00
	3	60.00	50.00	40.00	51.35
Government procurement	1	13.33	50.00	20.00	27.03
	2	0.00	0.00	0.00	0.00
	3	73.33	33.33	60.00	56.76
Faster processing of exports	1	80.00	75.00	70.00	75.68
	2	0.00	0.00	0.00	0.00
	3	13.33	16.67	20.00	16.22
Increased competition from imports	1	6.67	0.00	10.00	5.41
	2	40.00	41.67	40.00	40.54
	3	46.67	50.00	40.00	45.95
Better access to imported components	1	33.33	50.00	50.00	43.24
	2	6.67	0.00	0.00	2.70
	3	46.67	41.67	30.00	40.54
Other	1	0.00	0.00	0.00	0.00
	2	6.67	0.00	0.00	2.70
	3	0.00	0.00	0.00	0.00

Source: own estimates.

Note
Q10 : 1 = advantage; 2 = drawback; 3 = no effect.

way. In all three countries the faster processing of exports affected a high percentage of SMEs (80 per cent of the German SMEs, 75 per cent of the French and 70 per cent of the Italians). 75 per cent of the French SMEs considered that the harmonisation of technical standards was an advantage, whereas only 47 per cent of the German SMEs and 50 per cent of the Italians did so. For 47 per cent of the German SMEs the harmonisation of technical standards had no effect at all compared to only 17 per cent of the French SMEs. On the other hand, 50 per cent of the French SMEs perceived the facilitated access to government procurement as an advantage whereas only 13 per cent of the Germans and 20 per cent of the Italians did so. 73 per cent of the German SMEs and 60 per cent of the Italians felt no effect at all. 47 per cent of the German and 40 per cent of the Italian SMEs considered the adjustment of indirect tax payments as an advantage, whereas only 17 per cent of the French SMEs did so. 50 per cent of the French and Italian SMEs, but only 33 per cent of the Germans, perceived the better access to imported components as an advantage within the EU. In all three countries 40 per cent of the SMEs felt the drawbacks of increased competition from imports. But in all three countries the same percentage of SMEs or even more felt not affected at all. These percentages correspond to the results of the 1997 ENSR survey where 46 per cent of the SMEs felt the effects of higher competition due to the abolition of NTBs.[11]

One big hurdle – the removal of the different currencies within the EU countries – was investigated separately in question 11. 27 per cent of all SMEs felt no consequences at all. But it should be taken into consideration that several of them indicated some perceived additional advantages. Only 20 per cent of the German and 17 per cent of the French SMEs, but 50 per cent of the Italians, felt and expected no consequences at all.

49 per cent of the SMEs indicated a faster and easier handling of their international operations as a major effect of the introduction of the single currency. This was strongly perceived by German and French SMEs (53 per cent and 67 per cent). However, only 20 per cent of the Italian SMEs did so. 42 per cent of the French SMEs expected increased transactions within the EU due to the introduction of the single currency compared to only 20 per cent of the Germans and 10 per cent of the Italians. A low percentage of SMEs in all three countries under investigation expected no increased extra-EU transactions after the introduction of the euro. Altogether, 27 per cent of the SMEs felt a strong administrative burden during the changeover, but nearly 30 per cent saw less burden in the long term. In particular, German SMEs (47 per cent) felt the administrative burden in the beginning. But the Germans also saw a lessening of this burden in the long run. No German SME expected currency gains through the introduction of the euro compared to their French and Italian counterparts (50 per cent and 20 per cent), which would become

Table 8.6 Advantages and drawbacks of the introduction of the euro (% of enterprises)

Question 11	*Germany*	*France*	*Italy*	*Total*
No consequences	20.00	16.67	50.00	27.03
Faster and easier	53.33	66.67	20.00	48.65
Increased EU transactions	20.00	41.67	10.00	24.32
Increased transactions outside EU	13.33	16.67	10.00	13.51
Administrative burden	46.67	16.67	10.00	27.03
LT less burden	40.00	25.00	20.00	29.73
Currency gains	0.00	50.00	20.00	21.62
No currency gains	6.67	0.00	10.00	5.41
More transparency	53.33	50.00	30.00	45.95
Increased competition	33.33	16.67	20.00	24.32
Other	0.00	0.00	0.00	0.00
New software for euro preparation	40.00	83.33	40.00	54.05

Source: own estimates.

connected to the strong value and image of the German mark. Only about 5 per cent of all SMEs complained that they would be unable to benefit from currency gains after the introduction of the single currency. 46 per cent of the SMEs under investigation expected more transparency within the EU. This could be either positive, as they might benefit from cheaper inputs, or negative, due to increased competition for the final product. 24 per cent of all SMEs were afraid of increased competition. A relatively low percentage of French SMEs (17 per cent) were afraid of increased competition compared to the Germans and Italians (33 per cent and 20 per cent).

German and French SMEs seemed to perceive the challenges and opportunities of the euro to a larger extent than the Italians. In particular, French SMEs were very positive. Compared to German SMEs, for whom the introduction of the euro signified a strong administrative burden in the beginning, French SMEs could see fewer administrative problems. They even expected currency gains.

In general the advantages exceeded the drawbacks. Only 27 per cent of all SMEs expected no consequences at all. Negative effects, such as an initial administrative burden, were seen as outweighed by the advantage of less administrative burden in the longer run. If one connects the expectation of an increased transparency to that of growing competition it may be possible to estimate the positive and negative effects of transparency through the introduction of the single currency. 24 per cent of all SMEs were afraid of an increased competition and 46 per cent of more transparency. Perhaps half of all SMEs that expected more transparency will be positively affected through cheaper inputs.

In addition to the perceived influences of the introduction of the euro, SMEs were asked how they had prepared themselves for the new currency. 54 per cent indicated that they had taken this as an opportunity to introduce a new software system. Among them, French SMEs were at the top with 83 per cent, followed by the Germans and Italians with 40 per cent. This confirmed other empirical studies where German SMEs lagged behind their French counterparts in preparing for the introduction of the euro.[12] For some SMEs this constituted an opportunity to check the whole enterprise, while others had established working groups and education programmes for their employees. Even if a majority of them planned to introduce the euro as their main currency from 1999 onwards, they had left it up to their customers to choose the convenient currency.

The main results of the questionnaire research therefore show SMEs' increased export activities to other EU countries from 'before 1992' to the 'year 2000'. In addition, 43 per cent of the SMEs realised or planned cooperation agreements or FDI between 1992 and 2004, and out of this percentage the majority did or planned to do so within the EU. A large majority of SMEs felt affected by the 1992 removal of NTBs, and in particular the abolition of physical and technical barriers was strongly felt. It is therefore obvious that there is a connection between the 1992 market opening and SMEs' increased trans-border transactions within the EU. These increased trans-border transactions take the form of growing export activities and more sophisticated foreign-market entry strategies, such as joint ventures, FDI, licensing, etc. The reasons for these increased trans-border transactions are mostly driven by firm-specific factors or advantages. This explains in particular the growing number of trans-border cooperation agreements. One realises that traditional locational advantages became obsolete within the EU once the removal of barriers and the use of sophisticated communications and transport technology had facilitated increased internationalisation.

However, the questionnaire research shows its limits if one tries to connect firm age, the number of employees or even the product range to internationalisation strategies or the way the firms felt affected through the removal of NTBs. In addition, the sample was too small to reach any general conclusions regarding SMEs' strategies and attitudes in the different countries. Some strategies may also be industry-dependent and therefore generalisation becomes difficult.

Interpretation of the case studies

Case studies have emerged from various regions all over the world showing that clusters of small enterprises have broken into international markets. The best-known cases are the Italian industrial districts and similar cases come from other advanced, as well as less advanced, countries.[13]

The above case studies illustrate firms within the industrial districts of Tuttlingen in Germany and Nogent in France. This section is concerned with their ability to grow and to internationalise. First, the enterprises are analysed regarding their position in the industrial district. As clusters help to internationalise, it is assumed that this attitude is deepened through the establishment of the EMU. An attempt will be made to discover if this hypothesis is confirmed. Second, some conceptual and theoretical ideas will be developed to help to explain success or failure in internationalising, by drawing from our research into internationally competitive industrial districts.

Analysis of the enterprises

Our different case studies showed clearly the uniqueness of each enterprise in general and the uniqueness of their internationalisation strategies in particular. These are influenced by external factors such as national and European policy measures and the local infrastructure. But internal factors, such as the firm's history, its structure, the owner's or manager's character and the firm's competitive advantage(s), also played a major role. In this section an analysis is made of the impact of the establishment of the EMU on these firms, their internationalisation strategies and their competitive situation in the industrial district. The terms 'differentiation' and 'cost leadership' are used as defined by Porter.[14]

Impact of the EMU

Out of the seven SMEs, five felt affected by the establishment of the EMU. Four are located in Tuttlingen and one in Nogent. As the degree of internationalisation and the product range vary from one firm to another, they each felt affected in a different way.

SMEs producing R&D-intensive medical instruments not only felt the abolition of physical barriers. They were strongly affected by the harmonisation of technical standards. It meant a faster and less expensive handling of trans-border activities for high-tech instruments. Examples are ALTMANN, DEXTRA and MENTA, all of them located in Tuttlingen. ALTMANN and MENTA stated that the harmonisation of technical standards had increased demand for their high-tech instruments.

Even if TRAUBE is one of the market leaders of one or two highly specialised mechanical instruments, the firm has not been much affected by the removal of NTBs between the EU countries. The firm's major cooperation partners are large US distributors. Interestingly, the harmonisation of technical standards has had a positive impact on the firm's exports to the USA. US customers recognised the unified quality norms within the EU.

All SMEs, with the exception of MAISTRE and NUTRA, felt strongly affected by the abolition of physical barriers in the EU. The five SMEs and their cooperation partners or customers abroad realised that transactions within the EU had become faster and cheaper. One example is the case of MENTA. Before the abolition of physical border controls, it took about three or four weeks for the instruments to travel from Germany to their destination in Spain. After the removal of physical barriers, it took about three days.[15] This confirms the findings of the Cecchini Report.[16] Even SMEs with relatively low export rates in the EU quoted the advantages.

Also interesting is the case of the French producer DUPONT, which exports only through the intermediary of large French distributors. The firm imports 60 per cent of its hammer-forged instruments and 30 per cent of its final instruments from Tuttlingen. The abolition of physical barriers has speeded up and facilitated its imports. The small craft firm MAISTRE did not feel affected by the 1992 market opening due to its limited transactions within the EU. Its owner still complained about the high administrative burden and saw a lot of additional costs for his firm. Also NUTRA is rather indifferent regarding the removal of NTBs. It produces and distributes standardised surgical instruments[17] and competes for tenders. The firm's favoured markets for business transactions are developing countries.

ALTMANN, DEXTRA, MENTA and DUPONT considered the introduction of the single currency as a very important factor for facilitated transactions within the EU. For ALTMANN, DEXTRA and MENTA the main advantage of its introduction was the abolition of exchange-rate risk. All three SMEs expected an easier handling of their international activities within the EU. The three German SMEs had prepared for its introduction conscientiously. ALTMANN and DEXTRA had instituted working groups. MENTA and ALTMANN had sent out a questionnaire to major customers asking them if they were in favour of an early changeover. All SMEs in our sample had introduced price-lists in both euros and their respective national currency. This early preparation does not correspond to the theoretical findings of the literature survey.[18] Obviously, this early changeover is related to the high degree of internationalisation of SMEs in the MSE industry.

According to some SMEs the establishment of the EMU leads to increased competition (ALTMANN, MAISTRE, MENTA). This result is similar to that obtained by the ENSR survey of the European Commission where greater competition is considered to be a major threat to the EMU.[19] In particular, SMEs with a R&D-intensive production range (ALTMANN, DEXTRA, MENTA) are forced to grow and internationalise further to obtain the necessary economies of scale. Only by doing this can the firms exploit their competitive advantage in the form of R&D-intensive instruments and face the increased competition.

Others claim (in particular DEXTRA) that even the introduction of the single currency does not increase competition because of an existing high level of price transparency in the MSE industry. Strong competition comes from cheap-labour countries, but so far it has affected only standardised surgical instruments.

Internationalisation strategies

EXPORTS

SMEs' internationalisation strategies are strongly dependent on firm structure and size. All seven are doing direct and indirect exports. Independent of their different firm size both French SMEs are exporting more indirectly, through the intermediary of large French distributors, rather than directly. DUPONT'S contacts with firms or customers abroad are limited. By the use of indirect export channels the firm has lower costs and fewer risks. But it also reduces the firm's international learning experience and avoids international sophistication and commitment, as suggested by Root.[20] Indirect exporting demands little foreign-country and foreign-market knowledge and insulates the firm from foreign markets. The craft firm MAISTRE has also a low direct export rate of 1 per cent. The firm has only a limited influence on the marketing plan and therefore receives no feedback regarding promotion and pricing abroad.

Firms with a R&D-intensive product range prefer direct exports. Examples are ALTMANN, DEXTRA and MENTA. Despite their differences in firm size and structure, they cooperate with hospitals in the EU and the US to develop new products. DEXTRA and MENTA conduct their exports through commercial agents, SMEs as 'complementary equals'[21] being preferred.

Due to its relatively small firm size MENTA had not taken its internationalisation process much further. But the firm planned cooperation agreements with a Spanish and an Italian firm at the end of 1998. MENTA'S internationalisation process was therefore characterised by a step-by-step approach. Regarding its exports, the firm concentrated on markets it knew well from the owners' previous experience. As predicted by Johanson and Mattsson, already existing contacts and knowledge of the foreign language reduced uncertainty.[22] MENTA did not, however, start by exporting to neighbour countries or countries that were similar with regard to business practices as prescribed by the Uppsala model.[23]

Despite its firm's size, DEXTRA remains at stage one of the internationalisation process. Its structure plays an essential role in its attitude towards internationalisation. A decision in favour of FDI would be difficult to reach within the cooperative. From its foundation in 1941, the distribution centre has not changed its foreign-market entry strategy, with the exception of a distribution subsidiary in the US that closed with the death of its director. With increasing sophistication of its products, access to technology as a reason to internationalise has become important. In this sense the selection of appropriate commerical representatives abroad is increasingly based on their capacity to sell high-tech products. These cooperation agreements are long-term, based on trust, and are preferred to vertical integration by acquisition.

SUBCONTRACTING

All SMEs in the sample are subcontracting, are subcontractors, or both. However, firms with a R&D-intensive product range subcontract less compared to firms with standardised instruments.

Subcontracting is particularly pronounced for TRAUBE'S national and international transactions. In 1998, TRAUBE earned 80 per cent of its turnover from direct exports through large distributors, mostly to the US. But the strategy of staying a long time at stage one of the internationalisation process is common among SMEs acting as subcontractors. Only if the firm's competitive advantage(s) and its market visibility become high enough will some SMEs start to move beyond stage one. Even this is likely to be a timid step.[24] As a subcontractor, TRAUBE does not have to bother with promotion and can concentrate on highly specialised production and innovation, as predicted by Baglin.[25] This niche specialisation has made the firm into a market leader for some instruments.

It is also interesting to consider the case of DUPONT, which established a partnership with a firm in Sialkot to subcontract important parts of the value-chain for cost reasons. Transformation and assembling activities are cheaper in Pakistan. Despite this outsourcing, DUPONT is unable to compete at competitive prices. The French producer and distributor established the partnership in 1990, which is relatively late compared to German SMEs of the same sector who started to outsource in the 1970s. In addition, the firm left some final steps of the production process in-house, which increases costs.

FDI

Two of the seven SMEs invested abroad. Both SMEs are, however, very different regarding their product range and their objectives. NUTRA was founded together with its Pakistani joint venture for cost reasons. NUTRA'S cooperation partner receives its know-how and technology from the German SME and competes strongly for tenders in developing countries. Through the transfer of technology to the cooperation partner a serious competitor is created, confirming the hypothesis of Root.[26] It is a trade-off as the firm in the developed country gets the benefits of cheap labour in Pakistan, against the risk that the Pakistani partner firm will 'learn' to compete. But, in general, firms in the developed countries know very well the kind of technology they must not transfer. Difficult, secret processes must be kept at home.

The protection and continuous success of their technology was the main idea behind ALTMANN'S internationalisation. After the establishment of a distribution centre in the UK in 1987, ALTMANN founded its own subsidiary with production and service facilities in the USA in 1991. The main reason for this investment was market access and access to new technologies in this important market, characterised by high growth and invention rates.[27] Marketing advantages, a higher quality of supply in the target market and a better exploitation and protection of firm-specific advantage(s) were a consequence.[28]

ALTMANN'S Polish subsidiary started its operations in 1994. The reason for the establishment of the production plant was cheap labour costs. While the Polish investment was driven by location-specific factors, ALTMANN'S US investment was based on access to markets and new technologies and therefore driven by the firm's competitive advantage according to the paradigm of Dunning.[29] Despite relatively high labour costs in Germany, ALTMANN left the majority of R&D and production in Tuttlingen. This decision was driven by the pool of specialised and skilled workers, typical in an industrial district, as suggested by Krugman and Venables.[30] This constitutes a strong location-specific advantage. There emerges therefore a logical pattern: the investment in Poland is due to cheap labour, the investment in the USA for scientific inputs, and the headquarters in Tuttlingen offers the advantage of providing skilled labour.

As a result, one realises that SMEs in the MSE sector have leapfrogged a stage compared to large TNCs. SMEs in the industrial district outsourced parts of their value-chain to cheap-labour countries. But outsourcing is typically the SMEs' 'route' to internationalisation, a 'route' which even large TNCs now find attractive. It has been rendered possible because firms in less developed countries (LDCs) have acquired manufacturing technology and know-how from previous contacts with developed countries' TNCs which were the pioneers in LDCs. Local employees leave the TNC and start their own business. They export low-quality products to developed countries and are at the beginning of the learning curve. SMEs in developed countries have experienced the opportunity of getting SMEs in LDCs to do the labour-intensive part of their more complex production. In our example the SMEs in Tuttlingen realised the opportunity before the SMEs in Nogent. Their competitive situation is therefore much better.

Location in industrial districts

All seven SMEs maintain regular contacts with other SMEs in their industrial district. The number of contacts varies, however, from one firm to another.

ALTMANN is one of the larger SMEs in Tuttlingen and highly concentrated on R&D-intensive instruments. The firm integrated vertically to have long-term control over its prime technology. In this context it is important to mention that ALTMANN does compete for a few tenders and wishes to reduce this in the future. The firm's major strategy is one of product differentiation. It maintains regular contact with about twenty other firms in the industrial district. Increased internationalisation and growth led to intensified cooperation with their local cooperation partners. Each cooperation partner can reap more economies of scale and specialise further. It is a virtuous circle, leading to more growth for everybody.

Also, DEXTRA belongs to the larger SMEs in Tuttlingen. Even though the firm has about the same number of employees as ALTMANN, its firm structure is very different. As a cooperative, DEXTRA integrated some activities of the product's value-chain, but most fabrication stayed under the control of the manufacturing firms. Such a firm structure is possible only in an industrial district, which reduces transport costs to a minimum. Thanks to its structure the firm is able to reduce costs for standardised surgical instruments and is able to develop new and more sophisticated medical ones. As a cooperative, DEXTRA enjoys all the advantages of increased specialisation due to a high division of labour. The firm is successful in competing for tenders and at the same time R&D-intensive cooperation with medical centres and hospitals all over the world is possible. DEXTRA follows strategies of cost leadership and differentiation at the same time.

To avoid an overlapping of products,[31] DEXTRA has to coordinate not only between the surgeons and the manufacturing firms, but also between its eighteen manufacturing firms. Information flows between the members of DEXTRA are easier than in an arm's length relationship.[32] Even if coordination costs are relatively high and a certain overlapping takes place, DEXTRA retains a high degree of flexibility. Benefits from this part-internalisation arise through gains in time, since arm's length transactions would involve higher coordination efforts according to Hennart.[33] Members of the cooperative are all roughly the same size and each possesses its own area of specialisation. This reduces coordination costs as described by Bleeke and Ernst.[34] Each manufacturing firm is able to reach a high degree of specialisation, while the owners retain a relatively high degree of independence, which has a positive effect on their motivation. Flexibility and specialisation[35] are the competitive weapons of these SMEs and they do not lose their identities through their network, as would be the case in a vertically integrated firm.[36]

NUTRA and DUPONT both function as Pakistani connections for smaller SMEs. Both try to follow a strategy of cost leadership. This leads to a competitive advantage regarding costs for NUTRA, but not for DUPONT who cannot compete with competitive prices on a national and international level. NUTRA'S competitive advantage in the tender business is sustainable thanks to its central position in the industrial district. NUTRA is able to deliver standardised surgical instruments (transformed and assembled by the Pakistani partner firm) and some sophisticated instruments. These sophisticated instruments are bought from highly specialised firms in Tuttlingen. NUTRA maintains regular contact with about sixty small firms in the industrial district. These craft firms are too small to establish their own joint venture or partnership in Pakistan. The relationships are mutual. About 30 per cent of NUTRA'S annual turnover comes from its customers in Tuttlingen, which confirms the relatively high level of subcontracting in the industrial district. As suggested by Patry, both sides are able to reduce costs through specialisation.[37]

In both districts leader-firms take on a group configuration through a semi-integration, as in the case of DEXTRA, or through informal cooperation agreements, as in the case of DUPONT and NUTRA. In an article about Italian industrial districts, Corò and Grandinetti described the formation of groups through leader-firms.[38] According to the authors, the strategic reasons for the formation of such groups were:

1 a reduction of competition in the district and a better response to global competition
2 an increase in the firms' product range or diversification
3 rationalisation and control of the value-chain
4 development of specialised service activities
5 better international development of the firm.

DUPONT maintains regular contacts with six small firms in the region of Nogent. Each firm is specialised in the production of some specific instrument or part of the production process. In a majority of cases the instruments require a high percentage of skilled manual work. Important transformation processes and assembling are done by the Pakistani partner. In some cases, DUPONT subcontracts the final steps of the production process to differentiate an instrument through higher quality. The relationships between the firms are mutual and long-standing. One of their local cooperation partners is the small craft firm MAISTRE which also buys about 5 per cent of its surgical instruments from other highly specialised craft firms in Nogent. Subcontracting in production and service activities – a main characteristic of industrial districts – is used to reduce costs, leading to a high degree of specialisation by all partners, as investigated by Quinn.[39]

These subcontracting activities are very pronounced in the case of TRAUBE. 20 per cent of the firm's annual turnover is earned on the home market, 15 per cent of which comes from being subcontracted by firms in the industrial district of Tuttlingen. In turn, TRAUBE outsources parts of the production process that are too expensive to be done in-house. For this reason, it maintains regular contacts with about ten firms in Tuttlingen. TRAUBE thus constitutes a good example of 'network participation' which allows participants to focus and specialise on those activities where they are uniquely efficient.[40] TRAUBE subcontracts parts of the production process because it is unable to achieve enough volume in-house. By doing so, the firm is able to reduce costs. The proximity that supports more specialised suppliers of inputs and services, as well as a pool of specialised and skilled workers, promotes not only cooperation but also competition. In addition to the competition from countries with relatively low labour costs, the rivalry in the industrial district of Tuttlingen is felt strongly by TRAUBE. It is significant that each new employee has to be checked regarding his independence and loyalty.[41]

It is also interesting to note the case of MENTA, which remains in the general tender business alongside its specialisation in neurosurgery implants. All standardised surgical instruments are bought from three firms, located in Tuttlingen, with which the firm maintains close and regular contacts on a mutual basis. Even if MENTA has abandoned its own production of surgical instruments, it continues to compete for tenders (declining relatively in the long run) due to location-specific advantages in the industrial district of Tuttlingen. This arm's length, market-based coordination, by allowing each unit to specialise completely, appears to be cost-effective, since MENTA remains profitable and competitive. The high level of specialisation leads to improved capacity utilisation and increased economies of scale, confirming the hypothesis of Baglin.[42]

Cooperation in industrial districts goes hand in hand with competition. Proximity in the industrial districts, essential for inter-firm cooperation, also increases rivalry according to Porter.[43] In Tuttlingen, firms compete not only for market shares, but also for people and innovations. As suggested by Grant, this rivalry is important for quality improvements, cost reductions and innovations.[44] SMEs such as DEXTRA, ALTMANN and MENTA feel stimulated to improve through innovations, which enhance their strategy of differentiation. On the other hand, these firms strongly feel the competition of the market leader Aesculap.

In contrast to Tuttlingen, cooperation in Nogent is accompanied by a low degree of rivalry. The number of enterprises in the MSE industry has declined heavily in the industrial district of Nogent since World War II.[45] For the SMEs in this region, competition comes essentially from cheap-labour countries and from German firms.

In the following section the inter-firm relationships in both industrial districts are investigated in detail. An attempt is made to answer the question relating to why and when an industrial district is internationally competitive.

Internationally competitive industrial districts

Enterprises located in industrial districts realise efficiency gains which individual enterprises can seldom attain. The competitive advantage

Table 8.7 Comparison of the different enterprises

Name	*Products*	*Internationalisation*	*1992 Programme*	*Local cooperation*	*Strategy and competitive advantage*
ALTMANN	80% new products, stand. products reduced, less tender business	Direct export, little indirect export, FDI (in developed countries)	Phys./techn. barriers, euro: poss. influences on internationalisation	Rather integrated firm, but benefits from ID (info., labour, coop.), coop. with 20 firms	Product differentiation: new R&D-intensive instruments (niches)
DEXTRA	More new products, stand. instruments, more tender business	Direct export, little indirect export, little subcontracting (USA)	Phys./techn. barriers, euro: poss. influences on internationalisation	High coop. in the network, also coop. in the ID outside the network	Product differentiation and cost leadership: strategic network structure
NUTRA	Stand. surgical instr., new instr. bought, more tender business	Direct and indirect exports, J.V. (Pakistan), little subcontracting	No influence	High degree of cooperation with about 60 firms in ID	Cost leadership: central role in ID (Pakistan connection)
MENTA	More new products, stand. products bought, less tender business	Direct export, little indirect export, cooperation agreements planned	Phys./techn. barriers, euro: poss. influences on internationalisation	Little cooperation in ID (3 partners)	Product differentiation: new R&D-intensive instruments (niches)

TRAUBE	Mechanical surgical instruments	Direct and indirect exports, subcontracting	Phys./techn barriers, euro felt: but no strong influence	Strong cooperation in ID: components, production process	Product differentiation: concentration on some instruments (niches)
DUPONT	Standardised surgical instruments	Indirect export, little direct export, subcontr., partnership (Pakistan)	Phys. barriers, euro: poss. influence on imports	Cooperation with 6 firms in ID	Cost leadership: no long-term competitive advantage
MAISTRE	Mechanical surgical instruments, stand. instruments bought	Indirect export, little direct export	Negative influences	Cooperation with some firms in ID	Product differentiation: concentration on some instruments (niches)

Note
JV = joint venture; ID = industrial district.

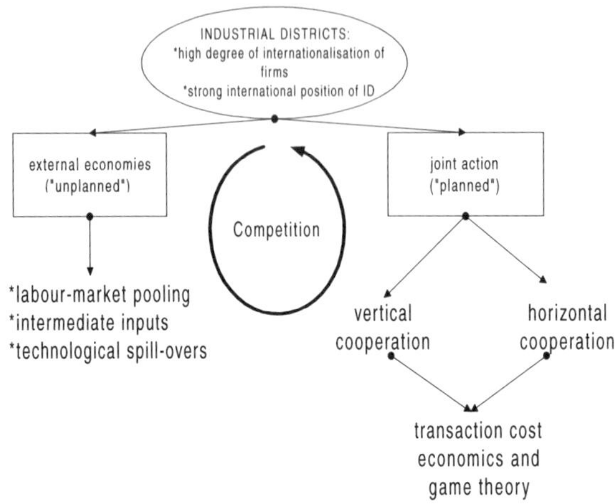

Figure 8.1 Dynamic of the industrial district.

(a combination of location-specific advantages) of an industrial district is therefore based on *collective efficiency*.[46] This collective efficiency is derived from *external economies* and *joint action*,[47] two factors that are essential for the international success of an industrial district. Schmitz describes external economies as 'unplanned' and joint action as 'planned'. By using the two terms in this section it is possible to predict whether the two districts of our sample will be internationally successful in the future. Through these two factors competition is affected in three ways: first, by increasing the productivity of the firms located in such agglomerations; second, by driving the direction and pace of innovation which supports future productivity growth; and third, by stimulating the formation of new businesses in the industrial district.[48] Industrial districts with a strong international position are therefore composed of highly internationalised firms. In this context, Italian researchers have found that export intensity is higher for a clustered than for an isolated firm.[49]

External economies

External economies occur where market prices do not fully incorporate certain benefits to economic agents. When social benefits are higher than private benefits we speak of external economies. The origin of localisation externalities lies within the firm's own industry. In this case, unit costs decrease with the output of all firms of the industry.[50] Based on Alfred Marshall, Krugman and Venables identify three reasons for localisation that create external economies: first, labour-market pooling; second, intermediate inputs; and third, technological spill-overs.[51] Even if external economies are difficult to measure, it is possible to investigate the importance of these three factors for the seven enterprises.

Almost all the firms we have investigated rely on local suppliers for steel and other inputs. The degree of *sourcing these local inputs* depends on the firms' product range. Firms that are specialised in sophisticated medical instruments, such as ALTMANN, are less dependent on local inputs. MENTA abandoned its strategy of relying on local inputs by focusing on sophisticated instruments.[52] Firms such as TRAUBE and DEXTRA (by their internal structure) rely strongly on intermediate inputs. Unlike firms in the industrial district of Nogent, the firms in Tuttlingen rely extensively on local suppliers for steel to produce standardised surgical instruments.

The presence of such specialised suppliers of inputs constitutes an important advantage for all firms in industrial districts. It guarantees competitive prices as well as the ready availability of a wide range of inputs. The existing networks among suppliers ensure that if one input is not available from a particular supplier it can be found elsewhere in the industrial district. As the suppliers are located close to the producers, the inputs can be delivered quickly to the factory gate, which diminishes not only time but also transport costs. As a maximum number of purchases can be made locally, the sum of the distances between industrial locations is minimised.[53] In addition, producers are not obliged to maintain large stocks of inputs if the local supplier market is well developed and specialised. Through this ready availability of intermediate inputs local producers are able to respond quickly to incoming orders.

NUTRA, for example, functions as a distribution centre, allowing its supplying firms to minimise the costs of storage. Delays and transportation costs are also reduced for the supplying firms. DEXTRA, with its special firm structure, internalises this important source of external economies. Despite overlapping in some cases, complementarities play an important role among the eighteen manufacturing partner firms. By limiting cooperation outside their strategic network DEXTRA diminishes rivalry.

Firms in Tuttlingen buy most of their new machinery from firms located in the industrial district, compared to firms in Nogent which source them from outside the cluster. The enterprise Chiron in Tuttlingen used to be a producer of surgical instruments, but abandoned this business completely in the 1970s to concentrate on machinery for the production of surgical instruments. The industrial district also possesses specialised service providers, such as machinery repair units.

In the MSE industry production processes are easily divisible and subcontracting activities are therefore widespread in Tuttlingen and Nogent. All firms interviewed in the industrial districts contracted out specific production processes and/or the production of particular instruments. The only firm that has relied less on subcontracting activities (they act more as a subcontractor for large multinationals) is ALTMANN, with its integrated firm structure. NUTRA subcontracts the production of sophisticated medical and surgical instruments to its respective local cooperation partners and MENTA buys all standardised surgical instruments from three trustworthy cooperation partners, located in the industrial district. TRAUBE subcontracts whole production processes, as does DUPONT.

Through the presence of a wide range of specialised subcontractors, economies of scale and scope can be reaped. Firms subcontracting whole production processes do not have to invest in expensive machinery. They are often small in size and do not have enough sales volume to optimise expensive machines. SMEs therefore save on costs, space and skills. By means of subcontracting, highly specialised firms can accept orders for a larger range of products and realise economies of scope. By doing so, relatively small firms in the network can successfully compete alongside larger, more integrated firms. This corresponds to the strategy of TRAUBE, which subcontracts important parts of the production process, but keeps the final steps in-house. The cooperation partners of NUTRA also follow such a strategy by using the distribution centre as a Pakistani connection and improving the transformed instruments by some final tasks.

The concentration of *highly skilled* labour is the locational advantage most cited in both Tuttlingen and Nogent. The clearly defined and limited market for specialised labour minimises labour search costs. Specialised workers find work without any difficulty, while firms looking for someone qualified can find the right person at short notice. The traditional three-year apprenticeship in Tuttlingen reinforces this location-specific advantage. The special apprenticeship as a medical technician consists of a simultaneous training in school and in the firm. In Nogent, the apprenticeship system is rather informal. The presence of a large number of skilled people in the industrial districts guarantees competition. In both industrial districts priority is given to employees with experience-based competence, rather than competence based on theoretical education, as suggested by Wiklund and Karlsson.[54]

Another source of external economies in industrial districts are *flows of technical and sector-specific knowledge*. All firms in both industrial districts confirmed the importance of such information flows. It is essential to have background information on an individual and his firm before engaging him as subcontractor or distributor. Information regarding prices, new markets and technical inventions is also important. Information is often gathered through informal gossip on the streets or in restaurants.[55] Firms are able to reduce transaction costs and uncertainties, due to the rapid flow of information. The speed and ease of information flow also facilitates the spread of new ideas or technologies within the industrial district. Keeping secrets is nearly impossible, particularly in Tuttlingen where investment in R&D is relatively high and where there are many more firms than in Nogent.

The ongoing ability of firms to *innovate* is essential for the competitive advantage of an industrial district, as described by Porter and

Audretsch.[56] Key factors include a high degree of human capital, a skilled labour-force and a high presence of scientists and engineers. In Tuttlingen, some innovative firms stimulate the growth of many others. The proximity of the firms helps to diffuse innovation which is the strength of a successful cluster. If the firms in an industrial district are both recipients and providers of external economies there is no lack of investment in R&D, as predicted by Schmitz.[57] Conversely we might argue that if all knowledge and in particular technological innovation comes from outside, the industrial district loses its dynamic and therefore its competitive advantage. In the industrial district of Tuttlingen leading firms keep their R&D activities at their headquarters, whereas the leading firm in the industrial district of Nogent had research centres elsewhere in France before being taken over. In the case of Tuttlingen, competition and innovation have remained vigorous, despite the firms outsourcing parts of their production to cheap-labour countries.

Even if the sources of external economies exist in both industrial districts, it is impossible to quantify them. These external economies are important for efficiency advantages that are reaped by small firms in industrial districts. Efficiency gains depend strongly on the intensity and depth of inter-firm division of labour. They can only be reaped if the industrial district evolves continually. If local competition is vigorous, new firms emerge and a self-reinforcing cycle promotes growth. The number of firms is higher in Tuttlingen than in Nogent and, therefore, the inter-firm division of labour is greater. In addition, more new firms have been created in Tuttlingen than in Nogent, where the number of firms had been declining before becoming relatively constant.[58]

In addition to external economies, according to Piore and Sabel, joint action is extremely important for the success of an industrial district[59] because external economies are not sufficient to explain its growth, its international competitiveness and the relatively high degree of internationalisation of its firms.

Joint action

Two principal forms of joint action can be observed in industrial districts. Individual firms establish horizontal or vertical cooperation agreements by sharing their equipment, improving components or developing new products. Vertical cooperation agreements include relationships between firms and their input suppliers, subcontractors and buyers. Horizontal cooperation agreements correspond to relationships between a few producers or a multilateral collaboration (business associations, producer consortia, etc.).[60]

The concept of *vertical cooperation* is commonly found in both Tuttlingen and Nogent. Firms such as TRAUBE, as well as the manufacturing partner firms of DEXTRA and NUTRA, use the same supplying firms for years, sometimes for decades (as in the case of TRAUBE). These long-term relationships within an industrial district lead to more mutual understanding and an improved handling of affairs. In addition, the response to incoming tenders is quicker.[61] The ties are particularly strong if the firms produce and distribute relatively standardised surgical instruments. Some of the larger firms in Tuttlingen, such as ALTMANN, are more integrated to protect their R&D, intensive products. While still located in the industrial district, they use local suppliers and subcontractors to a lesser extent than would be the case if they were smaller and less internationalised. Compared to Tuttlingen, firms located in Nogent rely not only on supplying firms in their industrial district, but also on other firms, located elsewhere in France or in Germany. Despite their specialisation in standardised surgical instruments and mechanical instruments with a high degree of skilled manual labour, their choice of local supplying firms is relatively limited.

In both Tuttlingen and Nogent, manufacturers and specialised subcontractors are strongly dependent on each other. Delivery times are reduced and quality is improved. Through vertical ties between manufacturer and subcontractor all parties are able to improve products and processes. DUPONT, TRAUBE, MENTA and NUTRA are in regular daily contact with their subcontractors. However, although subcontracting activities lower costs and lead to further specialisation, they also imply a loss of control. Forging, polishing and thermal treatment are important steps for the quality of a surgical instrument and a high level of trust is important between the manufacturer and the subcontractor. This kind of trust exists, for example, between DUPONT and their local subcontractors, but not between them and their Pakistani partner.

Having studied vertical joint action, it is also helpful to look at *horizontal collaboration* among producers in the industrial districts. By sharing capacity, joint research and product development and the pooling of marketing activities, firms can compete for large orders. The manufacturing partner firms of DEXTRA pool their marketing activities by concluding a cooperation agreement. By avoiding an arm's length relationship these firms have integrated their marketing activities while retaining a certain independence regarding production. But other firms, such as MENTA, NUTRA and DUPONT, also admitted sharing marketing information and know-how with their local partners.

Horizontal joint action is midway between cooperation and competition. For this reason, the notion of 'cooperative competition'[62] is closely connected to industrial districts. In both industrial districts there is a high degree of local competition. Competition in the industrial district of Tuttlingen is, however, more intense than in Nogent because of the large numbers of firms and high international involvement. Depending on the product range, firms compete on both product quality and prices. Growing price competition from cheap-labour countries encourages firms in the industrial districts to meet their rivals' prices.[63] Marketing and technological information are also closely guarded secrets. Larger firms such as ALTMANN or DEXTRA try to cope with the problem of confidentiality by integration or semi-integration. Smaller firms, such as MENTA, limit their contacts to a few firms for the same reason. Despite these attempts at secrecy, information flows easily within industrial districts due to proximity and existing networks.

This competition between the enterprises does not exclude joint action in the areas of training, services, local infrastructure improvements, etc. Firms in Tuttlingen are highly involved in multilateral joint action. The establishment of a special apprenticeship system as a medical technician constitutes a unique opportunity to train, research and advise young people. In addition, the well-known and much admired German system, of practical training combined with theoretical learning at school, has positive effects on the constitution of a pool of highly skilled manpower. A special formation in the area of MSE also existed in Nogent until 1990. During the 1990s firms realised that the industry-specific knowledge was lost and therefore reintroduced a special formation[64] that students can choose at the college of Nogent in 1999.

Another joint-action initiative in Tuttlingen is the publication of a brochure on quality requirements in the MSE industry. About twenty firms – sometimes complementary regarding their product range and sometimes competitors – published a small brochure, destined for their customers, on how to use instruments correctly. This joint action was decided upon in order to reduce the increasing number of complaints from customers due to incorrect use of the instruments.

The publication of a guide to firms producing surgical instruments is another example of joint action by about 200 SMEs in Tuttlingen. The customer arriving in Tuttlingen finds a guide to the firms and their specialisations at the reception desk in each hotel. An indication of their addresses and a map of the town helps the customer to orient himself. Such initiatives, reinforcing the position of smaller firms, are not supported by large firms such as Aesculap.

According to Schmitz, a large part of the external economies in an industrial district are due to 'planned' joint-action activities between the actors. Conversely, districts showing a low degree of joint action are expected to lose part of their competitive advantage.

Transaction-cost economics and game theory contribute to understanding the conditions under which joint action occurs. Through informal cooperation between the firms in the industrial districts of Tuttlingen and Nogent the costs of repeated transactions in the market place are reduced. In this context it is important to emphasise that the larger a cluster, the more privileged partners an SME can choose from within the cluster. This encourages more 'families' of complementary firms to flourish and each one becomes more efficient. Of course, costs are incurred through negotiating and maintaining an agreement between the firms in a cluster.[65] The transaction costs for maintaining an agreement, which include the costs of opportunistic behaviour, can be reduced through the generation of trust. All enterprises studied prefer informal cooperation agreements to reduce costs and market uncertainties. Of course, the number of informal cooperation agreements varies from one firm to another. Firms such as ALTMANN, DEXTRA and MENTA limit their contacts to protect their firm-specific advantage(s). The risk of losing a competitive advantage to a competitor is reinforced in an industrial district where technological spill-overs spread quickly. In general, collective joint action spanning many firms can only apply to non-sensitive ventures, such as the guide book for hotels mentioned above.

Joint actions in the industrial districts – and in particular observed vertical cooperation – rely strongly on trust between the actors. Bidault and Jarillo identify two sources of trust.[66] The *first source* is the similarity of ethical values. In both industrial districts the cooperation partners have known each other for decades. They have been to school together and have learnt their business in the same firms. In some cases there are family ties or other connections and outsiders require time to understand them.

People in the industrial district of Tuttlingen are connected through their South German dialect and their work ethic. Tuttlingen is located in Baden-Württemberg, well known for its successful 'Mittelstand' enterprises. People are known in the whole region as extremely hard-working, thrifty and wealthy. In a majority of cases, the enterprises are 'hidden' behind the owners' houses. Despite the high degree of internationalisation, together with a knowledge of foreign languages and an excellent education, people in Tuttlingen are anxious to keep their business secrets. In some cases their neighbour is their strongest competitor, nationally and internationally.

In the industrial district of Nogent firms are less concentrated in one place than in Tuttlingen. The firms in the MSE industry are located outside the villages in industrial zones. There is therefore a clear separation between the working and the living place.

Both industrial districts, but in particular the industrial district of Tuttlingen, limit entry to outsiders through informal restrictions. In the boundaries of an industrial district it is more important than elsewhere to know the right people in order to receive what you want. An outsider arriving in an industrial district has to spend a lot of time and energy in understanding the relations and functioning of the district.[67]

The *second source* of trust is time or experience, demonstrated by game theory. Trust is created through repeated and regular contacts between firms in an industrial district.[68] The repeated game of prisoner's dilemma produces a higher payoff from cooperation than from opportunism. This can be used to explain the long-standing cooperation between the same firms which we found to be common in both Tuttlingen and Nogent.

By their formal cooperation agreement DEXTRA captures benefits such as shared costs and risks, technological advantages through R&D spill-overs, fast market access and increasing market share. Opportunistic behaviour within this firm constellation would lead to sanctions. As the game is repeated an infinite number of times, it is necessary to include Axelrod's 'tit for tat' game.[69]

In the case of informal cooperation agreements, such as the relation between NUTRA and its customers or the relation between DUPONT and its supplying firms, the reputation of playing 'tit for tat' is essential. These long-term arrangements do not provide for formal sanctions as in the case of formal cooperation agreements. Informal sanction for misbehaviour would simply take the form of a cessation of orders, which signifies the death for a player in an agglomeration. Maintaining a reputation for trustworthiness is very important for firms located in industrial districts, due to their high local involvement. All seven firms in our sample emphasised the high level of trust between them and their partners.

Having a local reputation for being trustworthy is also extremely important for the firms' international operations. Foreign customers have different supplying firms in an industrial district. In addition, many foreign firms have established offices or production plants in Tuttlingen and Nogent, often by taking over a local player.[70] These firms have become a part of the local network, approaching the status of world-wide actors in this specific industry. A firm's reputation is therefore important not only for its local cooperation partners, but also for its international 'cooperations'. The removal of NTBs between the EU countries has reinforced this tendency as traditional comparative advantages became challenged. Markets were approached through advances in information technology, and acts of opportunism became easier to detect, at both a national and an international level.

The case studies and their analysis clearly demonstrate the uniqueness of each enterprise. Their internationalisation strategies are dependent on internal firm-specific factors and external environmental factors such as their local infrastructure and national or EU policies. But, compared to the SMEs located outside industrial districts, firms located inside districts develop easier firm-specific factors or advantages due to their position within the industrial district. In this sense, the majority of the SMEs that were studied (those involved in the development and production of 'new' products) have been positively affected by the 1992 removal of NTBs and have increased their international operations in other EU countries. Their initially higher degree of internationalisation (compared to the firms located outside industrial districts)[71] made them sensitive to improved market access. The local infrastructure supported their international competitiveness as described above.

But it is very important for a firm to belong to the 'right' and therefore successful cluster. Our examples of Tuttlingen and Nogent demonstrate this clearly. The cluster of Tuttlingen is larger and offers SMEs a wide choice of complementary firms that are highly efficient. Independent of the national and international environment, the local infrastructure offers fewer opportunities for a firm in the cluster of Nogent. There is less specialisation and efficiency and therefore less international success. The SMEs in the industrial district of Nogent did not react in the same positive manner to the establishment of the EMU as the SMEs in the industrial district of Tuttlingen.

Constraints of time and resources limited our empirical investigations, but we are confident that these seven firms are representative of the reality of the working of an industrial district. Further research, especially in Italy, would doubtless have allowed us to develop more insights. But we have at least been able to investigate one large and one small SME in each region. According to both interview partners, the small craft firm was representative for other small firms that specialised in one or two instruments or production processes.

9 General conclusions

New approaches towards internationalisation

This study confirms that, at least in the case of R&D-intensive medical instruments, the removal of NTBs has led to a deepening integration of international economic activity within the EU. The empirical part of this research shows that the liberalisation of cross-border markets has increased and intensified these SMEs' international activities. It can be taken as an example of how SMEs may have reacted to the Single Market of 1992 and to the single currency of 1999–2002. However, SMEs have to follow certain strategies in order to stay internationally successful.

First, the questionnaire research in France, Germany and Italy demonstrated that SMEs in the MSE industry, located outside industrial districts, were strongly affected by the removal of NTBs and in particular by the abolition of physical barriers. They increased not only their export volume, but also their further involvement in the EU through cooperation agreements or FDI.[1] By doing so, they were able to exploit their firm-specific advantages to a larger extent than before 1992.

Second, the case-study research showed how SMEs in the same industry benefited from being located in an industrial district. Through the advantage of proximity,[2] enterprises were able to gain in international competitiveness. SMEs producing specialised, R&D-intensive surgical instruments were the winners in the Single Market Programme. They increased their international operations to the EU and planned or realised other foreign-market entry strategies in addition to exports. However, firms producing standardised surgical instruments did not feel affected by the Single Market Programme.

A common experience for enterprises both inside and outside industrial districts is therefore the increased exploitation of their firm-specific advantages after the 1992 abolition of NTBs, when traditional comparative advantages were challenged. In the following section these firm-specific advantages will be focused on, to discover if hypotheses 1 and 2 of this research are rejected or not. In the second section the answer to hypothesis 3 is concentrated on. In the third section an attempt is made to show some strategies that lead to international success.

A central point: competitive advantage(s)

The description and analysis of the main internationalisation models in the first part of the research (chapters 1–5) and their usefulness in the empirical part (chapters 6 and 7) demonstrated the importance of having a concept that combines economic and business approaches. With the exception of Dunning, no scholar recognises this problem or tries to find a solution in drawing together economic and business concepts.[3] His method was to adapt the eclectic paradigm of international production to a world with fewer barriers and an increasing number of strategic alliances.

As described in the literature survey, economists such as Hymer[4] and Vernon[5] tried to theorise about MNE activity in the 1960s by assuming that firms went abroad to exploit their competitive advantage(s). The models were, however, based on monopolistic or oligopolistic assumptions. This was a time when cross-border trade and FDI was restrained by high barriers. In the 1970s internalisation theory went further by explaining that firms exist in a national and international context because they are able to coordinate complementary resources and capabilities at lower costs than by arm's length relationships. Geographical and location-specific factors play a minor role. In his eclectic paradigm Dunning distinguished between the nature of advantages possessed by the firm. The Uppsala model was finally spatially oriented. But the timing of the different steps of foreign-market entry were partly determined by the firms' competitive advantage(s). In the 1980s, the resource-based view and evolutionary theory tried to identify and evaluate the competitive advantage(s) of firms over time.[6] The upgrading of competitive advantages through continual innovation played a major role. These approaches influenced Dunning to update his eclectic paradigm which was originally based on existing competitive advantages.[7]

In the 1990s, market-oriented policies were introduced in many countries and the 1992 market opening within the EU reconfigurated locational priorities. Home-based competitive advantages were easier to export and complementary competitive advantages from foreign firms became more accessible through cooperation agreements. Dunning again updated his eclectic paradigm of international production by emphasising 'strategic-asset-seeking FDI' as a major reason for international involvement.[8]

Theoretical and empirical research demonstrated that it was essential for firms to possess or acquire dynamic competitive advantages.[9] However, such firms could only export and exploit these advantages efficiently after the 1992 abolition of NTBs. The exploitation of these advantages was very pronounced for firms with a high percentage of R&D-intensive products.

The questionnaire, and in particular the case-study research, demonstrated the importance of the firms' competitive advantage(s) for their internationalisation process. SMEs' reasons to internationalise are, irrespective of the country they belong to, increased market access, a higher turnover or access to a superior technology or business know-how. For certain production steps, especially those of standardised surgical instruments, cost reductions are still very important. For sophisticated, R&D-intensive instruments a firm's reason to internationalise is closely related to its firm-specific or competitive advantage(s). In explaining the growth of trans-border activities, economic and business theory shows that this is dependent on the firms possessing some kind of unique and sustainable competitive advantage (or a whole set of advantages) relative to their foreign competitors. Diminishing barriers between the countries lead to better exploitation of these competitive advantages.

Not all seven SMEs located inside the industrial district benefited from the 1992 removal of NTBs: only those producing sophisticated R&D-intensive instruments (ALTMANN, DEXTRA, MENTA) and those that have their major suppliers in the EU (DUPONT). These firms increased their international operations within the EU. In some cases their competitive advantage was therefore innovation-driven and in other cases it was due to a special organisational constellation. In cases where innovation and development absorb relatively high costs, the SMEs have to cover the growth of their fixed costs. They are faced with an increased minimum size of efficiency and have to specialise even more.

Also, the majority of SMEs located outside industrial districts strongly increased their cross-border transactions with other EU countries after the 1992 abolition of NTBs. Their reasons to internationalise were mostly market-driven and less resource- and efficiency-driven, which signifies that market access, growth and access to new technologies were very important for them. 78 per cent of all SMEs indicated new market access and 35 per cent the access to superior technology and business know-how as important reasons to internationalise.[10] These reasons are strongly connected to the growth of international transactions and this growth is dependent on the competitive advantage(s) of firms. Therefore it makes sense to claim that the majority of SMEs which responded to our questionnaire improved their competitive advantage(s) after the 1992 abolition of NTBs. Unfortunately, the questionnaire research was unable to establish a relationship between how SMEs' internationalisation strategies were affected by the abolition of NTBs and their product range.

Even if the SMEs located in industrial districts (in particular those in Tuttlingen) showed a higher degree of internationalisation than those located out of districts, the majority of both SME samples progressively increased their international transactions within the EU after the 1992 market opening. By doing so they were able to 'export' and improve their competitive advantage(s) in other EU countries.

The *first hypothesis* can therefore be confirmed. Decreasing NTBs led to an increased internationalisation of SMEs within the EU.

This increased internationalisation is based on the exploitation of their firm-specific competitive advantages rather than their country-specific advantages.

The confirmation of this first hypothesis can be considered as a pre-condition to analyse the second hypothesis.

In the discussion it became clear that the perception and importance of a firm's competitive advantage during the internationalisation differed from one model to another. Each internationalisation model must be considered in the context of the *time* it was developed. In the first models a firm's competitive advantage(s) was seen as something static and therefore as something that existed already. Due to the existence of various barriers to trade, comparative advantages played a major role in these models. From the 1980s on, business scholars, and also economists, concentrated their efforts on the dynamic aspects of these competitive advantages, but neglected all spatial concepts. The 1990s demonstrated that traditional comparative advantages were not sustainable. The 1992 market opening between the EU countries provided a good example. The removal or reduction of cross-border barriers to the movement of goods, people and services and technological advances promoted a new cross-border specialisation of production within the firms and between them. New forms of foreign-market entry strategies became attractive. The increasing number of alliances and cooperation agreements emphasised the firms' determination to get access to other firms' competitive advantages.

In this sense, one can claim that the different models try to explain different aspects and units of a firm's international production or of its internationalisation process. The models must therefore be considered more as *complementary* than as substitutes.

Both the questionnaire and the case-study research emphasised the role of a firm's competitive advantage(s) for its internationalisation. This role was clearly reinforced by the 1992 market opening within the EU. It was relatively easy to retrace SMEs' internationalisation in the case-study research due to the high quantity of information received. Some firms' internationalisation strategies corresponded to one of the models described. But, in general, the strategy is individual to each firm and modelling remains difficult.

It therefore became necessary to update existing models of internationalisation by adapting them to the changed environment of the 1990s. Dunning[11] reviewed his eclectic paradigm of international production by emphasising the importance of competitive advantages in cross-border transactions without neglecting changes regarding location and internalisation advantages. One can easily use his updated paradigm to explain each firm's internationalisation as an individual process, based in particular on its competitive advantage(s).

> Therefore, the *second hypothesis* can also be confirmed. Each SME's internationalisation is based on the exploitation of its firm-specific competitive advantage in the host countries. Because of the existence of different competitive advantages there are different models of internationalisation.

The majority of internationalisation models include foreign-market entry strategies such as exporting, contractual agreements and FDI. Closely connected with the development of the various internationalisation models over the decades and with empirical findings, the emphasis on the multiple foreign-market entry strategies differed. Early models concentrated more on FDI than on contractual agreements. But our research did not confirm the idea that exports lead to FDI. Rather, SMEs prefer long-term collaborative arrangements, involving lower fixed costs.

Then, the removal of cross-border barriers and technological progress made contractual agreements more attractive. A good example in this context is MENTA, which established contractual agreements with local partners in two EU countries. Also the results in the questionnaire research showed that a lot of SMEs planned or realised cooperation agreements with other enterprises located in developed countries between 1992 and 2004.[12] In a majority of cases the reasons to conclude such contractual agreements are expected complementarities and synergies, by benefiting from the competitive advantage(s) of the partner firm.

Firms located within industrial districts have the opportunity to develop stronger competitive advantages due to their proximity to other firms (external economies and joint action). The following section provides answers to hypothesis 3.

Location in industrial districts

It is clear that SMEs, producing R&D-intensive medical instruments strongly increased their transactions within the EU. This led to repercussions in the industrial district. All SMEs in both industrial districts maintained strong forward and backward linkages with other firms in their district. They subcontracted some steps of the production process, or bought some final or semi-finished products to compete for incoming tenders. This cooperation was dependent on the product range and on the firm structure. ALTMANN, for example, specialises in R&D-intensive

instruments, and therefore has a rather integrated firm structure and maintains fewer contacts than NUTRA and DUPONT, both of which function as Pakistani connections, one in the industrial district of Tuttlingen and the other in Nogent.

Both industrial districts possessed a local base of specialised suppliers (including labour with specialised skills). This local base in turn owed its existence to the local concentration of demand. The result of the specialisation was high product differentiation which constituted a strong 'pull' towards agglomeration.[13] This circular process of agglomeration was, however, more intense in Tuttlingen than in Nogent. The cluster of Tuttlingen is much larger than the cluster of Nogent and therefore offers a wider choice of privileged partners for the SMEs. We have seen that the number of firms in the MSE sector declined in the industrial district of Nogent after World War II, whereas in Tuttlingen the number expanded.

Increasing international transactions therefore led automatically to intensified forward and backward linkages with the respective partner firms to satisfy the demand, which intensified the degree of differentiation and specialisation in Tuttlingen. New firm foundations might be another positive consequence. All interviewed SMEs producing and distributing R&D-intensive instruments emphasised their increased transactions within the EU. In Nogent, the two SMEs of our sample did not increase their transactions with other EU countries. Even if DUPONT is in frequent contact with SMEs in Tuttlingen, they did not increase their transactions.

Increasing cooperation and consequently specialisation is, however, dependent on how strong the forward and backward linkages between the firms are. These linkages were more sophisticated in the industrial district of Tuttlingen than in Nogent. As described in chapter 8, external economies and joint action led to a strong competitive advantage in Tuttlingen. The *third hypothesis* can therefore only be confirmed for

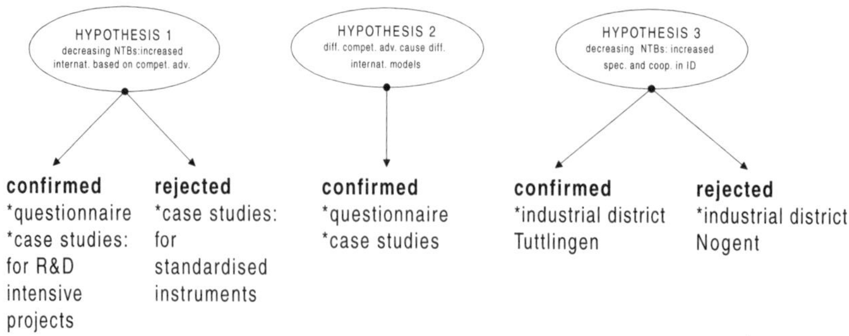

Figure 9.1 Results.

industrial districts with a strong local competitive advantage. For the industrial district of Tuttlingen it is therefore possible to confirm:

> Decreasing NTBs lead to increased international transactions of SMEs. This leads to an increasing specialisation and consequently to more cooperation between firms in industrial districts.

Towards an eclectic strategy of internationalisation

In this last section the aim is to go further regarding the internationalisation of firms. We know, however, that our research is rather limited as it covers firms of only one industry. In addition, our sample is too small to become a general model or lead to conclusions.

Whether SMEs are located inside or outside industrial districts, it is possible to argue that only those firms following an eclectic strategy of internationalisation are likely to be successful in the future. An eclectic strategy of internationalisation completes the rather dualistic approach of internationalisation that concentrates on labour- and capital-intensity. By doing so it may be possible to extend Dunning's eclectic paradigm of international production. One central point of an eclectic strategy of internationalisation is the firms' competitive advantage(s).

We know that, according to Dunning's eclectic paradigm of international production, a firm that benefits from OLI advantages makes an FDI or joint venture. On the one hand, firms invest in developed countries (DCs) to have access to a new technology or business know-how. We know that Porter distinguishes between the strategies of differentiation and cost leadership. The strategy behind this kind of investment is one of differentiation. On the other hand, firms invest in LDCs to reduce costs for some labour-intensive production processes. The strategy behind this kind of internationalisation is one of cost leadership.

Even if one or even both strategies are chosen, it is not certain that the firm will develop a competitive advantage. The SMEs that succeeded in our sample are ALTMANN and NUTRA. ALTMANN follows its strategy of product differentiation with success. The firm invested in the US to have access to new markets and technologies. The investment in Poland reduces costs for their less sophisticated product range. NUTRA also follows its strategy of cost leadership with success. The joint venture in Pakistan permits reducing transformation and assembling costs to a minimum.

The same reasoning is possible for contractual agreements and exports. Firms concluding contractual agreements with others in DCs follow a different strategy from those with firms in LDCs. MENTA planned cooperation agreements with Italian and Spanish firms. These contractual

Table 9.1 International strategies of SMEs located in industrial districts

	LDC/cost leadership	*DC/differentiation*
FDI/JV	NUTRA	ALTMANN
Cooperation agreement	DUPONT	MENTA
Exports/imports	NUTRA, DEXTRA, DUPONT	ALTMANN, DEXTRA, MENTA, TRAUBE, MAISTRE

agreements are destined to improve its competitive advantage in the form of R&D-intensive products. The strategy of differentiation has a chance of becoming a success. One SME that did not succeed with its strategy of cost leadership, despite its partnership with a Pakistani SME, is DUPONT. First, the French firm established its partnership late compared to its German competitors. And second, the firm has no control over the activities of its Pakistani partner compared to NUTRA.

Even for exports it became clear that the target market changes with the product range. Highly specialised R&D-intensive products are sold to DCs, where money is available to pay for these instruments. ALTMANN, MENTA, DEXTRA, TRAUBE and MAISTRE are SMEs that successfully follow a strategy of differentiation. On the other hand, NUTRA successfully follows a strategy of cost leadership to LDCs regarding tenders.

SMEs following both strategies seem to boost their advantages regarding their internationalisation if they are located in industrial districts. This is particularly relevant to the success of DEXTRA. Proximity advantages in the form of external economies and joint action reduce transaction costs. Without any exception, all SMEs of the sample would be unable to follow their current strategies if they were located outside the industrial district.[14] Their international success therefore owes a lot to their location in the industrial district. This confirms once again hypothesis 3 of our research.

Table 9.1 illustrates the firms of our two industrial districts. Independent of their international success, we placed all SMEs in the table according to the strategy(ies) they try to follow.

10 Conclusion

The increased regional integration within the EU has been one of the most powerful forces leading to the structural interdependence of the participating countries and firms. Traditional comparative advantages of the EU countries were challenged by the 1992 market opening. The dynamic in a firm's competitive advantage(s) became an essential factor in its internationalisation within the EU (and elsewhere).

The literature survey and the empirical part of this research demonstrated that there was considerable impact by the EMU on SMEs' international strategies, even if long-term effects – in particular due to the introduction of the single currency – were not known. The majority of SMEs in both samples increased their international transactions within the EU. The increased internationalisation can clearly be connected to a better exploitation of their competitive advantage(s).

The investigation of the different hypotheses demonstrated that SMEs within the same industry did not feel affected in the same way by the 1992 abolition of NTBs. SMEs producing R&D-intensive medical instruments felt strongly affected by increased integration within the EU, whereas SMEs producing standardised surgical instruments did not, or to a lesser extent. The benefits and the exploitation of increased market access depended on the dynamic of each firm's competitive advantage(s). Unfortunately, only the case-study research permits us to relate the R&D intensity of the products and the 1992 abolition of NTBs. The questionnaire research connected the 1992 market opening and SMEs' increased EU transactions, based on the better exploitation of their competitive advantage(s). Both the questionnaire and the case-study research showed the uniqueness of each SME's internationalisation. A firm's competitive advantage(s) played the central role in the choice of its foreign-market entry strategy.

The distinction between SMEs of the same industry located inside and outside industrial districts permitted us to find differences in the way they became affected through the establishment of the EMU. As SMEs located in industrial districts were more internationalised than SMEs outside such districts, it was interesting to analyse their local competitive advantages which constituted the basis of their international success in the EU and elsewhere.

Appendixes

Appendix 1 The why and where of clustering

	Why	*Where*
Krugman (1991)	• clusters arise by accident or due to self-fulfilling prophecies • clusters grow by interaction of increasing returns, transportation cost and demand	• in principle, clusters may arise at any location • existing clusters will grow and persist
Rauch (1993)	• clusters arise by accident; industrial developers may correct inefficiency • the relocation of firms depends on a tradeoff between investment cost and higher production cost	• in principle, clusters may arise at any location • some firms stay in old clusters; others locate in new, rising clusters
Scott (1986)	• clustering encourages vertical disintegration; vertical disintegration encourages clustering	• existing clusters will grow into clusters of small, specialised firms
Harrison (1992)	• clusters of small firms facilitate personal contacts and maximise trust	• existing, socially straight clusters will grow into clusters of small, specialised firms
Porter (1990)	• in clusters of highly competitive firms innovation is stimulated; only innovation creates the necessary competitive advantages to persist	• clusters of highly competitive firms will persist and may grow due to the entry of new competitors
Storper (1992)	• clustering leads to an effective management of the tradeoff between lock-in, technological flexibility and cost minimisation	• clustering should take place in highly innovative areas; firms within such a cluster must be small, specialised and flexible

Source: Meijboom, B.R. and Rongen, J.M.J. (1995), 'Clustering, logistics and spatial economics', p. 12.

Appendix 2 Questionnaire: SMEs' response to the European Single Market and beyond

OPTIONAL: **Name of the firm:**

1 Is your firm a:

☐ producer and/or ☐ distributor
of medical and surgical instruments?

2 Year of foundation of your firm: ....

3 Does your firm produce and/or distribute:

☐ 'new' products and/or ☐ standard products?

Please shortly describe your product range:

....
....
....

4 Please mark where your firm's activities are taking place and try to estimate the percentage of activities that take place at home and abroad:

Activity	*At home*	*Abroad*
Design/R&D		
Procurement of inputs		
Production/assembly		
Storage		
Distribution		
Service		
Other		

5 In how many countries is your firm represented directly or indirectly?

....

Out of these, how many are in EU countries (please note the countries below):

....
....
....

6 What proportion of the value-chain[1] does your firm provide (approximately)?

.........%

Describe the value-chain as you see it, identifying the sections which are accomplished by independent firms (as licensing or subcontracting firms, etc.):

....
....
....

7 Apart from exports (question 5) the following foreign-market entry strategies can be distinguished:

Contractual forms: licensing, subcontracting, franchising, assembly, R&D, etc.
Direct investment: joint venture, acquisition, greenfield . . . and other forms

Please note in the table below your actual and planned foreign-market entry strategies:

Country/location	*Date established*	*Date expected*	*Type*

8 Reasons for your international operations:

Reasons	*Very important*	*Less important*	*Not important*
Act as a subcontractor			
Chance: fax or offer from abroad			
New market access			

(*continued*)

Continued

Reasons	*Very important*	*Less important*	*Not important*
Gain access to superior technology and business know-how			
Cost reductions through cheaper inputs (taxes,. . .)			
Growth			
Saturated home market (through a niche strategy)			
Follow the customers			
Risk spreading			
Higher turnover			
Participation in EU programmes (ESPRIT, RACE, etc.)			
Other			

9 What percentage of your sales is made in the EU?

Before 1992

Less than 10%	10–20%	21–30%	31–50%	More than 50%

1998

Less than 10%	10–20%	21–30%	31–50%	More than 50%

Objective (year 2000)

Less than 10%	10–20%	21–30%	31–50%	More than 50%

10 The establishment of the European Single Market in 1992 meant a removal of non-tariff barriers between the EU countries. Please mark the points that provided an advantage or a drawback to your firm:

	Advantage	*Drawback*	*No effect*
Harmonisation of technical standards			
Adjustment of indirect tax payments			
Government procurement			
Faster processing of exports			
Increased competition from imports			
Better access to imported components			
Others			

11 In 1999 the single currency the euro will be introduced. Which consequences do you expect for your firm?

☐ no consequences at all
☐ faster and easier handling of international commercial operations
☐ increased transactions within the EU
☐ increased transactions outside the EU
☐ administrative burden during the period of adaptation
☐ less administrative burden in the long run
☐ currency gains
☐ no currency gains (exports when home currency is devalued)
☐ more transparency
☐ increased competition
☐ others:

What were/are your preparations for the introduction of the euro?
....
....
....

Appendix 3 Enterprises in the European Union 1992

Table A.3.1 Enterprises in the European Union 1992

	Enterprises with . . . employees									Total
	0[a]	*1–9*	*10–19*	*20–49*	*50–99*	*100–199*	*200–249*	*250–499*	*500 and more*	
Belgium	—	150,308	13,472	9,375	2,330	1,193	251	603	441	177,973
Denmark	79,836	65,554	8,321	4,999	1,346	682	118	219	168	161,243
Germany[b]	621,433	1,249,864	167,561	77,799	23,086	11,789	7,215		3,816	2,162,563
Finland	113,669	74,391	5,837	3,713	1,120	579	122	275	236	199,942
France	990,098	817,606	66,790	55,201	13,525	7,171	1,311	2,604	2,123	1,956,429
Greece	—	—	4,944	2,166	671	331	49	124	57	8,342
Italy (1991)	—	3,053,219	119,546	49,643	11,184	4,838	879	1,614	1,139	3,242,062
Luxembourg	5,297	7,236	1,093	735	242	123	68		24	14,818
The Netherlands	152,921	160,261	18,586	17,019	4,069	1,907	1,064		483	356,310
Austria[c]	1,266	3,248	1,711	3,808	1,670	909	203	358	220	13,393
Portugal	328,116	265,626	20,529	12,302	3,925	1,693	333	547	316	633,387
Sweden		176,921		8,191		986	572		422	187,092
Spain (1991)	1,604,245	652,491	65,521	36,384	8,446	3,505	682	1,237	868	2,373,379
United Kingdom (1991)	2,327,677		93,622	64,341	19,823	10,026	2,175	3,889	2,753	2,524,306
EUR 15[d]	7,845,241	6,782,689	640,246	331,470	91,460	45,569	9,437	17,757	13,681	15,777,551

Source: EUROSTAT, *Enterprises in Europe*, *Fourth Report*, Brussels (1996).

Table A.3.2 Enterprises in the European Union 1992 (%)

	Enterprises with . . . employees									*Total*
	0[a]	*1–9*	*10–19*	*20–49*	*50–99*	*100–199*	*200–249*	*250–499*	*500 and more*	
Belgium	—	84.5	7.6	5.3	1.3	0.7	0.1	0.3	0.2	100.0
Denmark	49.5	40.7	5.2	3.1	0.8	0.4	0.1	0.1	0.1	100.0
Germany[b]	28.7	57.8	7.7	3.6	1.1	0.5	0.3		0.2	100.0
Finland	56.9	37.2	2.9	1.9	0.6	0.3	0.1	0.1	0.1	100.0
France	50.6	41.8	3.4	2.8	0.7	0.4	0.1	0.1	0.1	100.0
Greece	—	—	59.3	26.0	8.0	4.0	0.6	1.5	0.7	100.0
Italy (1991)	—	94.2	3.7	1.5	0.3	0.1	0.0	0.0	0.0	100.0
Luxembourg	35.7	48.8	7.4	5.0	1.6	0.8	0.5		0.2	100.0
The Netherlands	42.9	45.0	5.2	4.8	1.1	0.5	0.3		0.1	100.0
Austria[c]	9.5	24.3	12.8	28.4	12.5	6.8	1.5	2.7	1.6	100.0
Portugal	51.8	41.9	3.2	1.9	0.6	0.3	0.1	0.1	0.0	100.0
Sweden		94.6		4.4		0.5	0.3		0.2	100.0
Spain (1991)	67.6	27.5	2.8	1.5	0.4	0.1	0.0	0.1	0.0	100.0
United Kingdom (1991)	92.2		3.7	2.5	0.8	0.4	0.1	0.2	0.1	100.0
EUR 15[d]	49.7	43.0	4.1	2.1	0.6	0.3	0.1	0.1	0.1	100.0

Source: EUROSTAT, *Enterprises in Europe*, *Fourth Report*, Brussels (1996).

Notes

[a]Craft firms or independents, where the owner is doing everything himself.

[b]Only the 'old Länder'.

[c]Only energy and water, mining and manufacturing, construction: value unknown, but estimated in the total amount.

[d]Without Ireland. EUR 15 = Ireland included (estimate).

Appendix 4 The most important Italian laws concerning foreign trade

Law n. 100/90/Law 212/92: creation of SIMEST to support the internationalisation of Italian SMEs, achieved by promotion and financial support to Italian enterprises in the development of joint ventures.

Law n. 227/77 (legge Ossola) for supporting exports. It provides an insurance for Italian exports of goods and services, to activities and financing associated with them, and to investments abroad and to programmes for trade expansion.

Law n. 394/81/Law n. 100/90 for the support of the internationalisation process. This law aims to promote the active participation of domestic enterprises on foreign markets, outside the EU, by granting financing of up to 80 per cent of the estimated investment. For this purpose, a fund was created at Mediocredito Centrale.

Law n. 49/87 concerning public support for international development. It provides for explicit intervention in favour of Italian enterprises for the establishment of joint ventures. In particular, Italian enterprises have access to financing at a lower rate in exchange for sharing the risk of capital investment in developing countries, both in the industrial and agriculture sectors.[1]

Appendix 5 Production steps in the fabrication of a surgical instrument

Example of tweezers:

1 the hammered forged instrument arrives from the swage forge[1]
2 control of cracks and manufacturing faults
3 boring (depending on the model)
4 polishing inside
5 bending (depending on the model)
6 welding
7 grinding
8 adjusting
9 polishing bright or matt
10 washing in ultrasonic bath[2]
11 final check

Notes

Introduction

1 According to Buckley and Brooke (1992), p. 144, 'a NTB is a government-imposed measure which has the effect of protecting domestic industry from competing imports or assisting the expansion of exports, or both'. The European Commission (1993b), p. 47, defines NTBs as rules, regulations or bureaucratic red tape that delay or preclude the purchase of foreign goods.
2 See paragraph 'Definitions', pp. 4–5.
3 In this context an agglomeration corresponds to a geographic concentration of firms in the same sector of activity. Another term for this phenomenon is 'industrial district'. It will be investigated in Part 1, chapter 4.
4 Reference is made to Porter (1985), pp. 33–228. Other authors call them competitive advantages (business literature) or proprietary advantages (Dunning).
5 See Puga and Venables (1997), pp. 347–68 and Brülhart and Torstensson (1996), pp. 9–29. See also Part I, chapter 1.
6 European Commission (1993a), p. 13.
7 Porter (1985), p. 26.

1 1992 and beyond – market opening within the EU?

1 European Commission (1988), p. 17 and Buigues and Sheehy (1995), p. 39.
2 Curzon Price (1996), p. 5.
3 Cecchini (1988), pp. 175–6.
4 Rugman and Hodgetts (1995), pp. 463–4.
5 Curzon Price (1996), p. 6.
6 Jovanovic (1992), pp. 218–21.
7 El-Agraa (1994), p. 161.
8 Curzon Price (1996), pp. 3–4.
9 Cecchini (1988), pp. 88–92.
10 The principle of mutual recognition has existed since 1978 (Cassis de Dijon) and is intended to be a transitional instrument while European standards are being developed. The countries of the EU have to accept in a reciprocal manner each others' products independent of existing national standards (Decision of 20.2.1979; ECJ. 120/78).
11 The CEN was set up in 1975 to manage cooperation among national standards bodies of the EU Member States, plus Iceland, Norway and Switzerland. Its main areas of activity include information technology, food, biotechnology, chemistry, mechanical engineering, energy, environment, consumer goods and services.

By May 1996, the CEN had published 2,600 standards, nearly 700 more were in the final stages of preparation and 2,400 were at the draft stage (EIU, 5 July 1997, p. 60).

12 The European committee for electrotechnical standards focuses on any equipment which uses electricity, from electronic components through household appliances to electricity generators. Its members are the eighteen countries of the EU and EFTA. Formed in 1973, they had published more than 2,000 standards by the end of 1995 (EIU, 5 July 1997, p. 60).

13 Cecchini (1988), p. 91.

14 European Strategic Programme for Research in Information Technology: the EU finances half of the cost of a project that is in line with EU terms of reference and that is proposed by two or more firms from different EU countries. The other part of the funds has to come from the participating firms or national sources (Jovanovic (1997), p. 194).

15 Basic Research in Industrial Technologies in Europe: this programme aspires to revitalise traditional industries within the EU. It has to be done through the introduction of new technologies in these industries (idem, pp. 194–5).

16 Krieger-Mytelka and Delapierre (1988), p. 251.

17 Joint European Venture.

18 To be eligible, any partner of the joint venture must have fewer than 250 employees, have an annual turnover not exceeding 40 million euros or an annual balance-sheet total not exceeding 27 million euros, and conform to the criterion of independence. The EC contribution is intended to cover some of the expenses relating to the setting up of the joint venture. The maximum amount is 100,000 euros per project.

19 EIU, 7 November 1997, p. 16.

20 EIU, 22 October 1997, pp. 24–5.

21 Regulation 2137/85 of 25.7.1985, O.J.L199, p. 1, of 31.7.1985: This existing opportunity is, however, largely unknown and does not enjoy a real autonomy. Nearly all employees are paid by the participating firms and important decisions have to be taken unanimously by all participating firms (Naulleau and Vasseur (1998), p. 77).

22 Panic (1991), p. 210.

23 United Nations (1997b), pp. 264–5.

24 Obstfeld (1997), pp. 1–4.

25 European Commission (1988), pp. 33–7 and Jovanovic (1992), pp. 344–8.

26 Cecchini (1988), p. 218.

27 Ibid., pp. 52–66.

28 European Commission (1988), p. 17.

29 European Commission (1996c), p. 1.

30 Jovanovic (1997), p. 199.

31 El-Agraa (1994), p. 164.

32 Baldwin (1989), p. 248.

33 Ibid., p. 249.

34 Peck (1989), p. 277.

35 European Commission (1996c), pp. 1–29.

36 Panic (1991), p. 208.

37 European Commission (1997b), pp. 265–90. The review consists of nineteen sectoral and nineteen horizontal studies, including a business survey carried out among 13,500 businesses in the EU.

38 European Commission (1996c), p. 11.

39 STRATEGOR (1993), pp. 186–7.

40 Jarillo and Martinez (1991), pp. 286–8.

41 In a questionnaire, firms were asked about their competitive advantage for their internationalisation process. The competitive advantages listed in the questionnaire were lower costs, higher quality, quality/price relation, superior technology, design and style, adaptation to clients, etc. At the beginning of their internationalisation 32 per cent of the firms indicated lower costs as an important competitive advantage, whereas in 1988 only 13 per cent of the firms did so. Superior technology was perceived by 6 per cent of the firms as their competitive advantage at the beginning of their internationalisation, and in 1988 by 10 per cent of the firms. For design and style, the percentages were 9 and 20 per cent.
42 Buckley and Brooke (1992), p. 387.
43 Aerts (1994), p. 67. 57 per cent of the sample indicated the induced growth as an initial reason for their international operations and 44 per cent found their domestic market too limited.
44 Root (1987), p. 1.
45 European Commission (1996c), p. 4.
46 Dunning (1991), pp. 41–74.
47 Ohlsson (1991), pp. 75–96.
48 European Commission (1996c), p. 3.
49 Buigues and Sheehy (1995), p. 52.
50 Ohlsson (1991), p. 79.
51 Buckley and Brooke (1992), pp. 384–5.
52 Buckley (1989), pp. 89–100.
53 Aerts (1994), p. 68. 67 per cent of the SMEs indicated quality as their main success factor and 40 per cent the advantage of inexpensive products.
54 Porter (1986), pp. 9–40.
55 Economies of scope cannot be realised, however, if the production takes place in different places and the goods have to be transported from one location to another.
56 Baldwin (1989), pp. 260–2.
57 Jenster and Jarillo (1994), pp. 9–16.
58 European Commission (1997b), p. 272.
59 Jovanovic (1998), p. 17.
60 Puga and Venables (1997), pp. 347–68.
61 Paci and Usai (1997), p. 3.
62 These policies favoured SMEs to a large extent by allowing cooperation agreements for joint R&D, by guaranteeing state aid up to a certain percentage of the investment costs (depending on the number of employees), by developing technological cooperation programmes and by improving the coordination of various structural funds (transfer of responsibilities to a local and regional level, automatic aid being replaced by discretionary aid, higher involvement of the Commission: competition policy).
63 Jenster and Jarillo (1994), pp. 9–16.
64 EIU, 11 March 1997, pp. 79–80.
65 The results are due to a review of nineteen sectoral and nineteen horizontal studies, including a business survey carried out among 13,500 businesses in the EU.
66 The Madrid Council of December 1995 decided upon a three-phase scenario for the introduction of the single currency. EMU started from 1 January 1999 when the exchange rates among the participating countries were fixed. It was planned that euro notes and coins would enter into circulation at the end of 2001 at the latest. Between 1999 and 2001 the former national currencies were to continue to circulate as sub-units of the euro, with economic agents being able to use the euro if they wished, but being under no obligation to do so.

67 Frankel and Rose (1997), p. 2.
68 Baldwin (1991), p. 22.
69 McKinnon (1963), pp. 717–25.
70 Molle and Morsink (1991), p. 98.
71 Baldwin (1991), p. 24.
72 Ahlberg *et al.* (1999), pp. 112–13. In the car industry these price differences were up to 50 per cent; for construction materials and large industrial equipment these price differences often exceeded 40 per cent. In pharmaceuticals the country-to-country price differences were often 50 per cent.
73 Claret-Tournier and Faijean (1998), p. 40.
74 In this context, the car industry is a good example of the variations of end prices, which can be up to 41 per cent from one EU country to another.
75 Lefebvre (1998), p. 206. Examples are enterprises offering software and micro-computers.
76 Ahlberg *et al.* (1999), p. 112.
77 Lefebvre (1998), pp. 208, 229.
78 Lefebvre (1998), p. 211.
79 Carr (1999), pp. 47–57.
80 EASDAQ stands for European Association of Securities Dealers Automated Quotation and is a private initiative, independent of any existing stock exchanges. Over ninety financial institutions from twelve countries (most EU Member States are included) are participating in the project as shareholders. The market opened on 30 September 1996 and the first Initial Public Offering took place on 27 November 1996 (European Commission (1997a), p. 2).
81 The Nouveau Marché began trading on 20 March 1996 and by the end of 1996 eighteen companies were listed (two non-French ones included). It disposed of a total market capitalisation of over 220 million euros and intends to become a Europe-wide equities market. To this end, the Nouveau Marché has linked up with other recently established nationally based SME stock markets to form a network of markets called Euro-NM. Euro-NM is a European Economic Interest Group, which would like to provoke synergies by the harmonisation of rules and regulations, the integration of commercial and technical activity and the establishment of common marketing activities (European Commission (1997a), p. 2).
82 European Commission (1997a), p. 1.
83 European Commission (1995c), p. 16.
84 European Commission (1996b), p. 173.
85 Claret-Tournier and Faijean (1998), p. 40.
86 Ibid., p. 38.
87 Jones (1998), p. 29.
88 Lefebvre (1998), pp. 232–3.
89 Nagorski and Theil (1998), pp. 16–18.
90 Raynal *et al.* (1999), p. 179.
91 Lefebvre (1998), pp. 224–5.

2 SMEs and internationalisation models

1 Hymer (1970), pp. 441–8.
2 Cantwell (1991), pp. 19–23.
3 Jovanovic (1997), p. 314.
4 Vernon (1966), pp. 190–207.
5 Vernon (1974), pp. 89–114.
6 Buckley and Brooke (1992), p. 60.

7 United Nations (1993), p. 8. It was found that 80 per cent of a sample of 735 SMEs' foreign affiliates were located in the developed countries in the late 1980s. Only Japanese and Australian SMEs directed more investments in the developing countries. Compared with large enterprises, SMEs have a net preference for developed countries.
8 Buckley *et al.* (1985).
9 Coase (1937), pp. 386–405.
10 Ibid., p. 392.
11 Demsetz (1997), p. 1.
12 Williamson (1975), pp. 82–105 and Williamson (1985), pp. 103–30.
13 Hennart (1991), p. 84.
14 Demsetz (1997), p. 20.
15 Ibid., p. 20.
16 Cantwell (1991), p. 25.
17 Hennart (1991), p. 105.
18 Jarillo (1993), p. 51–5.
19 Jovanovic (1997), p. 314.
20 Buckley and Brooke (1992), p. 69.
21 EIU, 10 April 1996, p. 33.
22 Jacquemot (1990), p. 121.
23 Dunning (1988b), pp. 2–4.
24 Ibid., pp. 4–5.
25 Ibid., p. 3.
26 Mucchielli (1985), pp. 17–19.
27 Buckley and Brooke (1992), pp. 68–9.
28 Dunning (1995), p. 481.
29 Teece (1986), pp. 21–45.
30 Johanson and Wiedersheim-Paul (1975), pp. 305–22.
31 Johanson and Mattsson (1988), pp. 209–17.
32 Bamberger and Evers (1994b), pp. 316–21.
33 Buckley (1989), pp. 89–100.
34 Joynt (1989), p. 352.
35 Aerts (1994), pp. 58–75.
36 Turnbull (1987), p. 173.
37 Petersen and Pedersen (1996), p. 16.
38 Zaby (1996), pp. 281–4.
39 Jarillo and Martinez (1991), pp. 283–302.
40 United Nations (1993), p. 6.
41 Johanson and Wiedersheim-Paul (1975), pp. 305–22.
42 Cavusgil (1984), pp. 195–208.
43 Petersen and Pedersen (1996), p. 16.
44 Ibid., pp. 4–15.
45 Porter (1985) and Bartlett and Goshal (1989). Business strategy literature bases the internationalisation process of the firm on economies of scale, which makes reference to the new theory. The different strategies for conquering a foreign market are cost leadership or differentiation.
46 Minimum size for efficiency signifies that from a certain size on a firm starts to realise economies of scale. Each firm that does not reach this minimum efficient scale risks encountering cost disadvantages *vis-à-vis* its competitors who produce larger volumes. This means a degradation of its competitive position.
47 United Nations (1993), pp. 11–12 and Fujita (1998), p. 89.
48 Jarillo (1990), pp. 84–7.

49 Prahalad and Doz (1987).
50 Bartlett (1986), pp. 367–401.
51 Jarillo and Martinez (1992), pp. 501–12. With respect to this topic, organisational questions of internationalisation are not further treated.
52 Jarillo and Martinez (1991), pp. 296–300.

3 The 'right' entry choice within the EMU

1 Buckley and Ghauri (1994), p. xii.
2 Kogut (1983), pp. 219–20 and Jovanovic (1997), pp. 141–2.
3 Root (1987), pp. 8–15.
4 Dunning (1988a), p. 54.
5 Ibid., p. 54.
6 Root (1987), pp. 13–14.
7 Buckley and Brooke (1992), pp. 398–9.
8 Molle and Morsink (1991), pp. 84, 97–8.
9 Hennart (1991), p. 105.
10 Caves (1996), pp. 208–12 and Jacquemot (1990), pp. 194–6.
11 Hennart (1991), pp. 92–3.
12 Stigler (1968), pp. 136–7. The author takes the example of raw-material cartels which had trouble with customers who wished to integrate backwards. Since the cartel members are limited in their output quotas, the discounted future profits of a cartel member need not be high, even with very high prices. Therefore it is profitable for buyers to integrate backwards by purchase and by seeking non-cartelised supply sources (see for example the Rhenish-Westphalian Coal Cartel).
13 Kogut (1983), p. 220.
14 Dunning (1988b), p. 2.
15 European Commission (1996c), p. 12.
16 Jarillo (1993), pp. 53–4.
17 Ibid., p. 69.
18 Jarillo and Martinez (1989), pp. 508–9.
19 Hennart (1991), p. 105.
20 Ibid., pp. 105–6.
21 See principal-agent theory.
22 Caves (1996), pp. 3–5. In management this corresponds to the strategies of product differentiation and cost leadership.
23 STRATEGOR (1993), p. 172 (scheme).
24 Root (1987), p. 124.
25 Buckley and Brooke (1992), pp. 398–404.
26 Dunning (1995), pp. 461–91.
27 Molle and Morsink (1991), pp. 81–5.
28 Sleuwagen (1988), pp. 153–70.
29 Doz (1991), pp. 309–18.
30 United Nations (1997b), p. 12.
31 Richardson (1972), pp. 883–7.
32 Moss Kanter (1994), p. 98.
33 Mariti and Smiley (1983), p. 437.
34 Porter and Fuller (1986), p. 325.
35 Bamberger and Bonacker (1994a), pp. 64–5 and Mucchielli (1991), pp. 36–57.
36 Gomes-Casseres (1994), pp. 62–74.
37 Lorange and Hakanson (1991), pp. 235–62.
38 Gammelsaeter and Guvag (1994), pp. 201–21.

39 There are different programmes, such as SPRINT, VALUE and THERMIE. SPRINT was adopted to stimulate innovation and technology transfer, especially in SMEs (patent or know-how licensing, technical cooperation, etc.). VALUE is aimed at promoting the spread and effective use of the results of research (preparation of business plans, market and feasibility studies). THERMIE is adopted for enterprises in the area of energy technologies. The majority of the projects involve SMEs, who are included as a selection criterion in the evaluation of technological tenders.
40 Porter and Fuller (1986), p. 325 and Duijnhouwer (1994), p. 182.
41 Duijnhouwer (1994), p. 183.
42 Hamel *et al.* (1989), pp. 133–9.
43 Jarillo (1993), p. 149.
44 Duijnhouwer (1994), pp. 174–200. The countries of the sample were The Netherlands, Austria, Switzerland, Denmark, Finland, Great Britain, Portugal and Ireland, and the industries were road transport and metal manufacturing.
45 Bronder and Pritzl (1992), pp. 17–44 and Moss Kanter (1994), pp. 98–102.
46 Lorange and Roos (1992), pp. 343–55, Lorange (1988), pp. 370–89 and Killing (1988), pp. 55–67.
47 BC-NET corresponds to a network of advisers and intermediaries at regional, national, EU and international levels who sign a renewable convention with the Commission each year. This network permits a fast identification of possible partners on the basis of specific propositions regarding a financial, commercial, industrial or technological cooperation. In 1994, 533 BC-NET advisers generated 10,349 cooperation profiles (European Commission (1995b), pp. 5–7).

BCC was created in 1973 and was the first EU instrument assisting SMEs to search for a partner abroad. Interested enterprises contact the central unit in Brussels and fill out a document of cooperation profile. The SMEs can then get in touch with each other through local intermediaries (European Commission (1995a), p. 36).

Europartenariat also stimulates transnational cooperation through the funds of the regional policy. It concerns especially less favoured regions (objective 1 of the regional policy), regions suffering industrial decline (objective 2 of the regional policy) and third countries. 300 to 400 enterprises of a special region were selected and put in contact with foreign partners through a fair. About 30 to 40 per cent of the participating enterprises concluded cooperation agreements (European Commission (1995b), pp. 5–7).

EICs were created in 1987 and have expanded from about 39 offices throughout Europe to 238 in 1996 (Jones (1996), p. 3). They are based on the regional chambers of commerce, on regional development agencies, professional associations, banks and regional authorities that have built up relations with their regional SMEs. Their main task is to advise firms that have no international experience about all questions relating to the establishment of the EMU.
48 Porter and Fuller (1986), p. 326.
49 Killing (1988), p. 61.
50 Root (1987), p. 113.
51 Bleeke and Ernst (1992), pp. 97–105 and Rugman and Hodgetts (1995), pp. 465–6.
52 Garrette (1998), p. 70. The author investigated 256 international alliances and stated that 84 per cent of intra-EU alliances were concluded on a horizontal level (*additive alliances*), compared to only 25 per cent on an international level.
53 Gomes-Casseres (1994), pp. 62–74.

54 Bamberger and Bonacker (1994a), pp. 64–5.
55 Lorenzoni and Baden-Fuller (1995), p. 150 and Hamel *et al.* (1989), pp. 133–9.
56 Lorange (1988), pp. 370–89.
57 Moss Kanter (1994), p. 100.
58 European Commission (1997b), pp. 113–14.
59 Buckley and Brooke (1992), pp. 43–7, defined licensing agreements as 'relating to a specific product and/or production process that incorporates inventions of the licensor (seller) that are made available to the licensee (buyer) in return for an agreed payment and on stipulated terms with regard to use'. Three types of licensing agreements are distinguished: (1) patent licences, (2) know-how licences, (3) trademark licences. Any licensing agreement usually includes two or more of these types in combination. Financial terms vary between agreements but usually involve a lump-sum payment at the start of the agreement and an annual payment of royalties related to the licensee's sales of the licensed products.
60 Buckley and Ghauri (1994), p. xii.
61 Buckley and Brooke (1992), pp. 412–17.
62 Caves (1996), p. 169.
63 Telesio (1979), p. 37.
64 Root (1987), pp. 86–7.
65 Buckley and Brooke (1992), pp. 413–14.
66 Caves (1996), p. 170.
67 Welch (1981), pp. 64–90.
68 Root (1987), pp. 98–103.
69 Welch (1981), pp. 64–90.
70 Root (1987), p. 89.
71 Hennart (1991), p. 87.
72 Root (1987), p. 120.
73 Paci and Usai (1997), p. 6. The high share of German patents is also related to the fact that the regulations of the European Patent Office closely follow the granting procedures of the German national system.
74 OECD (1982), p. 30.
75 Buckley and Prescott (1989), pp. 189–208.
76 Subcontracting means that a firm produces goods or services to the specifications of a customer who retains responsibilities for sales (Bamberger and Bonacker (1994a), p. 47).
77 Bourgault *et al.* (1994), p. 2.
78 Porter (1990), pp. 179–238 describes, for example, networks in Germany (printing press industry), in Italy (ceramic tile industry) and in Japan (robotics industry).
79 Bourgault *et al.* (1994), p. 2.
80 Patry (1994), p. 4.
81 Quinn *et al.* (1991), pp. 75–6.
82 Jarillo (1993), p. 80.
83 Baglin *et al.* (1990), p. 420.
84 Le Billon and Delluc (1995), pp. 88–9. Cadore, for example, is specialised in the production of glasses, Valdagno in textiles, Montebelluna in shoes, Sassuolo in ceramics, etc.
85 Nadvi (1998), p. 22.
86 Baglin *et al.* (1990), p. 423.
87 Jarillo (1993), p. 89.
88 Hovi (1994), p. 368.
89 United Nations (1997a), pp. 24–5.

4 Mechanisms of location

1 Mucchielli (1998), pp. 157–79.
2 Aharoni (1966), pp. 18–19.
3 Mucchielli (1998), pp. 173–9.
4 Porter (1985), pp. 12–16. An example is a relatively standardised product with high labour contribution that is produced in a country with cheap labour and must be re-imported as the highest proportion of demand is located in the home country (Mucchielli (1998), pp. 174–7).
5 Meijboom and Rongen (1995), pp. 4–7.
6 An example may be the existence of mining and rivers in England that initiated the creation of the whole cottage industry during the industrial revolution (Mucchielli (1998), p. 166).
7 For Meijboom and Rongen economic geography concepts are well explained by Krugman (1991) and Rauch (1993), organisational concepts by Scott (1986) and Harrison (1992) and strategic concepts by Porter (1990) and Storper (1992). See table, Appendix 1.
8 Humphrey and Schmitz (1996), p. 1863.
9 Porter (1998), p. 78.
10 The idea behind external economies is that economic agents are not able to capture in the price of their product all the benefits of their investment. The overlap is of benefit to other agents.
11 Marshall (1920), p. 316.
12 Schmitz (1998), p. 6.
13 Marshall (1920), pp. 225–6.
14 Lösch (1973), p. 124.
15 Krugman (1996), pp. 1–2.
16 Venables (1996), pp. 53–4.
17 Mucchielli (1998), p. 164.
18 Audretsch (1998), pp. 18–29 and Baptista (2000), pp. 515–35.
19 Porter (1998), pp. 81–3.
20 Wiklund and Karlsson (1994), pp. 123–4. The authors examined the industrial district of Gnosjö in Sweden. They found a high internal and external flexibility within the district. Internal flexibility is reached due to highly specialised employees with experience-based competence who often established their own firm. Network flexibility is achieved through specialised input subcontracting and sporadic short-term cooperation between firms. A greater variety of orders can therefore be accepted. Output flexibility is high as the firms are able to adapt quickly from one customer's requirements to another's.
21 Paci and Usai (1997), p. 2.
22 Porter (1998), p. 78.
23 Schmitz (1998), pp. 6–10 and Nadvi (1998), pp. 7–8.
24 Le Billon and Delluc (1995), p. 90.
25 Ibid., p. 91.
26 Porter (1990), p. 82.
27 Venables (1996), pp. 53–4.
28 Grant (1991), p. 538.
29 Porter (1990), p. 157.
30 Porter (1998), p. 80.
31 Corò and Grandinetti (1999), p. 118.
32 Mucchielli (1998), p. 167.
33 Petrucci and Quintieri (1998), p. 5.
34 Porter (1990), p. 210.

35 Tödtling (1994), p. 79.
36 Le Billon and Delluc (1995), p. 91.
37 The cluster's competitiveness may decline, for example, by the firms' outsourcing of major R&D activities or by a relatively late internationalisation compared to other firms in the sector.
38 Arino (1997), p. 217.
39 See the previous section on industrial districts, pp. 57–61.
40 Amin and Thrift (1994), p. 12.
41 For more details see Williamson (1985): questions of 'bounded rationality' are analysed on pp. 45–6, questions about 'uncertainty' on pp. 79–80 and pp. 56–9 and the question of 'opportunism' is treated on pp. 47–50.
42 Bidault and Jarillo (1995), pp. 1–2.
43 Benko *et al.* (1997), p. 308.
44 Lorenzoni and Baden-Fuller (1995), p. 155 and Benko *et al.* (1997), p. 310.
45 Gulati *et al.* (1994), pp. 8–16.
46 Axelrod (1984), pp. 11–24.
47 Ibid., pp. 27–54. The player using this rule is nice because he is never the first to act opportunistically, he is retaliatory because he retaliated in kind to the opportunism of the other player, he is forgiving because he reverts back to cooperation if the other player does and he is clear because he sends an unambiguous signal to the other player.
48 Granovetter (1992), pp. 25–57.
49 Jarillo and Ricart (1987), pp. 135–42.
50 Buckley and Casson (1988), pp. 34–7.
51 Blau and Alba (1982), pp. 363–79.
52 Hill (1990), pp. 506–7. Robert Axelrod delivered the foundations of the question of reputation between a group of players (pp. 150–5). Knowing other people's reputation allows one to know something about what strategy they use even before a player has to make his first choice.
53 Jarillo (1993), pp. 129–30, stated that it does not ensure the biggest share of the pie, but a good share of the biggest pie.
54 Piore and Sabel (1984), p. 265.
55 Bagella *et al.* (1998), pp. 1–34.
56 Demsetz (1997), p. 11.

5 Conclusions

1 Jovanovic (1992), p. 164.
2 The higher degree of internationalisation of SMEs within industrial districts is due to their locational advantage of proximity to other firms in the same sector of activity. In this context external economies and joint action are essential factors in sustaining their international competitive position, as will be investigated in chapter 8.

6 The European Medical and Surgical Equipment and orthopaedic appliances industry (MSE)

1 On 1 January 1995 Austria, Finland and Sweden entered the EU.
2 We subtracted the trade flows of Sweden, Finland and Austria in relation to the three countries under consideration in 1993 and 1997.
3 International Organisation for Standardisation : ISO 9001 proposed a model for quality assurance in design, development, production, installation and servicing; ISO 9002 proposed a model for quality assurance in production, installation and

servicing; and ISO 9003 proposed a model for quality assurance in final inspection and testing.

4 Euronorm.

5 The term 'medical device' is defined as any instrument, apparatus, appliance, material, software pertinent to it or other article intended to be used for human beings for the purpose of diagnosis, prevention, monitoring, treatment, alleviation of disease or compensation for an injury or handicap. It also applies to any device used for the investigation, replacement or modification of the anatomy or of a physiological process as well as for the control of conception (as defined in the European Directives 93/42/EEC and 90/385/EEC).

6 The EC mark means that medical devices must have been manufactured in conformity with the 'Essential Requirements' specified in the Directives applicable to it and with the national law. This procedure referred to as conformity assessment procedure comprises among other things for any medical device: safety, performance and benefit and surveillance.

7 European Commission (1996a), p. 12.

8 Ibid., p. 13.

9 A cluster is a group of firms concentrated in one geographic location and working in the same sector. The terms agglomeration and industrial district have also been used. For further information see chapter 4.

7 Field research

1 Porter (1990), pp. 358–67, 373.

2 Weimer (1990), p. 100.

3 Porter (1990), pp. 374–6.

4 Simon (1992), p. 56.

5 Porter (1990), p. 378.

6 Weimer (1990), pp. 135–6.

7 Voyer and Roy (1996), p. 228.

8 OECD (1997), p. 113. A general survey of the number of enterprises in the different EU countries is illustrated in Appendix 3. The firm size is based on the number of employees in the two tables.

9 OECD (1997), p. 115.

10 See Appendix 3 for further details.

11 United Nations (1996), p. 5.

12 Porter (1990), p. 154.

13 Becattini (1990), p. 161.

14 There is the traditional craft firm which dominates in industries such as clothing, shoe-making, leather goods, ceramics and furniture, and the high-technology firm which began to emerge in the late 1960s.

15 Goodman and Bamford (1989), p. 2.

16 Porter (1990), p. 443.

17 Le Billon and Delluc (1995), p. 89.

18 OECD (1997), pp. 184 and 187. In 1991, intra-EU trade represented 59 per cent of Italy's total trade. Four-fifths of Italian exports are destined for developed countries and the rest for Eastern European and developing countries. Within the EU, 21 per cent of Italy's exports are destined for Germany and 15 per cent for France. In 1990, about 48 per cent of Italian FDI was destined for EU countries and, with the exception of Japan, no other country had a comparably high percentage destined for developing countries.

19 Porter (1990), p. 446.

20 Ibid., pp. 436–7, 696.

21 United Nations (1996), pp. 9–10. The most important laws concerning foreign trade are illustrated in Appendix 4.

22 Porter (1990), p. 448. This explains the lower flows of intra-European trade compared to Germany and France in the industry description of MSE (chapter 6).

23 One firm was acting as a subcontractor, another firm was rather integrated and a third acted as a cooperative distribution centre for eighteen small manufacturing firms, etc. The questions had to be adapted very spontaneously to each constellation.

24 In 1980 there were 248 registered enterprises in Tuttlingen; in 1990, 264; and in 1998, 244. During the recession of 1992 many enterprises collapsed. The standardised surgical instrumentation industry was particularly hard hit (Handwerkskammer Konstanz, 26.4.1999).

25 Voyer and Roy (1996), pp. 224–5.

26 The birth of an industrial district can be traced to historical circumstances; they may arise from an unusual local demand or the prior existence of supplier industries. However, they may also arise due to the existence of one or two innovative firms that stimulate the growth of others.

27 Vocke (1987), pp. 304–29.

28 Handwerkskammer Konstanz, 26.4.1999.

29 ALTMANN GmbH (1998), *75 Jahre: Vom Patriarchen zum Pionier*, p. 11.

30 See industry description (chapter 6).

31 See industry description (chapter 6). Within the EU the UK was, after Germany and France, in the third place regarding the added value.

32 Food and Drug Administration.

33 eG: in German, *eingetragene Genossenschaft*. The legal form as a cooperative is based on the elaboration of 'welfare' for its member firms. Decisions about investments and future strategies are taken by the board of directors, although in certain cases they need the agreement of the executive board. The day-to-day business is the responsibility of the executive board. Extraordinary decisions in the day-to-day business are, however, discussed with the board of directors in order to achieve a broad acceptance (a positive experience within DEXTRA).

34 Ear, nose, throat.

35 Actually, DEXTRA 'recruits' its new members indirectly through already existing firms (generation changes, changes in the corporate form of a firm, etc.).

36 The subsidiary was founded in 1975 and closed in 1994.

37 The provincial town of Sialkot is Pakistan's leading centre, in per capita terms, for manufacturing exports. Sialkot's economy is dominated by SMEs. Among the leading export industries are the manufacture of sports goods, including hand-stitched footballs, and stainless-steel surgical instruments. Over 85 per cent of the exports are aimed at high-quality markets in North America and Western Europe (Nadvi (1998), p. 12).

Pakistani firms covered about 80 per cent of the world market in the MSE industry in 1999. This concerned, however, traditional instruments such as knives, scissors, forceps, etc. There were about 600 firms and 100,000 blue-collar staff in the MSE industry in Sialkot, according to the local chamber of commerce. White-collar staff have the advantage of speaking fluent English in addition to their mother language (Syndicat Mixte du Bassin d'Emploi de Nogent, 29 September 2000).

38 See industry note (chapter 6).

39 According to Mr Müller, these countries offer low quantities of stainless steel. For the production of surgical instruments the firms do not need large blocks of steel.

40 These instruments, belonging to product class 1, are not used in open heart operations and in the circulatory system. They do not stay a long time in the human body, in contrast to instruments belonging to product class 2.
41 Food Drug America.
42 Kreditanstalt für Wiederaufbau in Germany. This institution was established after World War II to facilitate reconstruction. The EU considers this institution as intermediary finance.
43 During World War II Chiron added compressors to their initial product range. In the 1970s they completely stopped their production of surgical instruments in order to concentrate on machines that were needed to produce surgical instruments. In 1998, nearly all manufacturing firms in the Tuttlingen region used Chiron machines for the production of surgical instruments.
44 In German: Technischer Überwachungsverein.
45 According to Mr Maistre from MAISTRE SA.
46 See industry description (chapter 6).
47 Banque de France (1991), pp. 24–5.

8 Results and interpretations

1 Chambre de commerce et d'industrie de Saint-Dizier et de la Haute-Marne (1 April 1999).
2 Porter (1990), p. 446.
3 About 60 per cent of the German SMEs had distribution activities abroad and 40 per cent of them their service activities. About 50 per cent of the Italian SMEs maintained distribution activities abroad and 40 per cent of them their service activities. In France the respective percentages were 41 per cent and 16 per cent.
4 The percentages in each country are calculated averages.
5 Cavusgil (1984), pp. 195–208.
6 Root (1987), p. 1; United Nations (1998), p. 37 and United Nations (1997a), p. 14.
7 Buckley and Brooke (1992), p. 387, estimated that around 40 per cent of first moves abroad are unplanned and take the form of faxes or other offers coming from abroad.
8 Dunning (1995), p. 481.
9 Porter (1990), p. 446.
10 European Commission (1997b), p. 271. See literature survey chapter 1, removal of NTBs, pp. 12–19.
11 See chapter 1, removal of NTBs, pp. 12–19. About 52 per cent of the medium-sized firms felt higher competition, 42 per cent of the small firms and 38 per cent of the very small firms.
12 Jones (1998), p. 29.
13 These case studies analyse, however, the industrial district as a case rather than the firm within the district. There are examples from Pakistan, from different South American countries, from the US, from Romania, etc.
14 Porter (1980), pp. 34–8.
15 See case study.
16 Cecchini (1988), pp. 52–66.
17 Standardised surgical instruments are not submitted to strict certification proceedings. They belong to EU product class 1.
18 Lefebvre (1998), pp. 232–3 and Jones (1998), p. 29.
19 European Commission (1997b), p. 268. See chapter 1, removal of NTBs, pp. 12–19.
20 Root (1987), p. 53.

21 Bleeke and Ernst (1992), pp. 97–105 and Gomes-Casseres (1994), pp. 62–74.
22 Johanson and Mattsson (1988), pp. 209–17.
23 Johanson and Vahlne (1990), pp. 11–14.
24 After fifty years, TRAUBE is only now thinking about plans for publishing its own catalogue.
25 Baglin *et al.* (1990), p. 420.
26 Root (1987), p. 113.
27 See industry description (chapter 6).
28 Root (1987), p. 124.
29 Dunning (1995), p. 481.
30 Krugman (1996), pp. 1–2 and Venables (1996), pp. 53–4.
31 In some cases, overlapping is welcome in order to dispatch special orders.
32 This information may consist of a special know-how or technology (privileged access to proprietary knowledge), the strategy of a competitor, etc.
33 Hennart (1991), p. 105.
34 Bleeke and Ernst (1992), pp. 97–105.
35 Piore and Sabel (1984), pp. 258–80. These authors were the first to introduce the term 'flexible specialisation' to describe industrial districts.
36 Jarillo (1993), p. 69.
37 Patry (1994), p. 4.
38 Corò and Grandinetti (1999), pp. 119–20.
39 Quinn *et al.* (1991), pp. 75–6.
40 Porter (1990), pp. 179–238. Porter describes such networks of supplying firms in different countries.
41 Information flows easily within industrial districts. Often it is inevitable that the relatives of an employee work in competing firms in Tuttlingen.
42 Baglin *et al.* (1990), p. 420.
43 Porter (1990), p. 82.
44 Grant (1991), p. 538.
45 See chapter 7, conduct of the case studies in the industrial city of Nogent, pp. 127–30.
46 The term 'collective efficiency' had already been used by Marshall (1920), pp. 262 and 267, without defining the expression clearly.
47 Schmitz (1998), p. 13.
48 Porter (1998), p. 80.
49 Bagella *et al.* (1998), pp. 1–34.
50 Junius (1997), p. 3.
51 Krugman (1996), pp. 1–2 and Venables (1996), p. 54. For further details see chapter 4, industrial districts, pp. 57–61.
52 It is important to remember that MENTA bought its titanium from Swiss or German agents who imported the titanium from Russia. The firm stopped producing standardised surgical instruments.
53 Lösch (1973), p. 124.
54 Wiklund and Karlsson (1994), p. 119.
55 For Mr Müller, the director of NUTRA, an important source of information is the 'Stammtisch'.
56 Porter (1998), p. 83 and Audretsch (1998), pp. 18–29.
57 Schmitz (1998), pp. 15–16.
58 See the descriptions of the two industrial districts (chapter 7, conduct of the case studies in the industrial districts of Tuttlingen (pp. 90–2) and Nogent (pp. 127–30)).
59 Piore and Sabel (1984), pp. 258–308.
60 Schmitz (1995), pp. 535–6. See Table 4.1, p. 59.

61 Mrs Traube, the director of TRAUBE, pointed out that she has confidence in the quality of the material provided. Everybody in the district uses the same quality of steel, which is very important for the further processing.
62 Schmitz (1995), p. 549.
63 Mrs Traube, the director of TRAUBE, pointed out that no firm in the industrial district wants to reveal its prices because of the high degree of local rivalry. When we wanted to buy an instrument she preferred to offer us one free.
64 CAP Instruments Coupants et de Chirurgie.
65 Williamson (1985), pp. 45–80.
66 Bidault and Jarillo (1995), pp. 1–2. See chapter 4.
67 In the beginning, it was not easy for Mr Schneider when he started to work at DEXTRA in the industrial district of Tuttlingen. He originated from Northern Germany, he speaks another dialect and did not know the network relations in the industrial district. Mrs Traube also encountered problems after her long absence from Tuttlingen and her work experience elsewhere.
68 Benko *et al.* (1997), p. 308.
69 Axelrod (1984), pp. 11–24.
70 In Nogent, for example, a firm such as Aesculap has a production/distribution plant. However, in Tuttlingen, too, large US firms have established offices. It is, however, important to use local people who have the necessary relationships. As already emphasised, entrepreneurs in industrial districts have prejudices *vis-à-vis* new market entrants not originating from the region or town. But they also see the necessity of opening their ‘closed world’ for FDI.
71 The sample of this thesis consists of only seven firms located inside industrial districts and thirty-seven located outside. But the firms inside an industrial district with a strong international position (Tuttlingen) have a higher degree of internationalisation than those located outside. This is confirmed by earlier studies on this subject (Bagella *et al.* (1998), pp. 1–34).

9 General conclusions: new approaches towards internationalisation

1 All SMEs that realised or planned cooperation agreements or FDI had done so or intended to do so between 1992 and 2002. Of these realised or planned strategies, 62 per cent were destined for EU countries. 60 per cent of the Italian, 50 per cent of the French and 20 per cent of the German SMEs realised or planned other foreign-market entry strategies in addition to exports (see chapter 8).
2 Under the form of external economies and joint action, as described in chapter 8.
3 Dunning (1995), pp. 461–91 and Dunning (1997).
4 Hymer (1970), pp. 441–8.
5 Vernon (1966), pp. 190–207.
6 Wernerfelt (1995), pp. 171–4.
7 Dunning (1997), pp. 68–98.
8 Dunning (1999), p. 12.
9 Dynamic competitive advantages evolve and adapt constantly to the changing environment. Innovation therefore plays a major role.
10 For further details see the section on the results of the questionnaire research (chapter 8, pp. 141–51).
11 Dunning (1995), p. 481.
12 See the section on the results of the questionnaire research (chapter 8, pp. 144–51).
13 Fujita and Thisse (1996), p. 369.
14 Reference is made to the high level of subcontracting activities in industrial districts. Due to these subcontracting activities firms such as NUTRA can buy

R&D-intensive medical instruments from their partner firms in the district to compete for tenders. Also firms such as MENTA, specialising in R&D-intensive projects, can buy traditional surgical instruments to complete tenders.

Appendix 2 Questionnaire

1 Value-chain = value of the finished product, without taxes.

Appendix 4 The most important Italian laws concerning foreign trade

1 OECD (1997), pp. 191–2.

Appendix 5 Production steps in the fabrication of a surgical instrument

1 There were two swage forges in Tuttlingen in 1999 compared to ten in the 1960s.
2 There were two small firms to galvanise in Tuttlingen.

Bibliography

Aerts, R. (1994), 'Becoming international: benefits and pitfalls for entrepreneurial SMEs: experiences from Belgium', in MaVeciana, J. (ed.), *SMEs: Internationalization, Networks and Strategy*, pp. 58–75 (Aldershot: Avebury).

Aharoni, Y. (1966), *The Foreign Investment Decision Process* (Boston: Harvard Business School).

Ahlberg, J., Garemo, N. and Nauclér, T. (1999), 'The Euro: how to keep your prices up and your competitors down', *The McKinsey Quarterly* 2: 112–18.

Amin, A. and Thrift, N. (1994), 'Living in the global', in Amin, A. and Thrift, N., (eds), *Globalization, Institutions, and Regional Development in Europe*, pp. 1–22 (Oxford: Oxford University Press).

Arino, A. (1997), 'Veracity and commitment', in Beamish, P.W. and Killing, J.P. (eds), *Cooperative Strategies – European Perspectives*, pp. 215–41 (San Francisco: The New Lexington Press).

Audretsch, D.B. (1998), 'Agglomeration and the location of innovative activity', *Oxford Review of Economic Policy* 14: 18–29.

Axelrod, R. (1984), *The Evolution of Cooperation* (New York: Basic Books).

Bagella, M., Becchetti, L. and Sacchi, S. (1998), 'The positive link between geographical agglomeration and export intensity: the engine of Italian endogenous growth?', *Economic Notes by Banca Monte dei Paschi di Siena SpA* 27: 1–34.

Baglin, G., Bruel, O., Garreau, A. and Greif, M. (1990), *Management Industriel et Logistique* (Paris: Ed. Economica).

Baldwin, R. (1989), 'The growth effects of 1992', *Economic Policy* 9: 248–81.

Baldwin, R. (1991), 'On the microeconomics of the European monetary union', *European Economy*, special edition no. 1: 21–36.

Bamberger, I. and Bonacker, R. (1994a), 'Strategies for small- and medium-sized enterprises and their measurement', in Bamberger, I. (ed.), *Product Market Strategies of Small- and Medium-sized Enterprises*, pp. 28–86 (Aldershot: Avebury).

Bamberger, I. and Evers, M. (1994b), 'Internationalization behaviour of small- and medium-sized enterprises – empirical results', in Bamberger, I. (ed.), *Product/Market Strategies of Small- and Medium-sized Enterprises*, pp. 310–63 (Aldershot: Avebury).

Banque de France (1991), 'L'industrie dans le bassin Nogentais', Paris.

Baptista, R. (2000), 'Do innovations diffuse faster within geographical clusters?', *International Journal of Industrial Organization* 18: 515–35.

Bartlett, C.A. (1986), 'Building and managing the transnational: the new organizational challenge', in Porter, M.E. (ed.), *Competition in Global Industries*, pp. 367–401 (Boston: Harvard Business School).

Bartlett, C.A. and Goshal, S. (1989), *Managing Across Borders* (Boston: Harvard Business School).

Becattini, G. (1990), 'Italy', in Sengenberger, W., Loveman, G. and Piore, M.J. (eds), *The Re-emergence of Small Enterprises: Industrial Restructuring in Industrialised Countries*, pp. 144–72 (Geneva: ILO).

Benko, G., Dunford, M. and Heurley, J. (1997), 'Districts industriels – Vingt ans de recherche', *Espaces et Sociétés* 88/89: 305–27.

Bidault, F. and Jarillo, C.J. (1995), 'Trust in economic transactions', Conference on industry structure and organizational networks (University of Geneva).

Blau, P.M. and Alba, R.D. (1982), 'Empowering nets of participation', *Administrative Science Quarterly* 27: 363–79.

Bleeke, J. and Ernst, D. (1992), 'Is your strategic alliance really a sale', *Harvard Business Review*, January/February: 97–105.

Bourgault, M., Lefevre, L.A. and Lefevre, E. (1994), 'Critical capabilities and performance of the small subcontracting firms in the aerospace industry', Research Paper (Montréal: CIRANO).

Bronder, C. and Pritzl, R. (1992), 'Ein konzeptioneller Ansatz zur Gestaltung und Entwicklung Strategischer Allianzen', in Bronder, C. and Pritzl, R. (eds), *Wegweiser für Strategische Allianzen*, pp. 17–44 (Wiesbaden: Gabler).

Brülhart, M. and Torstensson, J. (1996), 'Regional integration, scale economies and industry location in the European Union', Discussion Paper no. 1435 (London: CEPR).

Buckley, P.J. (1989), 'Foreign direct investment by small- and medium-sized enterprises: the theoretical background', *Small Business Economics* 1: 89–100.

Buckley, P.J. and Brooke, M.Z. (1992), *International Business Studies – An Overview* (Oxford: Blackwell).

Buckley, P.J. and Casson, M. (1979), 'A theory of international operations', in Anonymous, *European Research in International Business* (Amsterdam: North-Holland).

Buckley, P.J. and Casson, M. (1985), *The Economic Theory of the Multinational Enterprise* (London: Macmillan).

Buckley, P.J. and Casson, M. (1988), 'A theory of cooperation in international business', in Contractor, F.J. and Lorange, P. (eds), *Cooperative Strategies in International Business*, pp. 31–53 (Lexington: Heath & Co.).

Buckley, P.J. and Ghauri, P. (1994), *The Internationalization of the Firm: A Reader* (London: The Dryden Press).

Buckley, P.J. and Prescott, K. (1989), 'The structure of British industry's sales in foreign markets', *Managerial and Decision Economics* 10: 189–208.

Buigues, P. and Sheehy, J. (1995), 'The impact of the internal market programme on European integration', in Ems, E. (ed.), *35 Years of Free Trade in Europe: Messages for the Future*, pp. 38–63 (Geneva: EFTA).

Cantwell, J. (1991), 'A survey of theories of international production', in Pitelis, C.N. and Sugden, R. (eds), *The Nature of the Transnational Firm*, pp. 16–63 (London: Routledge).

Carr, N.G. (1999), 'Managing in the Euro zone', *Harvard Business Review* 1: 47–57.

Caves, R.E. (1996), *Multinational Enterprise and Economic Analysis* (Cambridge: Cambridge University Press).

Cavusgil, S.T. (1984), 'Differences among exporting firms based on their degree of internationalization', *Journal of Business Research* 12: 195–208.

Cecchini, P. (1988), *The European Challenge 1992: The Benefits of a Single Market* (Aldershot: Wildwood House).

Claret-Tournier, A. and Faijean, S. (1998), 'L'euro: c'est maintenant!', *L'Essentiel du Management*, Septembre, 36–41.

Coase, R. (1937), 'The nature of the firm', *Economica* 16: 386–405.

Corò, G. and Grandinetti, R. (1999), 'Evolutionary patterns of Italian districts', *Human Systems Management* 18: 117–29.

Curzon Price, V. (1996), 'Residual obstacles to trade in the Single European Market', *Euryopa* 1.

Demsetz, H. (1997), *The Economics of the Business Firm* (Cambridge: Cambridge University Press).

Doz, Y. (1991), 'Partnerships in Europe: the "soft" restructuring option?', in Mattsson, I.G. and Stymne, B. (eds), *Corporate and Industry Strategies for Europe*, pp. 303–26 (Amsterdam: North-Holland).

Duijnhouwer, A.L. (1994), 'Competitiveness, autonomy and business relationships', in MaVeciana, J. (ed.), *SMEs: Internationalization, Networks and Strategy*, pp. 174–200 (Aldershot: Avebury).

Dunning, J.H. (1988a), *Explaining International Production*, (London: Unwin Hyman).

Dunning, J.H. (1988b), 'The eclectic paradigm of international production: a restatement and some possible extensions', *Journal of International Business Studies* 19: 1–32.

Dunning, J.H. (1991), 'Governments, economic organization and international competitiveness', in Mattsson, I.G. and Stymme, B. (eds), *Corporate and Industry Strategies for Europe*, pp. 41–74 (Amsterdam: North-Holland).

Dunning, J.H. (1995), 'Reappraising the eclectic paradigm in an age of alliance capitalism', *Journal of International Business Studies* 26: 461–91.

Dunning, J.H. (1997), *Alliance Capitalism and Global Business* (London: Routledge).

Dunning, J.H. (1999), 'Globalization and the theory of MNE activity', Discussion Paper, Vol. II (Reading: University of Reading).

El-Agraa, A. (1994), *The Economics of the European Community* (New York: Harvester Wheatsheaf).

European Commission (1988), 'The European market, its barriers and methods of evaluation', *European Economy* 35: 17–39.

European Commission (1993a), *First Annual Report on SMEs' Activities* (Brussels: European Commission).

European Commission (1993b), 'The European Observatory for SMEs', First Annual Report, DG XXIII (Brussels: European Commission).

European Commission (1995a), 'Activités en faveur des PME et de l'artisanat', Report (Brussels: European Commission).

European Commission (1995b) 'Amélioration de la coopération et du developpement transnational des PME', Report (Brussels: European Commission).

European Commission (1995c), 'Rapport de la faisabilité de la création d'un marché européen des capitaux pour les jeunes sociétés entrepreneuriales de croissance rapide', COM(95) 498 final (Brussels: European Commission).

European Commission (1996a), 'Panorama', *European Communities*, ch. 16, pp. 9–15 (Brussels: European Commission).

European Commission (1996b), 'The European Observatory for SMEs', Fourth Annual Report (Brussels: European Commission).

European Commission (1996c), 'The impact and effectiveness of the Single Market', COM(96)520 final (Brussels: European Commission).

European Commission (1997a), 'European capital markets for small- and medium-sized enterprises: prospects and potential obstacles to progress', COM 187 final (Brussels: European Commission).

European Commission (1997b), 'The European Observatory for SMEs', Fifth Annual Report (Brussels: ENSR, Enterprise Survey).

Frankel, J.A. and Rose, A.K. (1997), 'Is EMU more justifiable ex post than ex ante?' research paper (Berkeley: University of California).

Fujita, M. (1998), *The Transnational Activities of Small- and Medium-Sized Enterprises* (Boston: Kluwer).

Fujita, M. and Thisse, J.-F. (1996), 'Economics of agglomeration', *Journal of the Japanese and International Economies* 10: 339–78.

Gammelsaeter, H. and Guvag, B. (1994), 'The small and middle-sized enterprise in cross-national joint-ventures: a way of inducing renewal and increasing viability', in MaVcciana, J. (ed.), *SMEs: Internationalization, Networks and Strategy*, pp. 201–21 (Aldershot: Avebury).

Garrette, B. (1998), 'Les Européens se trompent d'alliances', *L'Expansion Management Review* 88: 68–73.

Gomes-Casseres, B. (1994), 'Group versus group: how alliance networks compete', *Harvard Business Review*, July/August: 62–74.

Goodman, E. and Bamford, J. (1989), *Small Firms and Industrial Districts in Italy* (London: Routledge).

Granovetter, M. (1992), 'Problems of explanation in economic sociology', in Nohria, N. and Eccles, R.G. (eds), *Networks and Organizations*, pp. 25–56 (Boston: Harvard Business School Press).

Grant, R.M. (1991), 'Porter's "competitive advantage of nations": an assessment', *Strategic Management Journal* 12: 535–48.

Gulati, R., Khanna, T. and Nohria, N. (1994), 'Il n'y pas d'alliance réussie sans engagement', *Expansion Management Review*, winter: 7–16.

Hamel, G., Doz, Y.L. and Prahalad, C.K. (1989), 'Collaborate with your competitors – and win', *Harvard Business Review*, January/February: 133–9.

Hennart, J.-F. (1991), 'The transaction cost theory of the multinational enterprise', in Pitelis, C.N. and Sugden, R. (eds), *The Nature of the Transnational Firm*, pp. 80–136 (London: Routledge).

Hill, C.W.L. (1990), 'Cooperation, opportunism, and the invisible hand: implications for transaction cost theory', *Academy of Management Review* 15: 500–13.

Hovi, N. (1994), 'Internationalizing subcontractors: is co-operation an alternative?', in MaVeciana, J. (ed.), *SMEs: Internationalization, Networks and Strategy*, pp. 359–79 (Aldershot: Avebury).

Humphrey, J. and Schmitz, H. (1996), 'The triple C approach to local industrial policy', *World Development* 24: 1859–77.

Hymer, S. (1970), 'The efficiency (contradictions) of multinational corporations', *American Economic Review* 60: 441–8.

Jacquemot, P. (1990), *La Firme Multinationale: Une Introduction Economique* (Paris: Economica).

Jarillo, C.J. (1990), *Dirección Estratégica* (Madrid: McGraw-Hill).

Jarillo, C.J. (1993), *Strategic Networks* (Oxford: Butterworth-Heinemann).

Jarillo, C.J. and Martinez, J.I. (1989), 'The evolution of research on coordination mechanisms in multinational corporations', *Journal of International Business Studies*, fall: 489–513.

Jarillo, C.J. and Martinez, J.I. (1991), 'The international expansion of Spanish firms: towards an integrative framework for international strategy', in Mattsson, I.G. and Stymme, B. (eds), *Corporate and Industry Strategies for Europe*, pp. 283–302 (Amsterdam: North-Holland).

Jarillo, C.J. and Martinez, J.I. (1992), 'Different roles for subsidiaries: the case of multinational corporations in Spain', *Strategic Management Journal* 11: 501–12.

Jarillo, C.J. and Ricart, J.E. (1987), 'Sustaining networks', *Interfaces* September–October: 82–91.

Jenster, V. and Jarillo, C.J. (1994), *Internationalizing the Medium-sized Firm* (Copenhagen: Handelshojskolens Forlag).

Johanson, J. and Mattsson, L.-G. (1988), 'Internationalization in industrial systems – a network approach', in Hood, N. and Vahlne, J.-E. (eds), *Strategies in Global Competition*, pp. 201–23 (Beckenham: Croom Helm).

Johanson, J. and Vahlne, J.E. (1990), 'The mechanism of internationalisation', *International Marketing Review* 7: 11–24.

Johanson, J. and Wiedersheim-Paul, F. (1975), 'The internationalization of the firm – four Swedish cases', *Journal of Management Studies*, October: 305–22.

Jones, T. (1996), 'Info centres bid for extra funds', *European Voice*, 15 February, p. 31.

Jones, T. (1998), 'Paving the way for a smooth change-over', *European Voice*, 18–24 June, p. 29.

Jovanovic, M.N. (1992), *International Economic Integration* (London: Routledge).

Jovanovic, M.N. (1997), *European Economic Integration – Limits and Prospects* (London: Routledge).

Jovanovic, M.N. (1998), 'Economic integration and location of industries', Discussion Paper, Summer School, 31 August–10 September (Bressano).

Joynt, P. (1989), 'International strategy: a study of Norwegian companies', in Buckley, P. and Ghauri, P. (eds), *The Internationalization of the Firm – a Reader*, pp. 350–62 (London: The Dryden Press).

Junius, K. (1997), 'Economies of scale: a survey of the empirical literature', Working Paper no. 813 (Kiel Institute for World Economics).

Killing, J.P. (1988), 'Understanding alliances: the role of tasks and organizational complexity', in Contractor, F.J. (ed.), *Cooperative Strategies in International Business*, pp. 55–67 (Lexington: D.C. Heath & Co.).

Kogut, B. (1983), 'Foreign direct investment as a sequential process', in Kindleberger, C.P. and Audretsch, D. (eds), *Multinational Corporations in the 1980s* (Cambridge: MIT Press).

Krieger-Mytelka, L. and Delapierre, M. (1988), 'The alliance strategies of European firms and the role of ESPRIT', in Dunning, J.H. and Robson, P. (eds), *Multinational Corporations and European Integration*, pp. 231–53 (London: Routledge).

Krugman, P. (1996), 'Integration, specialisation, and adjustment', *European Economic Review*, forthcoming.

Le Billon, V. and Delluc, M. (1995), 'Le triomphe des réseaux à l'italienne', *L'Expansion* 505: 88–91.
Lefebvre, F. (1998), *L'Euro* (Levallois: Editions Francis Lefebvre).
Lorange, P. (1988), 'Co-operative strategies: planning and control considerations', in Hood, N. and Vahlne, J.E. (eds), *Strategies in Global Competition*, pp. 370–89 (London: Croom Helm).
Lorange, P. and Hakanson, L. (1991), 'R&D based cooperative ventures', in Mattson, L.-G. and Stymne, B. (eds), *Corporate and Industry Strategies for Europe*, pp. 235–62 (Amsterdam: North-Holland).
Lorange, P. and Roos, J. (1992), 'Stolpersteine beim Management Strategischer Allianzen', in Bronder, C. and Pritzl, R. (eds), *Wegweiser für Strategische Allianzen*, pp. 343–55 (Wiesbaden: Gabler).
Lorenzoni, G. and Baden-Fuller, C. (1995), 'Creating a strategic center to manage a web of partners', *California Management Review* 37: 146–63.
Lösch, A. (1973), *The Economic of Location* (New Haven: Yale University Press).
McKinnon, R. (1963), 'Optimum currency areas', *American Economic Review* 53: 717–25.
Mariti, P. and Smiley, R.H. (1983), 'Cooperative agreements and the organization of industry', *Journal of Industrial Economics* 31: 437–51.
Marshall, A. (1920), *Principles of Economics* (London: Macmillan).
Meijboom, B.R. and Rongen, J.M.J. (1995), 'Clustering, logistics, and spatial economics', Research Paper (University of Tilburg).
Molle, W. and Morsink, R. (1991), 'Intra-European direct investment', in Bürgenmeier, B. and Mucchielli, J.L. (eds), *Multinationals and Europe 1992: Strategies for the Future*, pp. 81–101 (London: Routledge).
Moss Kanter, R. (1994), 'Collaborative advantage: successful partnerships manage the relationship, not just the deal', *Harvard Business Review*, July–August: 96–108.
Mucchielli, J.L. (1985), *Les Firmes Multinationales: Mutations et Nouvelles Perspectives* (Paris: Economica).
Mucchielli, J.L. (1991), 'Strategic advantages for European firms', in Mucchielli, J.L. and Bürgenmeier, B. (eds), *Multinationals and Europe 1992*, pp. 36–57 (London: Routledge).
Mucchielli, J.L. (1998), *Multinationales et Mondialisation* (Paris: Editions du Seuil).
Nadvi, K. (1998), 'The cutting edge – collective efficiency and international competitiveness in Pakistan', Discussion Paper 360 (Brighton: Institute of Development Studies, University of Sussex).
Nagorski, A. and Theil, S. (1998), 'Building an engine run on Euros', *Newsweek*, 4 May: 16–18.
Naulleau, G. and Vasseur, J. (1998), 'Deux modèles d'alliance gagnants', *L'Expansion Management Review* 88: 74–81.
Obstfeld, M. (1997), 'A strategy for launching the Euro', NBER Working Paper 6233.
OECD (1982), *Innovation in Small and Medium Firms*, Background Reports (Paris: OECD).
OECD (1997), *PME et Mondialisation*, vol. 2 (Paris: OECD).
Ohlsson, L. (1991), 'Comparative advantage strategies for Swedish industry facing the 1990s', in Mattsson, I.G. and Stymme, B. (eds), *Corporate and Industry Strategies for Europe*, pp. 75–96 (Amsterdam: North-Holland).

Paci, R. and Usai, S. (1997), 'Technological enclaves and industrial districts. An analysis of the regional distribution of innovative activity in Europe', Research Paper (Centre for North/South Economic Research, Università di Cagliari.
Panic, M. (1991), 'The impact of multinationals on national economic policies', in Mucchielli, J.L. and Bürgenmeier, B. (eds), *Multinationals and Europe 1992*, pp. 204–25 (London: Routledge).
Patry, M. (1994), 'Faire ou faire faire: la perspective de l'économie des organisations', Research Paper (Montréal: CIRANO), 94c–1.
Peck, M.J. (1989), 'Industrial organization and the gains from Europe 1992', *Brookings Papers on Economic Activity* 2: 277–99.
Petersen, B. and Pedersen, T. (1996), 'Twenty years later – support and critique of the Uppsala Internationalisation Model', Workshop Paper for the presentation at the 22nd annual EIBA conference in Stockholm, 15–16 December.
Petrucci, A. and Quintieri, B. (1998), 'Globalization, quality and trade', 9–12 July (Bürgenstock: Conference on Globalization and International Trade).
Piore, M.J. and Sabel, C.F. (1984), *The Second Industrial Divide* (New York: Basic Books).
Porter, M.E. (1980), *Competitive Strategy: Techniques for Analyzing Industries and Competitors* (New York: The Free Press).
Porter, M.E. (1985), *Competitive Advantage: Creating and Sustaining Superior Performance* (New York: The Free Press).
Porter, M.E. (1986), 'Changing patterns of international competition', *California Management Review* 28: 9–40.
Porter, M.E. (1990), 'The competitive advantage of nations', *Harvard Business Review*, March–April: 73–93.
Porter, M.E. (1990), *The Competitive Advantage of Nations* (New York: The Free Press).
Porter, M.E. (1998), 'Clusters and the new economics of competition', *Harvard Business Review*, November–December: 77–90.
Porter, M.E. and Fuller, M.B. (1986), 'Coalitions and global strategy', in Porter, M.E. (ed.), *Competition in Global Industries,* pp. 315–43 (Boston: Harvard Business School Press).
Prahalad, C.K. and Doz, Y. (1987), *The Multinational Mission: Balancing Local Demands and Global Vision* (New York: Free Press).
Puga, D. and Venables, A.J. (1997), 'Preferential trading arrangements and industrial location', *Journal of International Economics* 43: 347–68.
Quinn, J.B., Doorley, T. and Paquette, P. (1991), 'Utilisez mieux la sous-traitance', *Harvard L'Expansion* 61: 71–9.
Raynal, S., Vermersch, F. and Carra-Pistollet, F. (1999), *Le Management du Projet Euro* (Paris: Editions d'Organisation).
Richardson, G.B. (1972), 'The organisation of industry', *Economic Journal* 82: 883–96.
Root, F.R. (1987), *Entry Strategies for International Markets* (Massachusetts: Lexington Books).
Rugman, A.M. and Hodgetts, R.M. (1995), *International Business – A Strategic Management Approach* (New York: McGraw-Hill).
Schmitz, H. (1995), 'Collective efficiency: growth path for small-scale industry', *Journal of Development Studies* 31: 529–66.

Schmitz, H. (1998), 'Collective efficiency and increasing returns', *Cambridge Journal of Economics* (forthcoming).

Simon, H. (1992), 'Les PME allemandes championnes du monde', *Harvard L'Expansion* 65: 50–7.

Sleuwagen, L. (1988), 'Multinationals, the European Community and Belgium: recent developments', in Dunning, J.H. and Robson, P. (eds), *Multinationals and the European Community*, pp. 153–70 (Oxford: Blackwell).

Stigler, G.J. (1968), 'The division of labour is limited by the extent of the market', in Stigler, G.J. (ed.), *The Organization of Industry*, pp. 129–41 (Chicago: University of Chicago Press).

STRATEGOR (1993), *Stratégie, Structure, Décision, Identité*, 2nd edn (Paris: Inter-Editions).

Teece, D.J. (1986), 'Transaction cost economics and the multinational enterprise: an assessment', *Journal of Economic Behavior and Organization* 7: 21–45.

Telesio, P. (1979), *Technology Licensing and Multinational Enterprises* (New York: Praeger).

Tödtling, F. (1994), 'The uneven landscape of innovation poles: local embeddedness and global networks', in Amin, A. and Thrift, N. (eds), *Globalization, Institutions, and Regional Development in Europe*, pp. 68–90 (Oxford: Oxford University Press).

Turnbull, P.W. (1987), 'A challenge to the stages theory of the internationalization process', in Buckley, P. and Ghauri, P. (eds), *The Internationalization of the Firm – a Reader* (London: The Dryden Press).

United Nations (1993), *Small- and Medium-sized Transnational Corporations* (New York and Geneva: UNCTAD).

United Nations (1996), 'Italian policies on small and medium-sized enterprises – national and regional initiatives in support of young and women entrepreneurs', Economic Commission for Europe (Geneva: UNCTAD, 20 November).

United Nations (1997a), *International Investment: Towards the Year 2001* (Geneva: UNCTAD).

United Nations (1997b), *World Investment Report* (New York and Geneva: UNCTAD).

United Nations (1998), *World Investment Report 1998* (New York and Geneva: UNCTAD).

Venables, A.J. (1996), 'Localization of industry and trade performance', *Oxford Review of Economic Policy* 12: 52–60.

Vernon, R. (1966), 'International investment and international trade in product cycle', *Quarterly Journal of Economics* 80: 190–207.

Vernon, R. (1974), 'The location of economic industry', in Dunning, J.H. (ed.), *Economic Analysis and the Multinational Enterprise*, pp. 89–114 (London: Allen & Unwin).

Vocke, H. (1987), *Die Chronik des Kreises Tuttlingen* (Waldshut: Städte- und Kreis-Chroniken-Verlag).

Voyer, R. and Roy, J. (1996), 'European high-technology clusters', in de la Mothe, J. and Paquet, G. (eds), *Evolutionary Economics and the New International Political Economy*, pp. 220–38 (London: Pinter).

Weimer, S. (1990), 'Federal Republic of Germany', in Sengenberger, W., Loveman, G. and Piore, M.J. (eds), *The Re-emergence of Small Enterprises: Industrial Restructuring in Industrialized Countries*, pp. 98–141 (Geneva: ILO).

Welch, L.S. (1981), 'Outward foreign licensing by Australian companies', in Buckley, P. and Ghauri, P. (eds), *The Internationalization of the Firm – a Reader*, pp. 64–90 (London: The Dryden Press).
Wernerfelt, B. (1995), 'The resource based view of the firm: ten years after', *Strategic Management Journal* 16: 171–4.
Wiklund, J. and Karlsson, C. (1994), 'Flexible companies in an industrial district: the case of the Gnosjö region in Sweden, in MaVeciana, J. (ed.), *SMEs: Internationalization, Networks and Strategy*, pp. 103–28 (Aldershot: Avebury).
Williamson, E.O. (1975), *Market and Hierarchies: Analysis and Antitrust Implications* (New York: The Free Press).
Williamson, E.O. (1985), *The Economic Institutions of Capitalism* (New York: The Free Press).
Zaby, A.M. (1996), 'Comparative analysis of export-oriented and foreign production-oriented firms' foreign market entry decisions: a comment', *Management International Review (MIR)* 36: 281–4.

Index